San Diego

Tijuana

Palm Springs

Publisher
Anthony S. Niskanen

Editor
Marilynn Boesky

Associate Editor
Mona Cacciari

RRN Inc. - New York

ISBN 0-9624223-1-2

DINING GUIDE
for
San Diego, Tijuana and Palm Springs

Published by

Flashfacts System
Division of RRN Inc.
22 West 21st Street
New York, NY 10010-6904

(212) 627-1733

CREDITS

DINING GUIDE Logotype created by Eileen Harte Design, Encino, CA
Maps created by Paul Niskanen of PEN Associates, Wynnewood, PA

Our thanks to San Diego Trolley Inc. and the San Diego Metropolitan Transit Development Board for permission to reproduce their map of the San Diego Trolley System, and to The South Coast Vintners Association for permission to reproduce their Temecula Valley Wine Country Tour Map.

RRN wishes to express its appreciation to the many restaurateurs and Southern California diners who have encouraged and assisted the creation of this Guide. Special thanks to Esther Whitney and Suzi Green of California Yacht Sales of San Diego for their assistance.

Flashfacts System℠ DINING GUIDES make unique client gifts. For inquiries about larger quantity orders or special editions, call or write:
Special Projects
RRN Inc.
at the above address and phone number.

Flashfacts System is a service mark of RRN Inc.

FROM THE EDITORS DESK

Where to go for lunch or dinner with a client or friend is rarely a simple decision. Even selecting a new place for Sunday Brunch can be a challenge. Most of us don't start out with a specific idea of where we want to eat. Some are more concerned with how far they want to drive, and others with the type of ambiance. Add to that the choice between the "tried and true" favorites, the newly opened restaurants, the "in" places, or the off-beat restaurants featuring unusual ethnic cuisines. Then add questions about the cost, the hours and the reservations policy and your decision process can get very complicated. In San Diego there are over 500 possibilities and when you add Tijuana the range of choices becomes international! Palm Springs with more than 150 restaurants is no easier, particularly if you're visiting for just a short time.

We hope our *Flashfacts System*℠ DINING GUIDE will make your selection process a lot easier. Information organization is its key strength. Its primary purpose is to help you identify and sort out the many options in a given geographical area (Dining Area) as quickly as possible. Once you have found a choice, you have at hand all the other practical information you'll need about the restaurant, such as its address, phone, meals served, days open, price level.

Although we do mention some of the awards restaurants have received, we have not formally rated them. Everyone's taste varies. Some of the restaurants listed are Mom and Pop operations, others are big and glitzy. Which one is better? That should be your choice. We've tried to keep our descriptions as factual as possible so you can make up your own mind.

Each of the three communities covered by this Edition has its own character. San Diego is well known for its casual dining and great views, but you may be amazed at the range of cuisines available -- from Afghan to Vietnamese.   Palm Springs has a more formal atmosphere that is reflected in some of their restaurants, but for the majority "desert casual" prevails after golf. And Tijuana.... is a world unto itself. A busy south-of-the border city only minutes away from San Diego. It has a variety and quality of restaurants that usually remain unknown to the casual visitor.

We'd like your feedback and suggestions about our Dining Guide. You'll find two Reply Postcards inside the back cover. One is designed to give us your reactions and to nominate additional restaurants for the next edition. The other is to order your complimentary copy of the new POCKET EDITION which covers the three Dining Areas of Tijuana.

Bon Appetit!

There is no charge to restaurants for a listing in this Guide and we have tried to be as comprehensive as possible. This information was gathered by telephone and mail surveys from the restaurants. Every effort has been made to confirm the accuracy of the data, but since changes do occur we recommend you call the restaurant to confirm any important details. This is particularly so in the Palm Springs area where off-season days and hours may vary significantly from these "normal" hours.

DEFINITIONS OF RESTAURANT PROFILE TERMS AND ABREVIATIONS

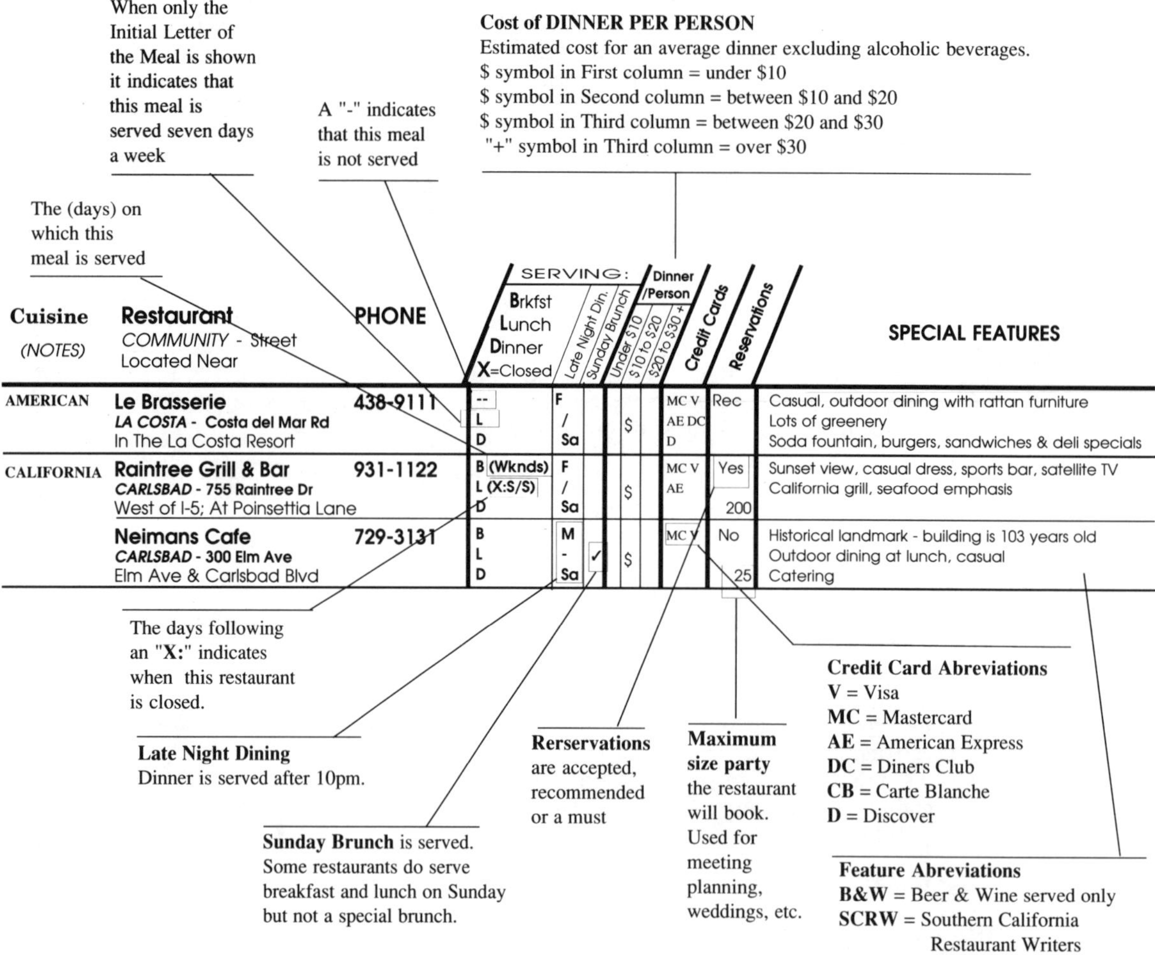

QUICK INDEX

FINDING INFORMATION IN THE GUIDE   The Guide is organized in three primary sections. The first profiles the restaurants of San Diego (starting on page 6), the second covers the restaurants of Tijuana, Mexico (starting on page 57) and the third the restaurants of Palm Springs and the Desert Communities (starting on page 65). In each section you'll find general alphabetic and cuisine indexes and overview maps showing the boundaries of the individual Dining Areas and their major roads. Most Dining Areas have local maps and an alphabetic index as well .

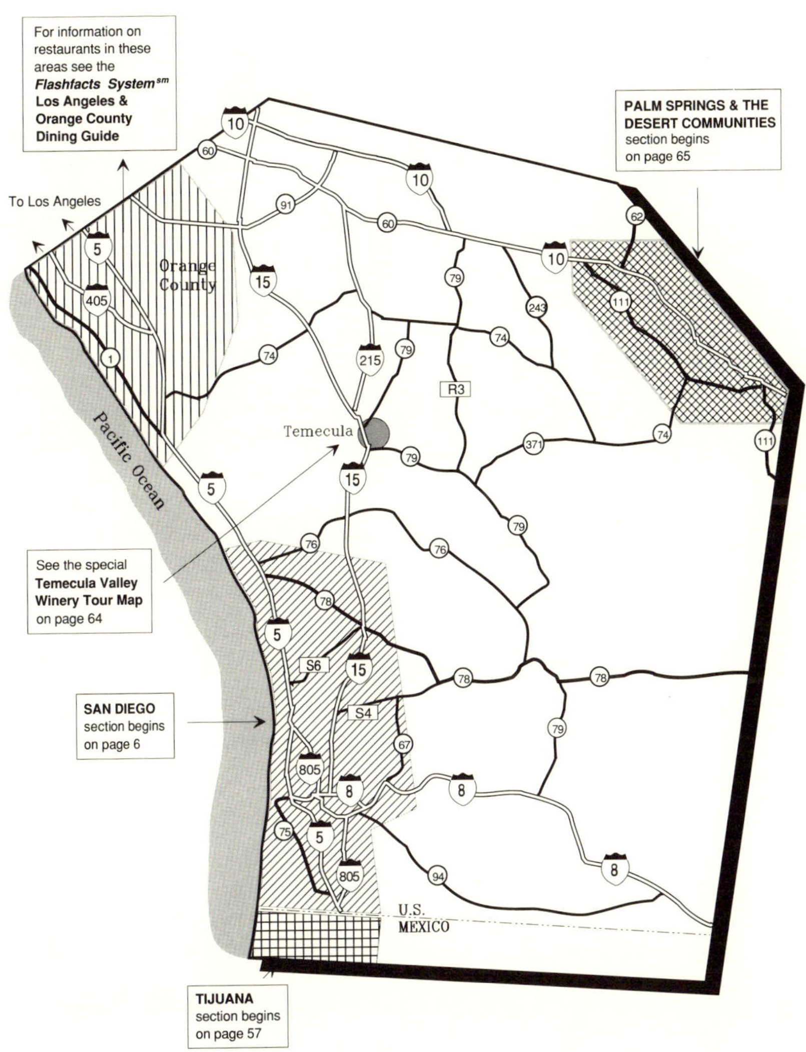

SAN DIEGO

Index to San Diego Dining Areas

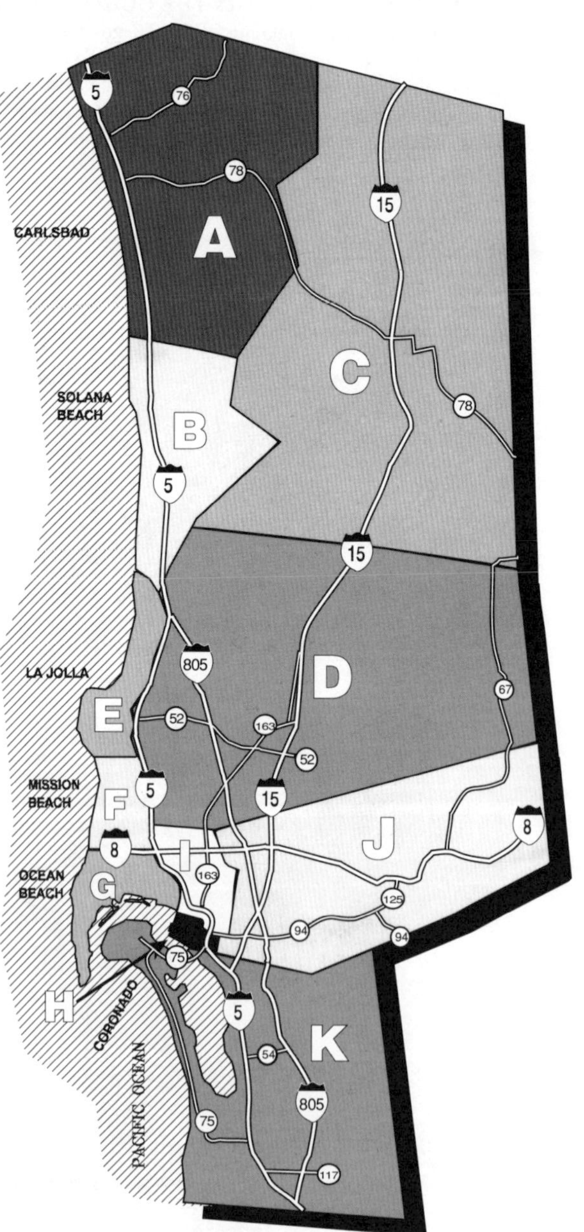

CUSINE INDEX

CUISINE
Restaurant........................ Found in Pages (Dining Area)

AFGHAN

Khyber Pass	D:24-25 (CLAIREMONT/MIRAMAR)
Pamir	B:16-20 (DEL MAR/LEUCADIA)
Pasha	E:26-31 (LA JOLLA)

AMERICAN

101 Diner, The	B:16-20 (DEL MAR/LEUCADIA)
Adam 'n' Albie's Beef Inn	I:46-50 (BALBOA PARK/OLD TOWN)
Alley Oops	F:32-35 (PACIFIC BEACH/MISSION BEACH)
Alpine Inn	J:51-53 (EAST COUNTY/EL CAJON)
B Street Cafe	H:40-44 (DOWNTOWN)
Barnett's Grand Cafe	H:40-44 (DOWNTOWN)
Barry's Cafe	H:40-44 (DOWNTOWN)
Bennigan's	I:46-50 (BALBOA PARK/OLD TOWN)
Bobby J's	B:16-20 (DEL MAR/LEUCADIA)
Bobby McGee's	J:51-53 (EAST COUNTY/EL CAJON)
Boll Weevil	E:26-31 (LA JOLLA)
Bonita Store Restaurant	K:54-56 (CORONADO/SOUTH BAY)
Boondocks, The	J:51-53 (EAST COUNTY/EL CAJON)
Bread Basket, The	J:51-53 (EAST COUNTY/EL CAJON)
Bull And Bear	J:51-53 (EAST COUNTY/EL CAJON)
Bully's	B:16-20 (DEL MAR/LEUCADIA)
Bully's	E:26-31 (LA JOLLA)
Bully's East	I:46-50 (BALBOA PARK/OLD TOWN)
Butcher Shop	D:24-25 (CLAIREMONT/MIRAMAR)
Butcher Shop	K:54-56 (CORONADO/SOUTH BAY)
Cafe 6th & K	H:40-44 (DOWNTOWN)
Cafe Broken Yolk	F:32-35 (PACIFIC BEACH/MISSION BEACH)
Cafe La Maze	K:54-56 (CORONADO/SOUTH BAY)
California Earthquake Cafe	C:21-23 (INLAND NORTH COUNTY)
California Earthquake Cafe	I:46-50 (BALBOA PARK/OLD TOWN)
Cass Street Bar & Grill	F:32-35 (PACIFIC BEACH/MISSION BEACH)
Chart House	A:14-15 (OCEANSIDE/CARLSBAD)
Chart House	B:16-20 (DEL MAR/LEUCADIA)
Chart House	E:26-31 (LA JOLLA)
Chart House/SD Rowing Club	H:40-44 (DOWNTOWN)
Chicken Pie Shop	I:46-50 (BALBOA PARK/OLD TOWN)
Chuck's Steak House	E:26-31 (LA JOLLA)
City Rock Cafe	H:40-44 (DOWNTOWN)
Clay's Texas Pit Bar-B-Q	E:26-31 (LA JOLLA)
Coco Palms	B:16-20 (DEL MAR/LEUCADIA)
College Restaurant, The	J:51-53 (EAST COUNTY/EL CAJON)
Corvette Diner, Bar & Grill, The	I:46-50 (BALBOA PARK/OLD TOWN)
Cotton Patch	G:36-38 (OCEAN BEACH/HARBOR ISLAND)
Country Inn Restaurant	B:16-20 (DEL MAR/LEUCADIA)
Crest Cafe	I:46-50 (BALBOA PARK/OLD TOWN)
D. Z. Akins	J:51-53 (EAST COUNTY/EL CAJON)
Daily Planet, The	F:32-35 (PACIFIC BEACH/MISSION BEACH)
Dini's	B:16-20 (DEL MAR/LEUCADIA)
Dobson's	H:40-44 (DOWNTOWN)
Dookies	J:51-53 (EAST COUNTY/EL CAJON)
Dooley McCluskey's	A:14-15 (OCEANSIDE/CARLSBAD)
Eggery, Etc., The	F:32-35 (PACIFIC BEACH/MISSION BEACH)
Flamingo's Bistro	H:40-44 (DOWNTOWN)
Frogg Lane Bar And Grill	H:40-44 (DOWNTOWN)
Galaxy Grill	H:40-44 (DOWNTOWN)
Gathering, The	I:46-50 (BALBOA PARK/OLD TOWN)
Gaucho Steak House, The	A:14-15 (OCEANSIDE/CARLSBAD)
Gellerosa Ranch Barbecue	H:40-44 (DOWNTOWN)
Gentleman's Choice, The	C:21-23 (INLAND NORTH COUNTY)
Golden Lion Tavern	H:40-44 (DOWNTOWN)
Good Egg, The	D:24-25 (CLAIREMONT/MIRAMAR)
Good Time Charlies	F:32-35 (PACIFIC BEACH/MISSION BEACH)
Gratzi	I:46-50 (BALBOA PARK/OLD TOWN)
Green Flash, The	F:32-35 (PACIFIC BEACH/MISSION BEACH)
Hard Rock Cafe	E:26-31 (LA JOLLA)
Harry's Cafe Gallery	E:26-31 (LA JOLLA)
Hennessey's Tavern & Pub	F:32-35 (PACIFIC BEACH/MISSION BEACH)
Hindquarter, The	D:24-25 (CLAIREMONT/MIRAMAR)
Hob Nob Hill	I:46-50 (BALBOA PARK/OLD TOWN)
Ida Bailey	H:40-44 (DOWNTOWN)
Improvision Comedy Club	F:32-35 (PACIFIC BEACH/MISSION BEACH)
Inn At Rancho Sante Fe	C:21-23 (INLAND NORTH COUNTY)
JR's	I:46-50 (BALBOA PARK/OLD TOWN)
Jake's Del Mar	B:16-20 (DEL MAR/LEUCADIA)
Jim's Hickory Wood Bar-B-Q	J:51-53 (EAST COUNTY/EL CAHON)
Julians	J:51-53 (EAST COUNTY/EL CAJON)
Kansas City Barbeque	H:40-44 (DOWNTOWN)
Kansas City Steakhouse	H:40-44 (DOWNTOWN)
Karl Strauss' Old Columbia Brewery	H:40-44 (DOWNTOWN)
Kelly's Steak House	I:46-50 (BALBOA PARK/OLD TOWN)
Kooky's Diner	D:24-25 (CLAIREMONT/MIRAMAR)
Kozak's	J:51-53 (EAST COUNTY/EL CAJON)
La Mont's Authentic Barbecue	B:16-20 (DEL MAR/LEUCADIA)
Las Cascadas	H:40-44 (DOWNTOWN)
Le Brasserie	A:14-15 (OCEANSIDE/CARLSBAD)
McDougal's	H:40-44 (DOWNTOWN)
Mercedes Room/Comedy Isle	F:32-35 (PACIFIC BEACH/MISSION BEACH)
Michael's Chicago Style Hot Dogs	C:21-23 (INLAND NORTH COUNTY)

CUSINE INDEX

CUISINE
Restaurant........................ Found in Pages (Dining Area)

Molly's	H:40-44 (DOWNTOWN)
Montana's American Grill	I:46-50 (BALBOA PARK/OLD TOWN)
Moose McGillycuddy's	F:32-35 (PACIFIC BEACH/MISSION BEACH)
Mystery Cafe	H:40-44 (DOWNTOWN)
Old Ocean Beach Cafe	G:36-38 (OCEAN BEACH/HARBOR ISLAND)
Old Ox	F:32-35 (PACIFIC BEACH/MISSION BEACH)
Old Pacific Beach Cafe	F:32-35 (PACIFIC BEACH/MISSION BEACH)
Other Place of Dale Anderson	E:26-31 (LA JOLLA)
Overlook Restaurant	H:40-44 (DOWNTOWN)
P. J. Wolf's	E:26-31 (LA JOLLA)
Pacifica Grill	H:40-44 (DOWNTOWN)
Packing House	C:21-23 (INLAND NORTH COUNTY)
Paradise Grill	B:16-20 (DEL MAR/LEUCADIA)
Pennant, The	F:32-35 (PACIFIC BEACH/MISSION BEACH)
Pepper's Cafe	H:40-44 (DOWNTOWN)
Pine Hills Lodge Julian	C:21-23 (INLAND NORTH COUNTY)
Putnam's	E:26-31 (LA JOLLA)
Quails Inn, The	C:21-23 (INLAND NORTH COUNTY)
Qwiig's Bar & Grill	G:36-38 (OCEAN BEACH/HARBOR ISLAND)
Raintree Grill & Bar	A:14-15 (OCEANSIDE/CARLSBAD)
Rainwater's Chop House	H:40-44 (DOWNTOWN)
Red Tracton's	B:16-20 (DEL MAR/LEUCADIA)
Remington's	B:16-20 (DEL MAR/LEUCADIA)
Renditions Restaurant	H:40-44 (DOWNTOWN)
Rory's	J:51-53 (EAST COUNTY/EL CAJON)
San Luis Rey Downs	C:21-23 (INLAND NORTH COUNTY)
Saska's	F:32-35 (PACIFIC BEACH/MISSION BEACH)
Schroder's	B:16-20 (DEL MAR/LEUCADIA)
Sheldon's Cafe	F:32-35 (PACIFIC BEACH/MISSION BEACH)
Spencer's	G:36-38 (OCEAN BEACH/HARBOR ISLAND)
Spice Rack	F:32-35 (PACIFIC BEACH/MISSION BEACH)
Spot, The	E:26-31 (LA JOLLA)
Stoneridge Country Club	C:21-23 (INLAND NORTH COUNTY)
Sunset Bar & Grill	G:36-38 (OCEAN BEACH/HARBOR ISLAND)
T-Bird Diner	C:21-23 (INLAND NORTH COUNTY)
T. D. Hays Restaurant	F:32-35 (PACIFIC BEACH/MISSION BEACH)
Terraces Cafe, The	C:21-23 (INLAND NORTH COUNTY)
Tony Roma's	F:32-35 (PACIFIC BEACH/MISSION BEACH)
Tony Roma's	J:51-53 (EAST COUNTY/EL CAJON)
Torrey Pines Inn	E:26-31 (LA JOLLA)
Torreyana Grille	E:26-31 (LA JOLLA)
Trents	C:21-23 (INLAND NORTH COUNTY)
Triple Crown	B:16-20 (DEL MAR/LEUCADIA)
Triton	B:16-20 (DEL MAR/LEUCADIA)
Valley Cafe	B:16-20 (DEL MAR/LEUCADIA)
Veranda, The	C:21-23 (INLAND NORTH COUNTY)
Vic's Restaurant	E:26-31 (LA JOLLA)
Whaling Bar/Cafe La Rue	E:26-31 (LA JOLLA)
Willy's American Bistro	I:46-50 (BALBOA PARK/OLD TOWN)
Yacht Club	H:40-44 (DOWNTOWN)

ARGENTINE

Tango Grill	H:40-44 (DOWNTOWN)

AUSTRALIAN

Sibyl's Down Under	H:40-44 (DOWNTOWN)

BASQUE

Chateau Basque	J:51-53 (EAST COUNTY/EL CAJON)

BELGIAN

Belgian Garden, The	I:46-50 (BALBOA PARK/OLD TOWN)
Belgian Lion	G:36-38 (OCEAN BEACH/HARBOR ISLAND)

CAJUN/CREOLE

Bayou Bar & Grill	H:40-44 (DOWNTOWN)
Chateau Orleans	F:32-35 (PACIFIC BEACH/MISSION BEACH)
Chez Orleans	C:21-23 (INLAND NORTH COUNTY)

CALIFORNIA

515 Fifth Avenue	H:40-44 (DOWNTOWN)
Atoll, The	F:32-35 (PACIFIC BEACH/MISSION BEACH)
Beach House, The	F:32-35 (PACIFIC BEACH/MISSION BEACH)
Cafe Champagne	C:21-23 (INLAND NORTH COUNTY)
Cafe Del Mar	B:16-20 (DEL MAR/LEUCADIA)
Cafe Del Rey Moro	I:46-50 (BALBOA PARK/OLD TOWN)
California Cafe	H:40-44 (DOWNTOWN)
California Cuisine	I:46-50 (BALBOA PARK/OLD TOWN)
Canes	I:46-50 (BALBOA PARK/OLD TOWN)
Chez Beat & Rolf	F:32-35 (PACIFIC BEACH/MISSION BEACH)
Falco	H:40-44 (DOWNTOWN)
George's at the Cove	E:26-31 (LA JOLLA)
Homeport Cafe	H:40-44 (DOWNTOWN)
La Boheme	I:46-50 (BALBOA PARK/OLD TOWN)
Lamont Street Grill	F:32-35 (PACIFIC BEACH/MISSION BEACH)
Malcolm's First Avenue	H:40-44 (DOWNTOWN)
Neimans Cafe	A:14-15 (OCEANSIDE/CARLSBAD)
Piret M Bistro/Gallery	B:16-20 (DEL MAR/LEUCADIA)

CUSINE INDEX

CUISINE
Restaurant .... Found in Pages (Dining Area)

Piret's .... E:26-31 (LA JOLLA)
Sammy's California Woodfired Pizza E:26-31 (LA JOLLA)
Tambo D'oro .... H:40-44 (DOWNTOWN)
Taryn's at The Track .... B:16-20 (DEL MAR/LEUCADIA)
Valle Rose Restaurant .... B:16-20 (DEL MAR/LEUCADIA)
Vincent/Four Seasons .... B:16-20 (DEL MAR/LEUCADIA)
Zodiac Restaurant, The .... I:46-50 (BALBOA PARK/OLD TOWN)

CAMBODIAN
Ly's Garden #1 .... I:46-50 (BALBOA PARK/OLD TOWN)

CHINESE
Chang, Cuisine of China .... J:51-53 (EAST COUNTY/EL CAJON)
China Camp .... H:40-44 (DOWNTOWN)
China Inn .... F:32-35 (PACIFIC BEACH/MISSION BEACH)
China Land Restaurant .... G:36-38 (OCEAN BEACH/HARBOR ISLAND)
Chu Dynasty .... I:46-50 (BALBOA PARK/OLD TOWN)
Chu Dynasty .... K:54-56 (CORONADO/SOUTH BAY)
Chung King Loh .... B:16-20 (DEL MAR/LEUCADIA)
Double Happiness .... B:16-20 (DEL MAR/LEUCADIA)
Fung Lin .... I:46-50 (BALBOA PARK/OLD TOWN)
George E. Wong .... E:26-31 (LA JOLLA)
Imperial Mandarin .... D:24-25 (CLAIREMONT/MIRAMAR)
Mandarin China .... G:36-38 (OCEAN BEACH/HARBOR ISLAND)
Mandarin Cove .... E:26-31 (LA JOLLA)
Mandarin Garden .... D:24-25 (CLAIREMONT/MIRAMAR)
Mandarin House .... E:26-31 (LA JOLLA)
Mandarin House .... I:46-50 (BALBOA PARK/OLD TOWN)
Miss China Restaurant .... E:26-31 (LA JOLLA)
North China .... G:36-38 (OCEAN BEACH/HARBOR ISLAND)
Panda Inn .... H:40-44 (DOWNTOWN)
Panda Inn .... J:51-53 (EAST COUNTY/EL CAJON)
Pei's of La Jolla .... E:26-31 (LA JOLLA)
Peking Palace .... E:26-31 (LA JOLLA)
Peking Wok .... C:21-23 (INLAND NORTH COUNTY)
Peter Chang's .... B:16-20 (DEL MAR/LEUCADIA)
Sau-Hy's Chinese Cuisine .... C:21-23 (INLAND NORTH COUNTY)
Shanghai Restaurant .... F:32-35 (PACIFIC BEACH/MISSION BEACH)
Shanghai Restaurant .... J:51-53 (EAST COUNTY/EL CAJON)
Szechuan .... F:32-35 (PACIFIC BEACH/MISSION BEACH)
Szechuan House .... E:26-31 (LA JOLLA)
Wei's Potsticker .... D:24-25 (CLAIREMONT/MIRAMAR)
Yet Wah Restaurant .... G:36-38 (OCEAN BEACH/HARBOR ISLAND)

CONTINENTAL
Abbey, The .... I:46-50 (BALBOA PARK/OLD TOWN)
Cafe Bon Appetit .... H:40-44 (DOWNTOWN)
Cambridge Inn, The .... C:21-23 (INLAND NORTH COUNTY)
Champagne Room, The .... A:14-15 (OCEANSIDE/CARLSBAD)
Chez Loma .... K:54-56 (CORONADO/SOUTH BAY)
Crown-Coronet Room .... K:54-56 (CORONADO/SOUTH BAY)
El Bizcocho .... C:21-23 (INLAND NORTH COUNTY)
Emil's .... I:46-50 (BALBOA PARK/OLD TOWN)
Frederick's .... B:16-20 (DEL MAR/LEUCADIA)
Frenchy Marseilles .... H:40-44 (DOWNTOWN)
Gourmet Room .... I:46-50 (BALBOA PARK/OLD TOWN)
Grant Grill & Lounge, The .... H:40-44 (DOWNTOWN)
Imperial House .... H:40-44 (DOWNTOWN)
Ironwoods, The .... I:46-50 (BALBOA PARK/OLD TOWN)
Jorg's Gourmet Cuisine .... J:51-53 (EAST COUNTY/EL CAJON)
La Tapenade .... B:16-20 (DEL MAR/LEUCADIA)
Le Bistro .... C:21-23 (INLAND NORTH COUNTY)
Le Corbier .... E:26-31 (LA JOLLA)
Lubach's .... H:40-44 (DOWNTOWN)
Mediterranean Room .... E:26-31 (LA JOLLA)
Mister A's .... I:46-50 (BALBOA PARK/OLD TOWN)
Mr. D's .... J:51-53 (EAST COUNTY/EL CAJON)
Orchids .... E:26-31 (LA JOLLA)
Palm Grill, The .... G:36-38 (OCEAN BEACH/HARBOR ISLAND)
Prince of Wales Room .... K:54-56 (CORONADO/SOUTH BAY)
Sculpture Garden Cafe .... I:46-50 (BALBOA PARK/OLD TOWN)
Sky Room .... E:26-31 (LA JOLLA)
Thee Bungalow .... G:36-38 (OCEAN BEACH/HARBOR ISLAND)
Top O' The Cove .... E:26-31 (LA JOLLA)
Tradewinds .... F:32-35 (PACIFIC BEACH/MISSION BEACH)
Tropical Patio, The .... E:26-31 (LA JOLLA)
Villa Carmel .... B:16-20 (DEL MAR/LEUCADIA)
Westgate Dining Room .... H:40-44 (DOWNTOWN)

CUBAN
Andres Cuban Restaurant ...... F:32-35 (PACIFIC BEACH/MISSION BEACH)

DELI
City Deli .... I:46-50 (BALBOA PARK/OLD TOWN)
Deer Park Winery .... C:21-23 (INLAND NORTH COUNTY)
Samsons Deli Restaurant .... H:40-44 (DOWNTOWN)
Samsons Deli-Restaurant ...... E:26-31 (LA JOLLA)

CUSINE INDEX

CUISINE
Restaurant .... Found in Pages (Dining Area)

DIET CUISINE
Spa Dining Room, The .... A:14-15 (OCEANSIDE/CARLSBAD)

ECLECTIC
Carlos & Annie's Cafe .... B:16-20 (DEL MAR/LEUCADIA)
El Crab Catcher .... E:26-31 (LA JOLLA)
Fat City .... H:40-44 (DOWNTOWN)
Grill on The Park .... H:40-44 (DOWNTOWN)
Jose Wong's .... A:14-15 (OCEANSIDE/CARLSBAD)
Kirby's Cafe & Bistro .... B:16-20 (DEL MAR/LEUCADIA)
Nancaro's Elephant Bar & Rest. ... E:26-31 (LA JOLLA)
St. Germain's Cafe .... B:16-20 (DEL MAR/LEUCADIA)
T. G. I. Friday's .... E:26-31 (LA JOLLA)
T. G. I. Friday's .... I:46-50 (BALBOA PARK/OLD TOWN)

ENGLISH
King's Grille .... I:46-50 (BALBOA PARK/OLD TOWN)
Piccadilly Line, The .... I:46-50 (BALBOA PARK/OLD TOWN)

ETHIOPIAN
Blue Nile .... J:51-53 (EAST COUNTY/EL CAJON)
Ethiopia .... F:32-35 (PACIFIC BEACH/MISSION BEACH)

FOOD-TO-GO
Asaggio Pizza, Pasta, Plus .... H:40-44 (DOWNTOWN)
El Indio .... I:46-50 (BALBOA PARK/OLD TOWN)
Pollo La Jolla .... E:26-31 (LA JOLLA)
Rubio's Deli-Mex .... C:21-23 (INLAND NORTH COUNTY)
Rubio's Deli-Mex .... F:32-35 (PACIFIC BEACH/MISSION BEACH)
Rubio's Deli-Mex .... J:51-53 (EAST COUNTY/EL CAJON)
Rubio's Deli-Mex .... K:54-56 (CORONADO/SOUTH BAY)
Sluggo's .... E:26-31 (LA JOLLA)

FRENCH
A La Francaise .... G:36-38 (OCEAN BEACH/HARBOR ISLAND)
Bistro Gardens, The .... B:16-20 (DEL MAR/LEUCADIA)
Cafe De Paris .... I:46-50 (BALBOA PARK/OLD TOWN)
Cafe Eleven .... I:46-50 (BALBOA PARK/OLD TOWN)
Cafe Toulouse .... F:32-35 (PACIFIC BEACH/MISSION BEACH)
Cindy Black .... E:26-31 (LA JOLLA)
Elario's .... E:26-31 (LA JOLLA)
Fontainebleau Restaurant .... H:40-44 (DOWNTOWN)
French Cafe .... D:24-25 (CLAIREMONT/MIRAMAR)
French Gourmet .... F:32-35 (PACIFIC BEACH/MISSION BEACH)
French Gourmet Too, The .... E:26-31 (LA JOLLA)
French Pastry Shop, The .... E:26-31 (LA JOLLA)
French Side of The West, The .. I:46-50 (BALBOA PARK/OLD TOWN)
L'Auberge .... E:26-31 (LA JOLLA)
L'Escale .... K:54-56 (CORONADO/SOUTH BAY)
La Bonne Bouffe .... B:16-20 (DEL MAR/LEUCADIA)
La Terrace .... E:26-31 (LA JOLLA)
Le Pavillon .... I:46-50 (BALBOA PARK/OLD TOWN)
Magic Pan .... E:26-31 (LA JOLLA)
Maitre D' .... E:26-31 (LA JOLLA)
Marius .... K:54-56 (CORONADO/SOUTH BAY)
Mille Fleurs .... C:21-23 (INLAND NORTH COUNTY)
Mirabelle .... A:14-15 (OCEANSIDE/CARLSBAD)
Palmier Bistro .... I:46-50 (BALBOA PARK/OLD TOWN)
Seafare .... C:21-23 (INLAND NORTH COUNTY)
St. James Bar .... E:26-31 (LA JOLLA)
Twelve Stars European Cafe .. I:46-50 (BALBOA PARK/OLD TOWN)
Upstairs Cafe at the Cove .... E:26-31 (LA JOLLA)
Village Cafe Francais, The .... B:16-20 (DEL MAR/LEUCADIA)
Winesellar & Brasserie .... D:24-25 (CLAIREMONT/MIRAMAR)

GERMAN
House of Munich .... K:54-56 (CORONADO/SOUTH BAY)
Kaiserhof .... J:51-53 (EAST COUNTY/EL CAJON)

GREEK
Aesop's Tables .... E:26-31 (LA JOLLA)
Athenian Gardens .... I:46-50 (BALBOA PARK/OLD TOWN)
Athens Market .... H:40-44 (DOWNTOWN)
Calliope's .... I:46-50 (BALBOA PARK/OLD TOWN)
Georgia's Greek Cuisine .... I:46-50 (BALBOA PARK/OLD TOWN)
Greek Town Restaurant .... H:40-44 (DOWNTOWN)
Jerry G. Bishop's .... H:40-44 (DOWNTOWN)

INDIAN
Ashoka .... E:26-31 (LA JOLLA)
Desmond's Cuisine Of India .... E:26-31 (LA JOLLA)
Star of India .... B:16-20 (DEL MAR/LEUCADIA)
Star of India .... E:26-31 (LA JOLLA)

INTERNAT'L
Cafe San Diego .... H:40-44 (DOWNTOWN)
Croce's .... H:40-44 (DOWNTOWN)

CUSINE INDEX

CUISINE
Restaurant........................ Found in Pages (Dining Area)

Esperanto	F:32-35 (PACIFIC BEACH/MISSION BEACH)
Henry's	A:14-15 (OCEANSIDE/CARLSBAD)
La Estancia Inn	C:21-23 (INLAND NORTH COUNTY)

IRISH

Blarney Stone Pub	H:40-44 (DOWNTOWN)
Callahan's Pub & Brewery	D:24-25 (CLAIREMONT/MIRAMAR)
Reidy O'Neil's	H:40-44 (DOWNTOWN)

ITALIAN

Avanti	E:26-31 (LA JOLLA)
Baci	F:32-35 (PACIFIC BEACH/MISSION BEACH)
Bonacci's Pizza & Pasta	I:46-50 (BALBOA PARK/OLD TOWN)
Borrelli's	B:16-20 (DEL MAR/LEUCADIA)
Bruno's	C:21-23 (INLAND NORTH COUNTY)
Busalacchi's Ristorante	I:46-50 (BALBOA PARK/OLD TOWN)
Cafe Roma	E:26-31 (LA JOLLA)
Chicago Brothers	F:32-35 (PACIFIC BEACH/MISSION BEACH)
Delmario's	B:16-20 (DEL MAR/LEUCADIA)
Falcone's	E:26-31 (LA JOLLA)
Figaro	I:46-50 (BALBOA PARK/OLD TOWN)
Filippi's Pizza Grotto	F:32-35 (PACIFIC BEACH/MISSION BEACH)
Filippi's Pizza Grotto	H:40-44 (DOWNTOWN)
Fio's	H:40-44 (DOWNTOWN)
Godfather, The	D:24-25 (CLAIREMONT/MIRAMAR)
Grazie E Prego	A:14-15 (OCEANSIDE/CARLSBAD)
Il Fornaio Cucina Italiana	B:16-20 (DEL MAR/LEUCADIA)
Issimo	E:26-31 (LA JOLLA)
John Tarantino's	G:36-38 (OCEAN BEACH/HARBOR ISLAND)
La Dolce Vita	B:16-20 (DEL MAR/LEUCADIA)
Lido's Italian Foods	J:51-53 (EAST COUNTY/EL CAJON)
Lino's Italian Restaurant	I:46-50 (BALBOA PARK/OLD TOWN)
Little Italy Pizza	G:36-38 (OCEAN BEACH/HARBOR ISLAND)
Little Italy Pizza	J:51-53 (EAST COUNTY/EL CAJON)
Little Joe's	H:40-44 (DOWNTOWN)
Luigi's	F:32-35 (PACIFIC BEACH/MISSION BEACH)
Manhattan	E:26-31 (LA JOLLA)
Merlano's	G:36-38 (OCEAN BEACH/HARBOR ISLAND)
Michelangelo Ristorante Italiano	G:36-38 (OCEAN BEACH/HARBOR ISLAND)
Nicolosi's	J:51-53 (EAST COUNTY/EL CAJON)
Old Trieste	F:32-35 (PACIFIC BEACH/MISSION BEACH)
Old Venice	G:36-38 (OCEAN BEACH/HARBOR ISLAND)
Olive Garden, The	A:14-15 (OCEANSIDE/CARLSBAD)
Papachinos	B:16-20 (DEL MAR/LEUCADIA)
Papachinos	E:26-31 (LA JOLLA)
Paparazzi	E:26-31 (LA JOLLA)
Pizza Nova	G:36-38 (OCEAN BEACH/HARBOR ISLAND)
Pizzeria Uno	F:32-35 (PACIFIC BEACH/MISSION BEACH)
Portofino	B:16-20 (DEL MAR/LEUCADIA)
Presto	E:26-31 (LA JOLLA)
Primavera	K:54-56 (CORONADO/SOUTH BAY)
Ricci's Ristorante Italiano	F:32-35 (PACIFIC BEACH/MISSION BEACH)
Ristorante Figaro	A:14-15 (OCEANSIDE/CARLSBAD)
Ristorante Galileo	C:21-23 (INLAND NORTH COUNTY)
Ristorante Pasta Al Dente	I:46-50 (BALBOA PARK/OLD TOWN)
Romano's Dodge House	C:21-23 (INLAND NORTH COUNTY)
Salvatore's Cucina Italiana	H:40-44 (DOWNTOWN)
Sante	E:26-31 (LA JOLLA)
Scalini	B:16-20 (DEL MAR/LEUCADIA)
Sorrentino's	F:32-35 (PACIFIC BEACH/MISSION BEACH)
Stephen Zolezzi's Stefano's	I:46-50 (BALBOA PARK/OLD TOWN)
Tep's Villa Roma	F:32-35 (PACIFIC BEACH/MISSION BEACH)
Valentino's	C:21-23 (INLAND NORTH COUNTY)
Villa D'este	B:16-20 (DEL MAR/LEUCADIA)
Villanis	I:46-50 (BALBOA PARK/OLD TOWN)
When In Rome	B:16-20 (DEL MAR/LEUCADIA)
Woodstock's Pizza	J:51-53 (EAST COUNTY/EL CAJON)

JAPANESE

Benihana of Tokyo	I:46-50 (BALBOA PARK/OLD TOWN)
Cafe Japengo	E:26-31 (LA JOLLA)
California Club Sushi Bar	J:51-53 (EAST COUNTY/EL CAJON)
Katsu Seafood & Steak House	C:21-23 (INLAND NORTH COUNTY)
Katzra	D:24-25 (CLAIREMONT/MIRAMAR)
Koto	K:54-56 (CORONADO/SOUTH BAY)
Mr. Noodle	D:24-25 (CLAIREMONT/MIRAMAR)
Mr. Sushi	F:32-35 (PACIFIC BEACH/MISSION BEACH)
Nobu Gourmet Japanese Rest.	B:16-20 (DEL MAR/LEUCADIA)
Restaurant Yae	C:21-23 (INLAND NORTH COUNTY)
Sakura-Bana	B:16-20 (DEL MAR/LEUCADIA)
Samurai Japanese Restaurant	B:16-20 (DEL MAR/LEUCADIA)
Shien Of Osaka	C:21-23 (INLAND NORTH COUNTY)
Shogun	E:26-31 (LA JOLLA)
Sushi Bar Nippon	H:40-44 (DOWNTOWN)
Sushi On The Rocks	E:26-31 (LA JOLLA)
Tengu	D:24-25 (CLAIREMONT/MIRAMAR)
Yakitori II	G:36-38 (OCEAN BEACH/HARBOR ISLAND)
Yoshino Japanese Restaurant	I:46-50 (BALBOA PARK/OLD TOWN)
Yumi	I:46-50 (BALBOA PARK/OLD TOWN)

CUSINE INDEX

CUISINE
Restaurant.......................... Found in Pages (Dining Area)

KOREAN

Korea House	D:24-25 (CLAIREMONT/MIRAMAR)

MEDITERRANEAN

Barcino	E:26-31 (LA JOLLA)

MEXICAN

Alfonso's	E:26-31 (LA JOLLA)
Alfonso's	H:40-44 (DOWNTOWN)
Alta Vista Mexican Restaurant	I:46-50 (BALBOA PARK/OLD TOWN)
Aztec	I:46-50 (BALBOA PARK/OLD TOWN)
Blue Bird Cafe	B:16-20 (DEL MAR/LEUCADIA)
Cabo Cabo Grill	H:40-44 (DOWNTOWN)
Cafe Ole	K:54-56 (CORONADO/SOUTH BAY)
Casa De Bandini	I:46-50 (BALBOA PARK/OLD TOWN)
Casa De Pico	I:46-50 (BALBOA PARK/OLD TOWN)
Casa Machado	D:24-25 (CLAIREMONT/MIRAMAR)
Casa Martinez	K:54-56 (CORONADO/SOUTH BAY)
Casa Salsa	K:54-56 (CORONADO/SOUTH BAY)
Chuey's Cafe	K:54-56 (CORONADO/SOUTH BAY)
Coyote Bar & Grill	A:14-15 (OCEANSIDE/CARLSBAD)
Crazy Burro	A:14-15 (OCEANSIDE/CARLSBAD)
Diego's Cafe Y Cantina	F:32-35 (PACIFIC BEACH/MISSION BEACH)
El Establo	C:21-23 (INLAND NORTH COUNTY)
El Tecolote	I:46-50 (BALBOA PARK/OLD TOWN)
Epazotes	B:16-20 (DEL MAR/LEUCADIA)
Fidel's	A:14-15 (OCEANSIDE/CARLSBAD)
Fidel's Little Mexico	B:16-20 (DEL MAR/LEUCADIA)
Garcia's	G:36-38 (OCEAN BEACH/HARBOR ISLAND)
Guadalajara Grill	I:46-50 (BALBOA PARK/OLD TOWN)
Hamburguesa	I:46-50 (BALBOA PARK/OLD TOWN)
Jose's Court Room	E:26-31 (LA JOLLA)
La Fonda Roberto's	K:54-56 (CORONADO/SOUTH BAY)
La Hacienda	I:46-50 (BALBOA PARK/OLD TOWN)
La Pinata	I:46-50 (BALBOA PARK/OLD TOWN)
La Playa Grill	E:26-31 (LA JOLLA)
La Salsa	K:54-56 (CORONADO/SOUTH BAY)
Mexican Village	K:54-56 (CORONADO/SOUTH BAY)
Miguel's Cocina	G:36-38 (OCEAN BEACH/HARBOR ISLAND)
Miguel's Cocina	K:54-56 (CORONADO/SOUTH BAY)
Nati's Mexican Restaurant	G:36-38 (OCEAN BEACH/HARBOR ISLAND)
Newport Annie's	F:32-35 (PACIFIC BEACH/MISSION BEACH)
Old Town Mexican Cafe	I:46-50 (BALBOA PARK/OLD TOWN)
Palenque	F:32-35 (PACIFIC BEACH/MISSION BEACH)
Red Onion, The	F:32-35 (PACIFIC BEACH/MISSION BEACH)
Rock Lobster	J:51-53 (EAST COUNTY/EL CAJON)
Senor Frog's	J:51-53 (EAST COUNTY/EL CAJON)
Su Casa	E:26-31 (LA JOLLA)
Taco Auctioneer	B:16-20 (DEL MAR/LEUCADIA)
Tony's Jacal	B:16-20 (DEL MAR/LEUCADIA)

MIDDLE EAST

Fairouz Cafe	G:36-38 (OCEAN BEACH/HARBOR ISLAND)
Sheik Cafe	I:46-50 (BALBOA PARK/OLD TOWN)

MOROCCAN

Marrakesh	J:51-53 (EAST COUNTY/EL CAJON)

NATURAL FOOD

Drowsy Maggie's	I:46-50 (BALBOA PARK/OLD TOWN)

PERUVIAN

El Chalan	F:32-35 (PACIFIC BEACH/MISSION BEACH)

POLISH

Stella's Hideaway	C:21-23 (INLAND NORTH COUNTY)

POLYNESIAN

Bali Hai	G:36-38 (OCEAN BEACH/HARBOR ISLAND)
Islands Restaurant, The	I:46-50 (BALBOA PARK/OLD TOWN)
Pacific Princess	F:32-35 (PACIFIC BEACH/MISSION BEACH)

SCANDINAVIAN

Dansk Restaurant	J:51-53 (EAST COUNTY/EL CAHON)

SEAFOOD

19th Buoy, The	G:36-38 (OCEAN BEACH/HARBOR ISLAND)
Aloha Louie's	E:26-31 (LA JOLLA)
Anthony's Fish Grotto	H:40-44 (DOWNTOWN)
Anthony's Fish Grotto	J:51-53 (EAST COUNTY/EL CAJON)
Anthony's Fish Grotto	K:54-56 (CORONADO/SOUTH BAY)
Anthony's Harborside	H:40-44 (DOWNTOWN)
Anthony's II	C:21-23 (INLAND NORTH COUNTY)
Anthony's La Jolla	E:26-31 (LA JOLLA)
Anthony's Star Of The Sea	H:40-44 (DOWNTOWN)
Baja Grill & Fish Market	B:16-20 (DEL MAR/LEUCADIA)
Barnacle Bill's	G:36-38 (OCEAN BEACH/HARBOR ISLAND)
Barrett Cafe	J:51-53 (EAST COUNTY/EL CAJON)
Basil St. Cafe	B:16-20 (DEL MAR/LEUCADIA)

CUSINE INDEX

CUISINE
Restaurant........................ Found in Pages (Dining Area)

SEAFOOD (Con't)

Restaurant	Pages (Dining Area)
Blue Crab Restaurant	G:36-38 (OCEAN BEACH/HARBOR ISLAND)
Boathouse, The	B:16-20 (DEL MAR/LEUCADIA)
Boathouse, The	F:32-35 (PACIFIC BEACH/MISSION BEACH)
Boathouse, The	G:36-38 (OCEAN BEACH/HARBOR ISLAND)
Brigantine, The	B:16-20 (DEL MAR/LEUCADIA)
Brigantine, The	C:21-23 (INLAND NORTH COUNTY)
Brigantine, The	G:36-38 (OCEAN BEACH/HARBOR ISLAND)
Brigantine, The	I:46-50 (BALBOA PARK/OLD TOWN)
Brigantine, The	J:51-53 (EAST COUNTY/EL CAJON)
Brigantine, The	K:54-56 (CORONADO/SOUTH BAY)
Cafe Pacifica	I:46-50 (BALBOA PARK/OLD TOWN)
Cecil's Cafe & Fish Market	G:36-38 (OCEAN BEACH/HARBOR ISLAND)
Charlie's	B:16-20 (DEL MAR/LEUCADIA)
D. B. Hacker's	B:16-20 (DEL MAR/LEUCADIA)
Dini's-by-the-sea	A:14-15 (OCEANSIDE/CARLSBAD)
Dockside Broiler	F:32-35 (PACIFIC BEACH/MISSION BEACH)
Fifth & Hawthorn	H:40-44 (DOWNTOWN)
Fish House Vera Cruz	C:21-23 (INLAND NORTH COUNTY)
Fish House West	B:16-20 (DEL MAR/LEUCADIA)
Fish Market, The	B:16-20 (DEL MAR/LEUCADIA)
Fish Market, The	H:40-44 (DOWNTOWN)
Fisherman's Grill	E:26-31 (LA JOLLA)
Harbor House	H:40-44 (DOWNTOWN)
Harbor House's Top of the Plaza	H:40-44 (DOWNTOWN)
Humphrey's	G:36-38 (OCEAN BEACH/HARBOR ISLAND)
Humphrey's La Jolla Grill	E:26-31 (LA JOLLA)
Islandia Bar & Grill, The	F:32-35 (PACIFIC BEACH/MISSION BEACH)
Jake's South Bay	K:54-56 (CORONADO/SOUTH BAY)
Marina Sea Grill	H:40-44 (DOWNTOWN)
Marine Room	E:26-31 (LA JOLLA)
McCormick & Schmick's	F:32-35 (PACIFIC BEACH/MISSION BEACH)
Monterey Whaling Company	I:46-50 (BALBOA PARK/OLD TOWN)
Mug-n-Mallet Restaurant-n-bar	G:36-38 (OCEAN BEACH/HARBOR ISLAND)
Neimans Sea Grill	A:14-15 (OCEANSIDE/CARLSBAD)
Pacifica Del Mar	B:16-20 (DEL MAR/LEUCADIA)
Papagayo	H:40-44 (DOWNTOWN)
Paradise Bay	F:32-35 (PACIFIC BEACH/MISSION BEACH)
Peohe's, The Landing	K:54-56 (CORONADO/SOUTH BAY)
Pisces	A:14-15 (OCEANSIDE/CARLSBAD)
Point Loma Seafoods	G:36-38 (OCEAN BEACH/HARBOR ISLAND)
Poseidon	B:16-20 (DEL MAR/LEUCADIA)
Rancho Vera Cruz	C:21-23 (INLAND NORTH COUNTY)
Red Ox	J:51-53 (EAST COUNTY/EL CAJON)
Red Sails Inn	G:36-38 (OCEAN BEACH/HARBOR ISLAND)
Reuben E. Lee	G:36-38 (OCEAN BEACH/HARBOR ISLAND)
Reuben's	H:40-44 (DOWNTOWN)
Rusty Pelican	E:26-31 (LA JOLLA)
Rusty Pelican	I:46-50 (BALBOA PARK/OLD TOWN)
Salmon House	F:32-35 (PACIFIC BEACH/MISSION BEACH)
San Diego Pier Cafe	H:40-44 (DOWNTOWN)
Shores at the Sea Lodge, The	E:26-31 (LA JOLLA)
Tickled Trout, The	I:46-50 (BALBOA PARK/OLD TOWN)
Tom Ham's Lighthouse	G:36-38 (OCEAN BEACH/HARBOR ISLAND)

SOUTHWEST

Restaurant	Pages (Dining Area)
Adobe Rose	K:54-56 (CORONADO/SOUTH BAY)
Cafe Coyote	I:46-50 (BALBOA PARK/OLD TOWN)
Cilantro's	B:16-20 (DEL MAR/LEUCADIA)
Kiva Grill	E:26-31 (LA JOLLA)
Restaurant Festival	H:40-44 (DOWNTOWN)

SPANISH

Restaurant	Pages (Dining Area)
Cafe' Sevilla	H:40-44 (DOWNTOWN)
La Gran Tapa	H:40-44 (DOWNTOWN)
Tablao Flamenco	F:32-35 (PACIFIC BEACH/MISSION BEACH)

SWEDISH

Restaurant	Pages (Dining Area)
Nordic Inn	G:36-38 (OCEAN BEACH/HARBOR ISLAND)

THAI

Restaurant	Pages (Dining Area)
Bangkok Thai Cuisine	F:32-35 (PACIFIC BEACH/MISSION BEACH)
Celadon	I:46-50 (BALBOA PARK/OLD TOWN)
Five Star Thai Cuisine	H:40-44 (DOWNTOWN)
Karinya Thai Cuisine	F:32-35 (PACIFIC BEACH/MISSION BEACH)
Lemon Grass	E:26-31 (LA JOLLA)
Saffron	I:46-50 (BALBOA PARK/OLD TOWN)
Taste of Thai	I:46-50 (BALBOA PARK/OLD TOWN)
Tawana Siamese Cuisine	D:24-25 (CLAIREMONT/MIRAMAR)
Thai Chada	I:46-50 (BALBOA PARK/OLD TOWN)

VEGETARIAN

Restaurant	Pages (Dining Area)
Cornucopia	I:46-50 (BALBOA PARK/OLD TOWN)
Kung Food	I:46-50 (BALBOA PARK/OLD TOWN)

VIETNAMESE

Restaurant	Pages (Dining Area)
A-Dong	J:51-53 (EAST COUNTY/EL CAJON)
Le Bambou	B:16-20 (DEL MAR/LEUCADIA)
Pho Pasteur	D:24-25 (CLAIREMONT/MIRAMAR)
Phoung Nam	I:46-50 (BALBOA PARK/OLD TOWN)

ALPHABETIC INDEX

This index is provided to help you locate the information for a restaurant whose name you know. After you find the name, just turn to the Dining Area pages and look for the restaurant in its Cuisine category section.

Restaurant................. Dining Area: Pages (Cuisine Category)

Restaurant	Dining Area: Pages (Cuisine Category)
101 Diner, The	B:16-20 (AMERICAN)
19th Buoy, The	G:36-38 (SEAFOOD)
515 Fifth Avenue	H:40-44 (CALIFORNIA)

--- A ---

Restaurant	Dining Area: Pages (Cuisine Category)
A La Francaise	G:36-38 (FRENCH)
A-Dong	J:51-53 (VIETNAMESE)
Abbey, The	I:46-50 (CONTINENTAL)
Adam 'n' Albie's Beef Inn	I:46-50 (AMERICAN)
Adobe Rose	K:54-56 (SOUTHWEST)
Aesop's Tables	E:26-31 (GREEK)
Alfonso's	E:26-31 (MEXICAN)
Alfonso's	H:40-44 (MEXICAN)
Alley Oops	F:32-35 (AMERICAN)
Aloha Louie's	E:26-31 (SEAFOOD)
Alpine Inn	J:51-53 (AMERICAN)
Alta Vista	I:46-50 (MEXICAN)
Andres Cuban Restaurant	F:32-35 (CUBAN)
Anthony's Fish Grotto	H:40-44 (SEAFOOD)
Anthony's Fish Grotto	J:51-53 (SEAFOOD)
Anthony's Fish Grotto	K:54-56 (SEAFOOD)
Anthony's Harborside	H:40-44 (SEAFOOD)
Anthony's II	C:21-23 (SEAFOOD)
Anthony's La Jolla	E:26-31 (SEAFOOD)
Anthony's Star Of The Sea	H:40-44 (SEAFOOD)
Asaggio Pizza, Pasta, Plus	H:40-44 (FOOD-TO-GO)
Ashoka	E:26-31 (INDIAN)
Athenian Gardens	I:46-50 (GREEK)
Athens Market	H:40-44 (GREEK)
Atoll, The	F:32-35 (CALIFORNIA)
Avanti	E:26-31 (ITALIAN)
Aztec	I:46-50 (MEXICAN)

--- B ---

Restaurant	Dining Area: Pages (Cuisine Category)
B Street Cafe	H:40-44 (AMERICAN)
Baci	F:32-35 (ITALIAN)
Baja Grill & Fish Market	B:16-20 (SEAFOOD)
Bali Hai	G:36-38 (POLYNESIAN)
Bangkok Thai Cuisine	F:32-35 (THAI)
Barcino	E:26-31 (MEDITERRANEAN)
Barnacle Bill's	G:36-38 (SEAFOOD)
Barnett's Grand Cafe	H:40-44 (AMERICAN)
Barrett Cafe	J:51-53 (SEAFOOD)
Barry's Cafe	H:40-44 (AMERICAN)
Basil St. Cafe	B:16-20 (SEAFOOD)
Bayou Bar & Grill	H:40-44 (CAJUN/CREOLE)
Beach House, The	F:32-35 (CALIFORNIA)
Belgian Garden, The	I:46-50 (BELGIAN)
Belgian Lion	G:36-38 (BELGIAN)
Benihana of Tokyo	I:46-50 (JAPANESE)
Bennigan's	I:46-50 (AMERICAN)
Bistro Gardens, The	B:16-20 (FRENCH)
Blarney Stone Pub	H:40-44 (IRISH)
Blue Bird Cafe	B:16-20 (MEXICAN)
Blue Crab Restaurant	G:36-38 (SEAFOOD)
Blue Nile	J:51-53 (ETHIOPIAN)
Boathouse, The	B:16-20 (SEAFOOD)
Boathouse, The	F:32-35 (SEAFOOD)
Boathouse, The	G:36-38 (SEAFOOD)
Bobby J's	B:16-20 (AMERICAN)
Bobby McGee's	J:51-53 (AMERICAN)
Boll Weevil	E:26-31 (AMERICAN)
Bonacci's Pizza & Pasta	I:46-50 (ITALIAN)
Bonita Store Restaurant	K:54-56 (AMERICAN)
Boondocks, The	J:51-53 (AMERICAN)
Borrelli's	B:16-20 (ITALIAN)
Bread Basket, The	J:51-53 (AMERICAN)
Brigantine, The	B:16-20 (SEAFOOD)
Brigantine, The	C:21-23 (SEAFOOD)
Brigantine, The	G:36-38 (SEAFOOD)
Brigantine, The	I:46-50 (SEAFOOD)
Brigantine, The	J:51-53 (SEAFOOD)
Brigantine, The	K:54-56 (SEAFOOD)
Bruno's	C:21-23 (ITALIAN)
Bull And Bear	J:51-53 (AMERICAN)
Bully's	B:16-20 (AMERICAN)
Bully's	E:26-31 (AMERICAN)
Bully's East	I:46-50 (AMERICAN)
Busalacchi's Ristorante	I:46-50 (ITALIAN)
Butcher Shop	D:24-25 (AMERICAN)
Butcher Shop	K:54-56 (AMERICAN)

ALPHABETIC INDEX

Restaurant................. Dining Area: Pages (Cuisine Category)

--- C ---

Restaurant	Dining Area: Pages (Cuisine Category)
Cabo Cabo Grill	H:40-44 (MEXICAN)
Cafe 6th & K	H:40-44 (AMERICAN)
Cafe Bon Appetit	H:40-44 (CONTINENTAL)
Cafe Broken Yolk	F:32-35 (AMERICAN)
Cafe Champagne	C:21-23 (CALIFORNIA)
Cafe Coyote	I:46-50 (SOUTHWEST)
Cafe De Paris	I:46-50 (FRENCH)
Cafe Del Mar	B:16-20 (CALIFORNIA)
Cafe Del Rey Moro	I:46-50 (CALIFORNIA)
Cafe Eleven	I:46-50 (FRENCH)
Cafe Japengo	E:26-31 (JAPANESE)
Cafe La Maze	K:54-56 (AMERICAN)
Cafe Ole	K:54-56 (MEXICAN)
Cafe Pacifica	I:46-50 (SEAFOOD)
Cafe Roma	E:26-31 (ITALIAN)
Cafe San Diego	H:40-44 (INTERNAT'L)
Cafe Toulouse	F:32-35 (FRENCH)
Cafe' Sevilla	H:40-44 (SPANISH)
California Cafe	H:40-44 (CALIFORNIA)
California Club Sushi Bar	J:51-53 (JAPANESE)
California Cuisine	I:46-50 (CALIFORNIA)
California Earthquake Cafe	C:21-23 (AMERICAN)
California Earthquake Cafe	I:46-50 (AMERICAN)
Callahan's Pub & Brewery	D:24-25 (IRISH)
Calliope's	I:46-50 (GREEK)
Cambridge Inn, The	C:21-23 (CONTINENTAL)
Canes	I:46-50 (CALIFORNIA)
Carlos & Annie's Cafe	B:16-20 (ECLECTIC)
Casa De Bandini	I:46-50 (MEXICAN)
Casa De Pico	I:46-50 (MEXICAN)
Casa Machado	D:24-25 (MEXICAN)
Casa Martinez	K:54-56 (MEXICAN)
Casa Salsa	K:54-56 (MEXICAN)
Cass Street Bar & Grill	F:32-35 (AMERICAN)
Cecil's Cafe & Fish Market	G:36-38 (SEAFOOD)
Celadon	I:46-50 (THAI)
Champagne Room, The	A:14-15 (CONTINENTAL)
Chang, Cuisine of China	J:51-53 (CHINESE)
Charlie's	B:16-20 (SEAFOOD)
Chart House	A:14-15 (AMERICAN)
Chart House	B:16-20 (AMERICAN)
Chart House	E:26-31 (AMERICAN)
Chart House/SD Rowing Club	H:40-44 (AMERICAN)
Chateau Basque	J:51-53 (BASQUE)
Chateau Orleans	F:32-35 (CAJUN/CREOLE)
Chez Beat & Rolf	F:32-35 (CALIFORNIA)
Chez Loma	K:54-56 (CONTINENTAL)
Chez Orleans	C:21-23 (CAJUN/CREOLE)
Chicago Brothers	F:32-35 (ITALIAN)
Chicken Pie Shop	I:46-50 (AMERICAN)
China Camp	H:40-44 (CHINESE)
China Inn	F:32-35 (CHINESE)
China Land Restaurant	G:36-38 (CHINESE)
Chu Dynasty	I:46-50 (CHINESE)
Chu Dynasty	K:54-56 (CHINESE)
Chuck's Steak House	E:26-31 (AMERICAN)
Chuey's Cafe	K:54-56 (MEXICAN)
Chung King Loh	B:16-20 (CHINESE)
Cilantro's	B:16-20 (SOUTHWEST)
Cindy Black	E:26-31 (FRENCH)
City Deli	I:46-50 (DELI)
City Rock Cafe	H:40-44 (AMERICAN)
Clay's Texas Pit Bar-B-Q	E:26-31 (AMERICAN)
Coco Palms	B:16-20 (AMERICAN)
College Restaurant, The	J:51-53 (AMERICAN)
Cornucopia	I:46-50 (VEGETARIAN)
Corvette Diner, Bar & Grill, The	I:46-50 (AMERICAN)
Cotton Patch	G:36-38 (AMERICAN)
Country Inn Restaurant	B:16-20 (AMERICAN)
Coyote Bar & Grill	A:14-15 (MEXICAN)
Crazy Burro	A:14-15 (MEXICAN)
Crest Cafe	I:46-50 (AMERICAN)
Croce's	H:40-44 (INTERNAT'L)
Crown-Coronet Room	K:54-56 (CONTINENTAL)

--- D ---

Restaurant	Dining Area: Pages (Cuisine Category)
D. B. Hacker's	B:16-20 (SEAFOOD)
D. Z. Akins	J:51-53 (AMERICAN)
Daily Planet, The	F:32-35 (AMERICAN)
Dansk Restaurant	J:51-53 (SCANDINAVIAN)
Deer Park Winery	C:21-23 (DELI)
Delmario's	B:16-20 (ITALIAN)
Desmond's Cuisine Of India	E:26-31 (INDIAN)
Diego's Cafe Y Cantina	F:32-35 (MEXICAN)
Dini's	B:16-20 (AMERICAN)
Dini's-by-the-sea	A:14-15 (SEAFOOD)
Dobson's	H:40-44 (AMERICAN)

ALPHABETIC INDEX

Restaurant................. Dining Area: Pages (Cuisine Category)

Restaurant	Dining Area: Pages (Cuisine Category)
Dockside Broiler	F:32-35 (SEAFOOD)
Dookies	J:51-53 (AMERICAN)
Dooley McCluskey's	A:14-15 (AMERICAN)
Double Happiness	B:16-20 (CHINESE)
Drowsy Maggie's	I:46-50 (NATURAL FOOD)

--- E ---

Restaurant	Dining Area: Pages (Cuisine Category)
Eggery, Etc., The	F:32-35 (AMERICAN)
El Bizcocho	C:21-23 (CONTINENTAL)
El Chalan	F:32-35 (PERUVIAN)
El Crab Catcher	E:26-31 (ECLECTIC)
El Establo	C:21-23 (MEXICAN)
El Indio	I:46-50 (FOOD-TO-GO)
El Tecolote	I:46-50 (MEXICAN)
Elario's	E:26-31 (FRENCH)
Elephant Bar & Restaurant	E:26-31 (ECLECTIC)
Emil's	I:46-50 (CONTINENTAL)
Epazotes	B:16-20 (MEXICAN)
Esperanto	F:32-35 (INTERNAT'L)
Ethiopia	F:32-35 (ETHIOPIAN)

--- F ---

Restaurant	Dining Area: Pages (Cuisine Category)
Fairouz Cafe	G:36-38 (MIDDLE EAST)
Falco	H:40-44 (CALIFORNIA)
Falcone's	E:26-31 (ITALIAN)
Fat City	H:40-44 (ECLECTIC)
Fidel's	A:14-15 (MEXICAN)
Fidel's Little Mexico	B:16-20 (MEXICAN)
Fifth & Hawthorn	H:40-44 (SEAFOOD)
Figaro	I:46-50 (ITALIAN)
Filippi's Pizza Grotto	F:32-35 (ITALIAN)
Filippi's Pizza Grotto	H:40-44 (ITALIAN)
Fio's	H:40-44 (ITALIAN)
Fish House Vera Cruz	C:21-23 (SEAFOOD)
Fish House West	B:16-20 (SEAFOOD)
Fish Market, The	B:16-20 (SEAFOOD)
Fish Market, The	H:40-44 (SEAFOOD)
Fisherman's Grill	E:26-31 (SEAFOOD)
Five Star Thai Cuisine	H:40-44 (THAI)
Flamingo's Bistro	H:40-44 (AMERICAN)
Fontainebleau Restaurant	H:40-44 (FRENCH)
Frederick's	B:16-20 (CONTINENTAL)
French Cafe	D:24-25 (FRENCH)
French Gourmet	F:32-35 (FRENCH)
French Gourmet Too, The	E:26-31 (FRENCH)
French Pastry Shop, The	E:26-31 (FRENCH)
French Side of The West, The	I:46-50 (FRENCH)
Frenchy Marseilles	H:40-44 (CONTINENTAL)
Frogg Lane Bar And Grill	H:40-44 (AMERICAN)
Fung Lin	I:46-50 (CHINESE)

--- G ---

Restaurant	Dining Area: Pages (Cuisine Category)
Galaxy Grill	H:40-44 (AMERICAN)
Garcia's	G:36-38 (MEXICAN)
Gathering, The	I:46-50 (AMERICAN)
Gaucho Steak House, The	A:14-15 (AMERICAN)
Gellerosa Ranch Barbecue	H:40-44 (AMERICAN)
Gentleman's Choice, The	C:21-23 (AMERICAN)
George E. Wong	E:26-31 (CHINESE)
George's at the Cove	E:26-31 (CALIFORNIA)
Georgia's Greek Cuisine	I:46-50 (GREEK)
Godfather, The	D:24-25 (ITALIAN)
Golden Lion Tavern	H:40-44 (AMERICAN)
Good Egg, The	D:24-25 (AMERICAN)
Good Time Charlies	F:32-35 (AMERICAN)
Gourmet Room	I:46-50 (CONTINENTAL)
Grant Grill & Lounge, The	H:40-44 (CONTINENTAL)
Gratzi	I:46-50 (AMERICAN)
Grazie E Prego	A:14-15 (ITALIAN)
Greek Town Restaurant	H:40-44 (GREEK)
Green Flash, The	F:32-35 (AMERICAN)
Grill on The Park	H:40-44 (ECLECTIC)
Guadalajara Grill	I:46-50 (MEXICAN)

--- H ---

Restaurant	Dining Area: Pages (Cuisine Category)
Hamburguesa	I:46-50 (MEXICAN)
Harbor House	H:40-44 (SEAFOOD)
Harbor House's Top of the Plaza	H:40-44 (ITALIAN)
Hard Rock Cafe	E:26-31 (AMERICAN)
Harry's Cafe Gallery	E:26-31 (AMERICAN)
Hennessey's Tavern & Pub	F:32-35 (AMERICAN)
Henry's	A:14-15 (INTERNAT'L)
Hindquarter, The	D:24-25 (AMERICAN)
Hob Nob Hill	I:46-50 (AMERICAN)
Homeport Cafe	H:40-44 (CALIFORNIA)
House of Munich	K:54-56 (GERMAN)
Humphrey's	G:36-38 (SEAFOOD)
Humphrey's La Jolla Grill	E:26-31 (SEAFOOD)
Ida Bailey	H:40-44 (AMERICAN)

If by some chance we've missed your favorite restuarant and you'd like to nominate it to be included in the next edition, please fill out and return the postage-paid NOMINATION POSTCARD you'll find at the back of the book.

If the Postcard is missing, you can enter your nominations by writing to us at :

Flashfacts System
Division of RRN Inc.
One Madison Ave (27A)
New York, NY 10010

Thanks.

The Editors

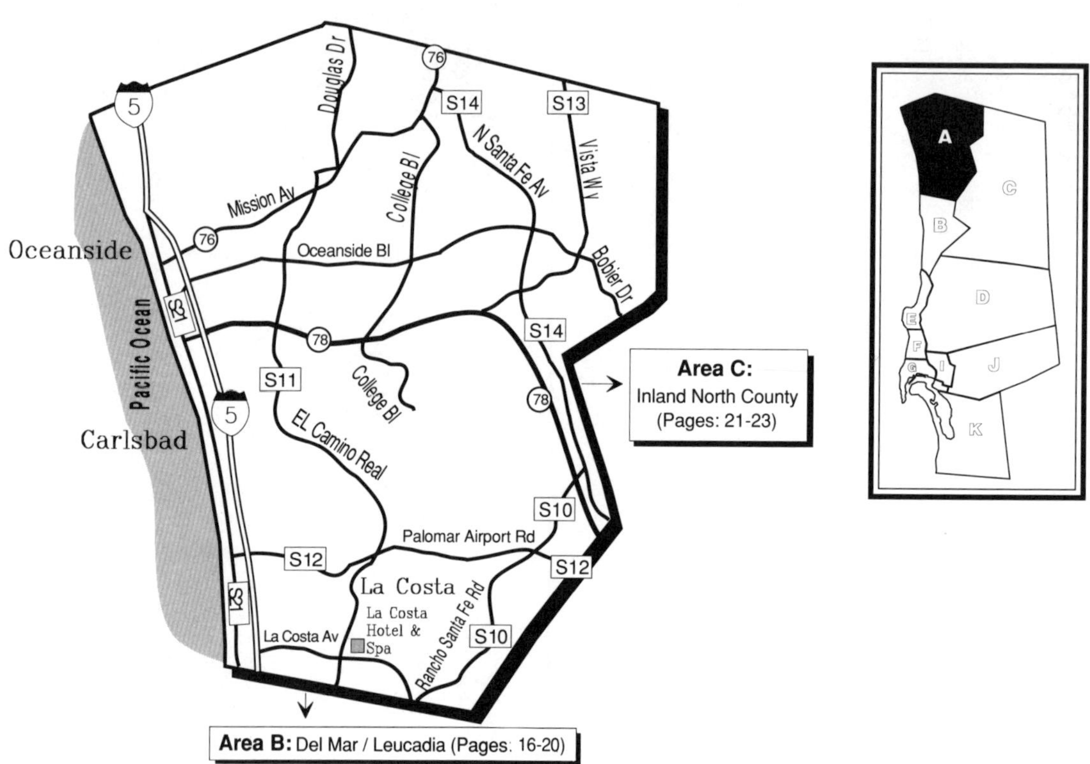

Area C:
Inland North County
(Pages: 21-23)

Area B: Del Mar / Leucadia (Pages: 16-20)

ALPHABETIC LISTINGS

RESTAURANT (CUISINE Category)	RESTAURANT (CUISINE Category)	RESTAURANT (CUISINE Category)
Champagne Room, The (CONTINENTAL)	Gaucho Steak House, The (AMERICAN)	Neimans Sea Grill (SEAFOOD)
Chart House (AMERICAN)	Grazie E Prego (ITALIAN)	Olive Garden, The (ITALIAN)
Coyote Bar & Grill (MEXICAN)	Henry's (INTERNAT'L)	Pisces (SEAFOOD)
Crazy Burro (MEXICAN)	Jose Wong's (ECLECTIC)	Raintree Grill & Bar (AMERICAN)
Dini's-by-the-sea (SEAFOOD)	Le Brasserie (AMERICAN)	Ristorante Figaro (ITALIAN)
Dooley McCluskey's (AMERICAN)	Mirabelle (FRENCH)	Spa Dining Room, The (DIET CUISINE)
Fidel's (MEXICAN)	Neimans Cafe (CALIFORNIA)	

Cuisine (NOTES)	Restaurant COMMUNITY - Street Located Near	PHONE (619)	Serving Brkfst / Lunch / Dinner X=Closed	Late Night Din.	Sunday Brunch	Under $10	$10 to $20	$20 to $30+	Credit Cards	Reservations	SPECIAL FEATURES
AMERICAN	Chart House OCEANSIDE - 314 Harbor Dr South West of I-5	722-1345	-- -- D	F / Sa				$	MC V AE DC D	Yes	Ocean view dining, Bar overlooks the water Seafood, Beef, Large salad bar Multiple locations
	Dooley McCluskey's CARLSBAD - 640 Grand Av, Suite A Roosevelt St & Grand Ave	434-3114	-- L D	Y			$		MC V	Rec (D) 40	Lively. popular, oak & brass English Pub A favorite with the locals Prime rib, pasta, chocolate rum pie
	Gaucho Steak House LA COSTA - Costa Del Mar Rd In The La Costa Resort	438-9111	-- -- D	F / Sa				$	MC V AE DC	Rec	Dark, cozy, candlelight, Menu features Argentine-style aged beef, game & fowl Jacket preferred
	Le Brasserie LA COSTA - Costa del Mar Rd In The La Costa Resort	438-9111	-- L D	F / Sa			$		MC V AE DC D	Rec	Casual, outdoor dining with rattan furniture Lots of greenery Soda fountain, burgers, sandwiches & deli specials
	Raintree Grill & Bar CARLSBAD - 755 Raintree Dr West of I-5; At Poinsettia Lane	931-1122	B (Wknds) L (X:S/S) D	F / Sa			$		MC V AE	Yes 200	Sunset view, casual dress, sports bar, satellite TV California grill, seafood emphasis
CALIFORNIA	Neimans Cafe CARLSBAD - 300 Elm Ave Elm Ave & Carlsbad Blvd	729-3131	B L D	M - Sa	✓		$		MC V	No 25	Historical landmark - building is 103 years old Outdoor dining at lunch, casual Right next door to Neiman's Sea Grill, catering
CONTINENTAL	Champagne Room, The LA COSTA - Costa Del Mar Rd In The La Costa Resort	438-9111	-- D (X:Su-Tu)					+	MC V AE DC	Must	Formal setting, with old world French decor Gourmet dining with European service Jacket and tie required
DIET CUISINE	Spa Dining Room, The LA COSTA - Costa Del Mar Rd In The La Costa Resort	438-9111	B L D				$		MC V	Yes	Bright, airy atmosphere, pastel colors, casual Low calorie and Low cholesterol dishes Non-alcoholic beverages
ECLECTIC	Jose Wong's LA COSTA - Costa Del Mar Rd In The La Costa Resort	438-9111	B (X:M-W) L (X:Su-W) D (X:M-W)		✓		$		MC V AE DC	Rec	Fun, unusual decor mixing Mexican & Chinese accents Menu offers a wide variety, Sunday champagne brunch F/Sa Scottish buffet breakfast, Seafood buffet nightly
FRENCH	Mirabelle LA COSTA - 7720 El Camino Real South of La Costa Rd	753-0040	-- -- D (X:Su)				$		MC V AE	Rec 80	Family run, elegant, yet casual surroundings Gourmet veal and beef specials Catering, carry-out, B&W only
INTERNAT'L	Henry's CARLSBAD - 264 Elm Av West of Carlsbad Blvd	729-9244	-- L D					$	MC V AE DC	Rec	Intimate, formal setting, Italian accent Entertainment nightly
ITALIAN	Grazie E Prego OCEANSIDE - 1733 S. HILL STREET	433-5811	-- L (X:Su/M) D (X:Su/M)				$		MC V AE	Rec 8p+	Comfortable European-style dining room with fireplace, patio dining, Southern specialties: veal, chicken pasta, pizza, calzone, catering
	Olive Garden, The CARLSBAD - 1884 Marron Rd West of El Camino Real	434-1016	-- L D	F / Sa			$		MC V AE DC	No	Unlimited salad refills, garlic breaksticks Non-alcoholic beverages, northern & southern cuisine Carry-out
	Ristorante Figaro LA COSTA - Costa del Mar Rd In The La Costa Resort	438-9111	-- -- D (X:Su/T)	Y				+	MC V AE DC	Rec	Elegant, formal setting, Italian decor, oil paintings Traditional Northern Italian dishes Jacket required,
MEXICAN	Coyote Bar & Grill CARLSBAD - 300 Carlsbad Village Dr	729-HOWL	-- L D	Y			$		MC V	No	Sante Fe decor, Large patio with open fire pits Casual, 75 different types of tequillas Carry-out, catering
	Crazy Burro LA COSTA - 6996 El Camino Real North of Alga Rd	438-3373	-- L D		✓	$			MC V AE	Yes	View of La Costa area, Festive feeling Seafood specialties with a Mexican emphasis Carry-out, catering
	Fidel's CARLSBAD - 3001 Carlsbad Blvd South of Elm Av	729-0903	-- L D			$			MC V	Rec (L)	Sister restaurant of the Solana Beach Fidel's Patio dining, very casual, relaxed, festive feeling Traditional Mexican dishes
SEAFOOD	Dini's-by-the-sea CARLSBAD - 3290 Carlsbad Blvd South of Pine Av	434-6000	-- L (X:S/S) D	F / Sa			$		MC V AE	Rec	Ocean view, daily specials, prime rib, seafood Popular with the locals
	Neimans Sea Grill CARLSBAD - 300 Elm Avenue Corner of Carlsbad Blvd & Elm Ave	729-3131	-- D (X:Su)		✓	$			MC V	No 150	Ocean view dining Piano music nightly Catering, banquet facilities
	Pisces LA COSTA - Costa Del Mar Rd In The La Costa Resort	438-9111	-- D (X:W)					+	MC V AE DC	Rec	Elegant setting, haute cuisine, gourmet seafood Featuring: Dover Sole, Abalone, and more Jacket required

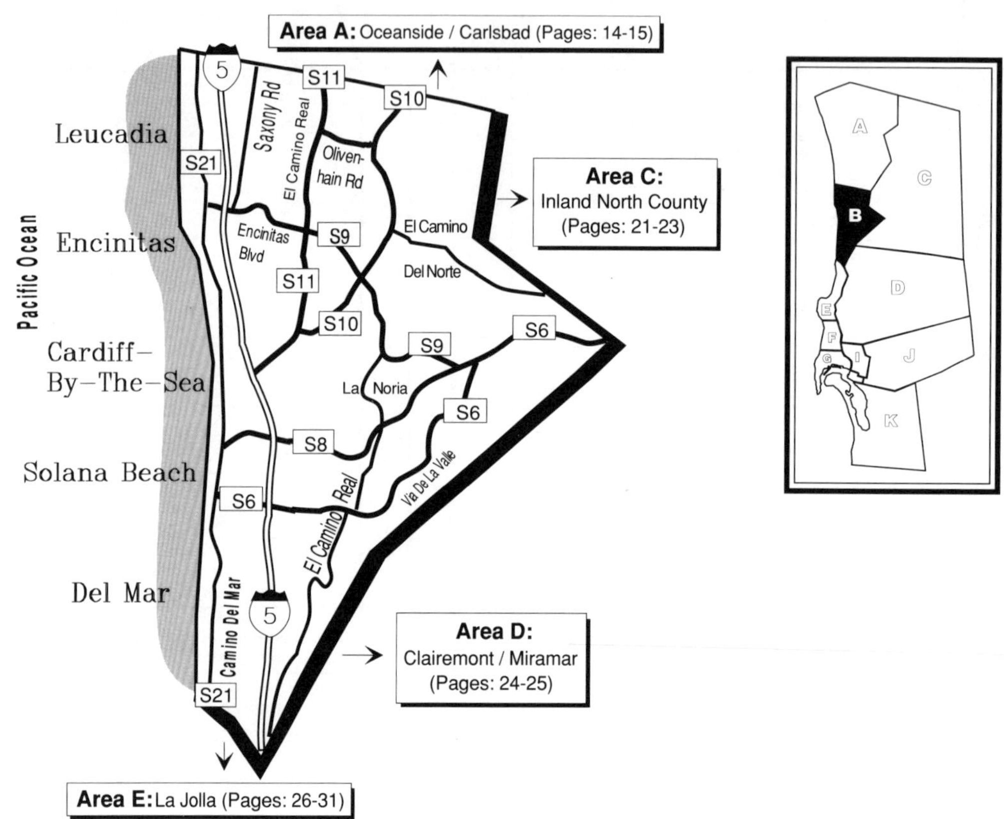

ALPHABETIC LISTINGS

RESTAURANT (CUISINE Category)	RESTAURANT (CUISINE Category)	RESTAURANT (CUISINE Category)
101 Diner, The (AMERICAN)	Epazotes (MEXICAN)	Red Tracton's (AMERICAN)
Baja Grill & Fish Market (SEAFOOD)	Fidel's Little Mexico (MEXICAN)	Remington's (AMERICAN)
Basil St. Cafe (SEAFOOD)	Fish House West (SEAFOOD)	Sakura-Bana (JAPANESE)
Bistro Gardens, The (FRENCH)	Fish Market, The (SEAFOOD)	Samurai Japanese Restaurant (JAPANESE)
Blue Bird Cafe (MEXICAN)	Frederick's (CONTINENTAL)	Scalini (ITALIAN)
Boathouse, The (SEAFOOD)	Il Fornaio Cucina Italiana (ITALIAN)	Schroder's (AMERICAN)
Bobby J's (AMERICAN)	Jake's Del Mar (AMERICAN)	St. Germain's Cafe (ECLECTIC)
Borrelli's (ITALIAN)	Kirby's Cafe & Bistro (ECLECTIC)	Star of India (INDIAN)
Brigantine, The (SEAFOOD)	La Bonne Bouffe (FRENCH)	Taco Auctioneer (MEXICAN)
Bully's (AMERICAN)	La Dolce Vita (ITALIAN)	Taryn's at The Track (CALIFORNIA)
Cafe Del Mar (CALIFORNIA)	La Mont's Authentic Barbecue (AMERICAN)	Tony's Jacal (MEXICAN)
Carlos & Annie's Cafe (ECLECTIC)	La Tapenade (CONTINENTAL)	Triple Crown (AMERICAN)
Charlie's (SEAFOOD)	Le Bambou (VIETNAMESE)	Triton (AMERICAN)
Chart House (AMERICAN)	Nobu Gourmet Japanese Rest. (JAPANESE)	Valle Rose Restaurant (CALIFORNIA)
Chung King Loh (CHINESE)	Pacifica Del Mar (SEAFOOD)	Valley Cafe (AMERICAN)
Cilantro's (SOUTHWEST)	Pamir (AFGHAN)	Villa Carmel (CONTINENTAL)
Coco Palms (AMERICAN)	Papachinos (ITALIAN)	Villa D'este (ITALIAN)
Country Inn Restaurant (AMERICAN)	Paradise Grill (AMERICAN)	Village Cafe Francais, The (FRENCH)
D. B. Hacker's (SEAFOOD)	Peter Chang's (CHINESE)	Vincent/Four Seasons (CALIFORNIA)
Delmario's (ITALIAN)	Piret M Bistro/Gallery (CALIFORNIA)	When In Rome (ITALIAN)
Dini's (AMERICAN)	Portofino (ITALIAN)	
Double Happiness (CHINESE)	Poseidon (SEAFOOD)	

Cuisine (NOTES)	Restaurant / COMMUNITY - Street / Located Near	PHONE (619)	Serving (Brkfst / Lunch / Dinner / X=Closed)	Late Night Din.	Sunday Brunch	Under $10	$10 to $20	$20 to $30+	Credit Cards	Reservations	SPECIAL FEATURES
AFGHAN	**Pamir** / *SOLANA BEACH* - 524 Stevens Av / South of Lomas Sante Fe Rd	481-4040	-- / L (X:S/S) / D			$			MC V	Rec	Dining room is like a sultan tent, exotic rugs / Paintings / Afghan staples, rice, chicken, lamb & beef, B&W only
AMERICAN	**101 Diner, The** / *ENCINITAS* - 552 1st St / On Old Hwy 101	753-2123	B / L / --		$			None		No / 6	Art deco and counter seating in this casual setting / Daily specials / Catering, No Bar
	Bobby J's / *ENCINITAS* - 745 First St / In The Lumberyard	944-1447	-- / L / D		$				MC V	No	Fun, casual, great old pictures, patio dining, / Gourmet burgers, hot dogs, pastas, salads, fajitas / Even Stir Fry, B&W only
	Bully's / *DEL MAR* - 1404 Camino del Mar / North of 14th St	755-1660	B / L / D	Y			$		MC V / AE DC	No	Packed with the sporting crowd, exciting & lively / Some of the best prime-rib, seafood, burgers too / Locations throughout San Diego
	Chart House / *CARDIFF-BY-THE-SEA* - 2588 S. Hwy 101 / South of Montgomery Ave	436-4044	-- / -- / D		F / / Sa			$	MC V / AE DC / D	Yes / 40	Relaxed, comfortable setting, oyster & salad bar / Simple grilled preparations of beef, chicken & seafood / Multiple locations
	Coco Palms / *ENCINITAS* - 1950 Hwy. 101	942-1444	-- / -- / D		✓	$			AE MC / DC CB	Yes	Art decor, Tropical, Beautiful view of the ocean / Outdoor dining, Menu offers blackened prime rib, crab / seafood, Live entertainment (F/Sa)
	Country Inn Restaurant / *ENCINITAS* - 1486 Encinitas Blvd / East of El Camino Real	942-9166	B / L / D			$			MC V	Yes / 40	Relaxed country decor, Daily specials / Menu offers selection from salads to sandwiches / Large choice of entrees
	Dini's / *DEL MAR* - 526 Camino del Mar / In Sea Horse and Stratford Inn	481-9111	-- / L (X:Sa/Su) / D		F / / Sa	$			MC V / AE DC	Rec / 6p+	Unpretentious spot in the Stratford Inn / A favorite with the locals / Seafood and Mexican specials
	Jake's Del Mar / *DEL MAR* - 1660 Coast Blvd / South of 17th St	755-2002	-- / L (X:Sa-M) / D (X:M)		F / / Sa			$	MC V / AE	Rec	Located on the beach, fabulous ocean/sunset view / Fresh seafood, beef & poultry, lobster(F/Sa) / Premium California wines
	La Mont's Authentic Barbecue / *ENCINITAS* - 392 El Camino Real / South of Encinitas Blvd	753-1251	-- / L (X:Sa-M) / D (X:M)			$			MC V / DC	Rec / 6p+	Down-home cooking, family recipes / Southern style BBQ / Cookbook available with family recipes
	Paradise Grill / *ENCINITAS* - 1476 Encinitas Blvd / East of El Camino Real	943-9997	B / L (X:Su) / D			$			MC V / AE DC	Rec	Casual, counters, booths, Texas style hickory BBQ / Fresh seafood, honey fried, chicken, pork / Carry-out
	Red Tracton's / *SOLANA BEACH* - 550 Via de la Valle / Across from Del Mar Racetrack	755-6600	-- / L (X:Su) / D		F / / Sa			$	MC V / AE DC	Rec	Masculine decor, hunter green theme & brass fixtures / Friendly staff, steak, prime rib, seafood specialties
	Remington's / *DEL MAR* - 2010 Jimmy Durante Blvd / South of Via de la Valle	755-5104	-- / L (X:Sa/Su) / D	Y				+	MC V / AE	Rec / 100	Fine elegant dining, table phones, Down to earth / American fare, lobster by the pound, beef, chicken / Very large portions, Jackets preferred
	Schroder's / *OCEANSIDE* - 1903 South Hill St / At Vista Way	433-5424	-- / L / D			$			MC V	Rec / 50	Sportsman bar, pool tables, big screen TV, satellite / Setting is relaxed, comfortable, low-key, small / Dining room serves hamburgers, sandwiches, BBQ ribs
	Triple Crown / *DEL MAR* - 15575 Jimmy Durante Blvd. / In the Del Mar Hilton	792-5200	-- / L (X:Su/M) / D (X:Su/M)				$		AE D / MC V	Rec	Elegant, romantic dining to classical music, comfortable / oversize furniture creates cozy feeling, Menu offers / steaks, seafood, prime rib, pastas, Jacket required
	Triton / *CARDIFF-BY-THE-SEA* - 2530 S. Hwy 101 / South of Montgomery Ave	436-8877	-- / L (X:Su) / D			$			MC V / AE DC	Rec	On the water, outdoor dining, specialty is seafood / chicken & beef dishes, oyster bar / Popular with locals
	Valley Cafe / *DEL MAR* - 15575 Jimmy Durante Blvd.	729-5200	B / L / D			$			MC V / AE	Yes	Open sun-filled, garden setting, over looks a patio / Light & hearty menu, lunch buffet
CALIFORNIA	**Cafe Del Mar** / *DEL MAR* - 1247 Camino del Mar / 13th & Camino Del Mar	481-1133	-- / L (X:Sa/Su) / D		✓	$			MC V / AE	Yes	Glass enclosed patio, Cafe setting, Outdoor dining / Menu changes every two weeks, Homemade desserts
	Piret M Bistro/Gallery / *ENCINITAS* - 897 First St / In The Lumberyard	942-5152	-- / L (X:Su) / D (X:Su/M)		✓	$			MC V / AE	Rec / 50	Bistro & gallery rooms, spectacular displays of flowers / Private dining facilities / Daily specials, Operated by Piret and George Munger
	Taryn's at The Track / *DEL MAR* - 514 Via de La Valle / Near Del Mar Race Track	481-8300	-- / -- / D			$			MC V / AE / DIS	Yes	Southwest, contemporary setting with painted tiles / Wide selection of seafoods, pastas, gourmet pizzas / Prime steaks, Banquet facilities & Catering

Cuisine (NOTES)	Restaurant / PHONE / COMMUNITY - Street / Located Near	SERVING: Brkfst Lunch Dinner X=Closed	Late Night Din.	Sunday Brunch	Under $10	$10 to $20	$20 to $30+	Credit Cards	Reservations	SPECIAL FEATURES
CALIFORNIA (Con't)	**Valle Rose Restaurant** 481-8861 / DEL MAR - 2660 Via de la Valle / In The Flower Hill Mall	-- L (X:Su) D	F / Sa	✓		$		MC V AE DC	Rec	Classic California setting, warm & friendly menu offers seafood, salads, soups & the chef's daily specials
	Vincent/Four Seasons 720-9788 / SOLANA BEACH - 731 So Hwy 101 / Mercado del Sol Shopping Center	-- -- D				$		MC V AE DC	Rec	Fixed menu, daily specials Appetizers at the bar from 4p Catering
CHINESE	**Chung King Loh** 481-0184 / SOLANA BEACH - 552 Stevens Av / South of Lomas Sante Fe Dr	-- L D				$		MC V AE	Rec 64	Comfortable setting featuring Chinese screens and antiques, Mandarin & Szechuan cuisine, Wide selection of vegetarian dishes, Catering & Banquet facilities
	Double Happiness 481-8584 / DEL MAR - 1011 Camino del Mar / North of 11th St	-- L (X:S/S) D			$			MC V AE	Rec	Atmosphere is intimate with dark surroundings Outdoor dining in enclosed patio Mandarin & Szechuan dishes
	Peter Chang's 942-5159 / ENCINITAS - 1441 Encinitas Blvd	-- L (X:Su) D			$			MC V AE	Yes	Superior lunch buffet, natural style Chinese cooking With French influence
CONTINENTAL	**Frederick's** 755-2432 / SOLANA BEACH - 128 South Acacia Av / West of Hwy 101	-- -- D (X:Su/M)					+	MC V	Rec 50	Intimate atmosphere, but not pretentious, candlelight Country French emphasis, prix-fixe, daily menu
	La Tapenade 756-1123 / RANCHO SANTA FE - 5921 Valencia / In Fairbanks Ranch Resort	B L (X:Su) D		✓		$		MC V AE	Yes	Elegant Spanish influence with open beam ceilings Outdoor dining, beef, seafood and chicken Lavish Sunday Buffet, Claude Segal is the chef
	Villa Carmel 943-7597 / ENCINITAS - 1010 First Street	B L (X:Su/M) D (X:Su/M)				$		MC V AE	Yes	Romantic, quiet setting featuring roast duck, chicken dishes, nightly specials B&W only
ECLECTIC	**Carlos & Annie's Cafe** 755-4601 / DEL MAR - 1454 Camino del Mar / North of 15th St	B L D			$			MC V AE DC	No	Ocean view, casual sidewalk cafe setting features Mexican & Southwestern dishes A favorite with the locals, Carry-out
	Kirby's Cafe & Bistro 481-1001 / DEL MAR - 215 15th St	B L D (X:M/Tu)				$		MC V AE	Yes	Casual outdoor dining w/ocean view, romantic at night Menu features a little of everything Some Mexican dishes, B&W only
	St. Germain's Cafe 753-5411 / ENCINITAS -1010 First St	B L ---				$		MC V AE DIS	Rec	Cafe setting, intimate, cozy atmosphere featuring outdoor dining, waffles, omelettes, fresh seafood, Imported beers & wine only
FRENCH	**Bistro Gardens, The** 259-1515 / DEL MAR - 1540 Camino del Mar / In the Inn at Del Mar	B L D	F / Sa			$		MC V AE	Yes	Patio dining in this quaint restaurant with waterfalls Intimate atmosphere serving traditional French fare Dancing F & Sa
	La Bonne Bouffe 436-3081 / ENCINITAS - 471 Encinitas Blvd / In The Town & Country Shop Ctr	-- -- D (X:Su-M)				$		MC V	Rec 40	Charming atmosphere, good wine list Country/Provencal cuisine
	Village Cafe Francais 942-5968 / ENCINITAS - 1524 Encinitas Blvd / East of El Camino Real	-- -- D (X:M)					+	MC V AE DC	Must 26	Charming, quaint bistro feeling, country French Prix-fixe, changing menu No corkage fee
INDIAN	**Star of India** 632-1113 / ENCINITAS - 927 First St / In Lumberyard Shopping Center	-- L (X:S/S) D	F / Sa	✓			$	MC V DC D	Rec 30	Casual, table & booths, Indian wall decor, northern Indian dishes, Tandoori & vegetarian items Lunch buffet
ITALIAN	**Borrelli's** 436-1501 / ENCINITAS - 1409 Encinitas Blvd / East of El Camino Real	-- L (X:Su) D	F / Sa		$			MC V	No 30	Similar to the old-time pizza parlors Lively casual relaxed atmosphere Wide choice of pizza and pasta
	Delmario's 792-1131 / DEL MAR - 2010 Jimmy Durante Blvd / North of Camino Del Mar	-- -- D				$		MC V	Rec	Relaxed old world decor, Large hand-painted scene of Venice's Grand Canal, Outdoor dining Italian specialties with traditional Italian desserts
	Il Fornaio Cucina Italiana 755-8876 / DEL MAR - 1555 Camino del Mar / In The Plaza Shopping Ctr	B L D	F / Sa			$		MC V	Rec	Beautiful ocean view, From San Francisco, northern Italian emphasis, homemade pasta, pizza & breads Retail store for carry-out
	La Dolce Vita 759-9011 / FAIRBANKS RANCH - 349 N. Pacific Av	-- L (X:M) D (X:M)					+	MC V	Yes	Rustic Mediterranean atmosphere with outdoor dining White jacketed waiters, seafood, veal, pasta Antipasto display, pastries made on the premises
	Papachinos 481-7171 / DEL MAR - 2650 Via de la Valle / In The Flower Hill Mall	-- L D	Y		$			MC V	No (L) 60	Family style with outrageous portions, pizza & pasta Patio dining Carry-out

Cuisine (Notes)	Restaurant COMMUNITY – Street Located Near	Phone	Serving Brkfst / Lunch / Dinner (X=Closed)	Late Night Din.	Sunday Brunch	Under $10	$10 to $20	$20 to $30+	Credit Cards	Reservations	Special Features
ITALIAN (Con't)	**Portofino** ENCINITAS - 1108 First St North of I St	942-8442	-- --- D	F / Sa				$	MC V AE DC	Must 165	Mediterranean garden atmosphere, relaxing & comfortable Patio with roll back roof Northern Italian dishes, Daily specials
	Scalini NORTH CITY WEST - 3790 Via de la Valle East of I-5	259-9944	-- -- D				$		MC V AE DC	Rec 50	Elegant atmosphere, view of the Polo Fields Open kitchen, Northern Italian cuisine, gourmet pizza Private room, entertainment(T-Sa), Silver Medal/SCRW
	Villa D'este DEL MAR - 2282 Carmel Valley Road	259-2006	-- L (X:S/S) D				$		AE MC V	Yes	Elegant, Italian villa setting, specialties include homemade pastas, Northern Italian cuisine ''Best Italian Restaurant'' SD Magazine
	When In Rome LEUCADIA - 828 North Hwy 101 In Leucadia Plaza	944-1771	-- L (X:Sa-M) D					$	MC V AE	Rec	Chic atmosphere, candlelight, romantic, cosmopolitan menu, homemade pasta, breads, seafoood specials Silver Award/SCRW
JAPANESE	**Nobu** SOLANA BEACH - 315 S. Hwy 101	755-0113	-- L D						MC V		Teppan Bar, Sushi Bar & Tatami room Elegant Dining, Traditional Japanese dishes plus filet mignon and lemon chicken
	Sakura-Bana ENCINITAS - 1031 First St In the Lumberyard Shopping Center	942-6414	-- L (X:Su) D			$			MC V AE	No	Contemporary decor, generous portions Sushi bar B&W only
	Samurai Japanese Restaurant SOLANA BEACH - 979 Lomas Santa Fe Dr East of I-5	481-0032	-- L D	F / Sa			$		MC V AE	Rec	Traditional Japanese setting, relaxed feeling, outdoor dining, Sushi bar, Tatami room, Teppan grills Popular with north county residents
MEXICAN	**Blue Bird Cafe** SOLANA BEACH - 646 Valley Ave North of Stevens Ave	755-4426	B (X:M) L (X:M) D (X:M)			$			MC V	Rec 8p+	Friendly, casual atmosphere, traditional Mexican dishes A North County favorite Mexican breakfasts served all day
	Epazotes DEL MAR - 1555 Camino Del Mar North of 15th St	259-9966	-- L D	F / Sa			$		MC V AE	Yes	Sister restaurant to the acclaimed Cilantro's Beautiful ocean view, baja bar & grill, unique Mexican dishes with a Southwest flavor
	Fidel's Little Mexico SOLANA BEACH - 607 Valley Ave North of Stevens Ave	755-5292	-- L D			$			MC V	Rec 8p+ 100	Authentic, quaint atmosphere Popular beach spot, family-owned, casual, fun, warm Patio dining, Carry-out, Silver Award/SCRW
	Taco Auctioneer CARDIFF-BY-THE-SEA - 1951 San Elijo Av At Birmingham Dr	942-8226	-- L (X:S/S) D	F / Sa			$		MC V	Must	South of the border atmosphere Regional dishes from areas throughout Mexico Silver medal/SCRW, B&W only
	Tony's Jacal SOLANA BEACH - 621 Valley Av North of Stevens Av	755-2274	-- L (X:Su) D			$			MC V AE	Rec 10p+	Casual, family eatery, generous portions, booths Favorites are fish tacos & turkey tamales, menu also offers other Mexican specialties
SEAFOOD	**Baja Grill & Fish Market** DEL MAR - 1342 Camino del Mar	792-6551	-- L D		✓		$		MC V	Rec 6p+	Relaxed, outdoor dining on the patio which is split level, garden setting, awnings Menu features Baja-style cuisine, Fish market
	Basil St. Cafe LEUCADIA - 576 North Hwy 101 South of Leucadia Blvd	942-5145	-- -- D (X:Su-T)				$		MC V	Rec	Patio dining, Vegetarian dishes Fresh natural foods using home grown herbs Guitarist F & Sa, Catering, B&W only
	Boathouse, The ENCINITAS - 87 Encinitas Blvd West of Hwy 101	944-1338	-- L (M-F) D	F / Sa			$		MC V AE DC D	Rec	Ocean view creates a relaxed atmosphere Emphasis is seafood, steak, prime rib & pasta Multiple locations
	Brigantine, The DEL MAR - 3263 Camino del Mar South of Via de la Valle	481-1166	-- L D				$		MC V AE	Rec	Ocean view, outdoor seating on the deck overlooking the Racetrack, nautical atmosphere, seafood specials Oyster bar, Multiple locations
	Charlie's CARDIFF-BY-THE-SEA - 2526 S. Hwy 101 South of Montgomery Ave	942-1300	-- -- D		✓		$		MC V AE	Rec 50	Located on the beach, watch the waves and the people Daily specials, grilled beef and poultry specials Private parties
	D. B. Hacker's ENCINITAS - 101 Hwy 101 North of Encinitas Blvd	436-3162	-- L D				$		MC V	No	Casual, cafe feeling, candlelight dining Beachy & relaxed with a menu offering a variety of seafood dishes
	Fish House West CARDIFF-BY-THE-SEA - 2633 S. Hwy 101 South of Montgomery Av	753-6438	-- L (X:S/S) D	F / Sa			$		MC V	Rec	On restaurant row, nautical decor, across from the ocean, seafood & lobster specials, beef & chicken
	Fish Market, The DEL MAR - 640 Via de la Valle	755-2277	-- L D				$		MC V AE	8p+	Very casual, fish house setting wharf feeling Fresh seafoods & pastas, own fishing fleets Multiple locations

Cuisine (NOTES)	Restaurant COMMUNITY - Street Located Near	PHONE	Brkfst Lunch Dinner X=Closed	Late Night Din.	Sunday Brunch	Under $10	$10 to $20	$20 to $30 +	Credit Cards	Reservations	SPECIAL FEATURES
SEAFOOD (Con't)	**Pacifica Del Mar** *DEL MAR* - 1555 Camino del Mar North of 15th St	792-0476	-- L (X:Su) D	F / Sa			$		MC V AE DC	Rec 12	Ocean view, daily changing menu serving regional American cuisine with Southwestern and Oriental flair Sister restaurant to award-winning Pacifica Grill
	Poseidon *DEL MAR* - 1670 Coast Blvd South of 15th St	755-9345	B (Sa-Su) L (X:S/S) D	F / Sa	✓			$	MC V AE	Rec 30	Unique beach experience, located on the sand Outdoor seating, inside fireplace, local hang-out Fresh fish, meats, salads sandwiches
SOUTHWEST	**Cilantro's** *DEL MAR* - 3702 Via de la Valle	259-8777	-- L (X:S/S) D				$		MC V AE	Yes	Sante Fe style decor, contemporary relaxed, comfortable Upscale, menu features marinated garlicchicken, chiles & cilantro, chili spiced filet mignon, fajitas
VIETNAMESE	**Le Bambou** *DEL MAR* - 2634 Del Mar Heights Road	259-8183	-- L (X:M-Su) D (X:M)			$			MC V		Contemporary, quiet setting with a menu offering authentic Vietnamese cuisine, chicken with lemon grass cinnamon-scented curries, shrimp & port, B&W only

ADDITIONS

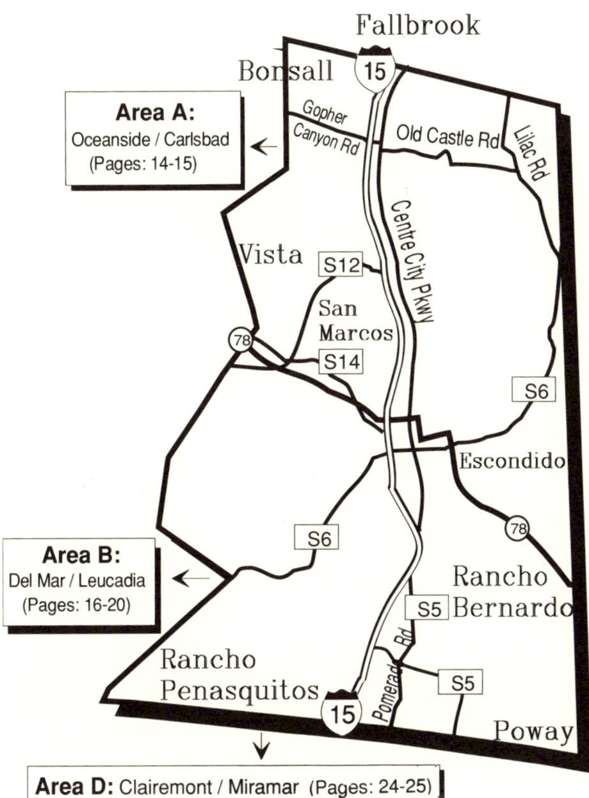

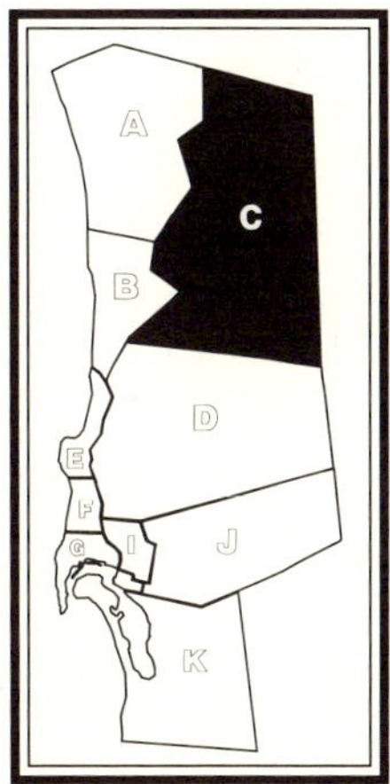

ALPHABETIC LISTINGS

RESTAURANT (CUISINE Category)

Anthony's II (SEAFOOD)
Brigantine, The (SEAFOOD)
Bruno's (ITALIAN)
Cafe Champagne (CALIFORNIA)
California Earthquake Cafe (AMERICAN)
Cambridge Inn, The (CONTINENTAL)
Chez Orleans (CAJUN/CREOLE)
Deer Park Winery (DELI)
El Bizcocho (CONTINENTAL)
El Establo (MEXICAN)
Fish House Vera Cruz (SEAFOOD)
Gentleman's Choice, The (AMERICAN)
Gentleman's Choice, The (AMERICAN)

RESTAURANT (CUISINE Category)

Inn At Rancho Sante Fe (AMERICAN)
Katsu Seafood & Steak House (JAPANESE)
La Estancia Inn (INTERNAT'L)
Le Bistro (CONTINENTAL)
Michael's Chicago Style Hot Dogs (AMERICAN)
Mille Fleurs (FRENCH)
Packing House (AMERICAN)
Peking Wok (CHINESE)
Pine Hills Lodge Julian (AMERICAN)
Quails Inn, The (AMERICAN)
Rancho Vera Cruz (SEAFOOD)
Restaurant Yae (JAPANESE)
Ristorante Galileo (ITALIAN)

RESTAURANT (CUISINE Category)

Romano's Dodge House (ITALIAN)
Rubio's Deli-Mex (FOOD-TO-GO)
San Luis Rey Downs (AMERICAN)
Sau-Hy's Chinese Cuisine (CHINESE)
Seafare (FRENCH)
Shien Of Osaka (JAPANESE)
Stella's Hideaway (POLISH)
Stoneridge Country Club (AMERICAN)
T-Bird Diner (AMERICAN)
Terraces Cafe, The (AMERICAN)
Trents (AMERICAN)
Valentino's (ITALIAN)
Veranda, The (AMERICAN)

Cuisine (NOTES)	Restaurant COMMUNITY - Street Located Near	PHONE (619)	Serving Brkfst/Lunch/Dinner X=Closed	Late Night Din.	Sunday Brunch	Under $10	$10 to $20	$20 to $30+	Credit Cards	Reservations	SPECIAL FEATURES
AMERICAN	California Earthquake Cafe SAN MARCOS-1020 W. San Marcos Blvd Old California Restaurant Row	471-1222	-- L D			$			MC V AE	YES	Lively diner, nostalgic decor, fun, family oriented Soda fountain, burgers, meatloaf, daily specials Entertainment & dancing nightly
	Gentleman's Choice ESCONDIDO - 1511-13 E. Valley Pkwy In The Vineyard Shopping Ctr	480-9922	-- L (X:S/S) D	F / Sa			$		MC V AE DC	Rec 100	18th century decor, formal feeling but casual, seafood Prime rib, banquet facilities & off-premises catering
	Gentleman's Choice SAN MARCOS - 1020 W. San Marcos Blvd In Old California Market	744-5215	-- L (X:S/S) D	F / Sa			$		MC V AE DC	Rec 40	Voted "Best Prime Rib Inland"; 18th century decor formal yet relaxed and comfortable, Prime rib & seafood Entertainment(F/Sa)
	Inn At Rancho Sante Fe RANCHO SANTA FE - 5951 Linea Del Cielo	756-1131	B L D					$	MC V AE DC	Yes	Elegant country inn in a quiet setting, intimate bar Dining room is modeled after a traditional tap room Garden room setting also
	Michael's Chicago Style Hot Dogs ESCONDIDO - 150 W. El Norte Pkwy East of Centre City Pkwy	747-3399	-- L D			$			NONE	No	Diner atmosphere, very casual, fun, family oriented Menu offers: milk shakes, cheese fries, Italian sausage sandwiches, burgers
	Packing House FALLBROOK - 125 S. Main St South of Alvarado St	728-5458	-- L (X:Su) D (X:Su)		✓		$		MC V	6p+	Rustic, comfortable atmosphere, booths Beef & daily seafood specials, salad bar Entertainment(F/Sa)
	Pine Hills Lodge Julian PINE HILLS - 2960 La Posada Way Blue Jay Drive	765-1100	-- -- D (F-Sa)		✓		$		MC V AE DC	Rec 100	Country style dining room Barbeque Dinner theater(F-Sa)
	Quails Inn, The LAKE SAN MARCOS - 1035 La Bonita Dr In Lake San Marcos Resort	744-2445	-- L (X:Su) D	F / Sa	✓		$		MC V	Rec 8p+	Lake view from most seats, surroundings are subtle in colors of mauve, coral, & light blue-green Quiet and relaxed, basic American menu
	San Luis Rey Downs BONSALL - 31474 Golf Club Dr In San Luis Rey Downs Resort	758-3762	B L D				$		MC V AE	Rec	Rustic atmosphere with quiet, relaxed dining Prime rib & seafood are the specialties Entertainment(F-Su)
	Stoneridge Country Club POWAY - 17166 Stoneridge CC Lane In Stoneridge Country Club	487-2138	B (X:M) L (X:M) D (X:M)				$		MC V	Rec	Elegant, country atmosphere, expansive golf course view Menu features chicken, steak, seafood, Dancing(F/Sa) to live music
	T-Bird Diner ESCONDIDO - 601 N.Broadway	480-2473	-- L D			$			AE MC V	No	Nostalgic diner playing '50's music, a variety of memorabilia on the walls, authentic soda fountain Typical diner menu
	Terraces Cafe, The PENASQUITOS - 14455 Penasquitos Dr.	672-9100	B L D		✓		$		MC V AE	Yes	Relaxed, casual Sits on the Carmel Highland Golf Course Live jazz on the green Sunday afternoons
	Trents PENASQUITOS - 14455 Penasquitos Dr. See Terraces Cafe	672-9100	- -- D				$		AE MC V	Yes	Elegant setting Find dining featuring Regional/American cuisine Entertainment & dancing(Th-Su)
	Veranda, The RANCHO BERNARDO - 17550 Bernardo Oaks Dr North of Rancho Bernardo Rd	487-1611	B L D					$	MC V AE DC	Rec	Early California country house feeling, relaxed, comfortable, seafood & prime rib
CAJUN/CREOLE	Chez Orleans ESCONDIDO - 302 North Midway Dr North of Valley Pkwy.	743-1772	-- -- D (X:Su-M)		✓			$	MC V AE DC	Rec	New Orleans style decor featuring poultry, seafood, steaks, prime rib, lamb & veal Banquet facility & catering
CALIFORNIA	Cafe Champagne RANCHO CALIFORNIA In Culbertson Winery (see map page 64)	699-0088	-- L D					$	MC V	Rec 20	Patio seating that overlooks valley's vineyards, soft, comfortable setting, California menu with southwest accent, fresh herb gardens, Wine tasting, Private room
CHINESE	Peking Wok VISTA - 1241 East Vista Way South of Bobier Dr	724-8078	-- L (X:S/S) D				$		MC V AE DC	Rec 6p+	San Diego magazine awards '87,'88, '89 San Diego Union '88, '89 Edible art, seafood specialties, piano music
	Sau-Hy's FALLBROOK - 909 South Main St South of Aviation Rd	728-1000	-- L (X:Su-M) D(X:Su-M			$			MC V AE DC	Yes	Interior features Chinese lanterns and shelves of authentic Ming vases; Szechuan, Hunan, Peking & Cantonese dishes
CONTINENTAL	Cambridge Inn, The VISTA - 1280 East Vista Way In Mesa Vista Center	726-2303	-- L(X:Sa-M D (X:M)			$			MC V	Rec 5p+ 85	Homey English decor with a continental touch, homecooked roast, lamb, seafood Piano bar(W-Sa), Banquet facilities, Senior specials
	El Bizcocho RANCHO BERNARDO-17550 Bernardo Oaks Dr In The Rancho Bernardo Inn	487-1611	-- -- D		✓			+	MC V AE DC	Must 40	Reminiscent of a turn-of-the-century luxury resort Golf course view,low calorie, prix-fixe menus available Jacket required, piano bar

Cuisine (NOTES)	Restaurant / COMMUNITY - Street / Located Near	PHONE	Serving: Brkfst/Lunch/Dinner X=Closed	Late Night Din.	Sunday Brunch	Under $10	$10 to $20	$20 to $30+	Credit Cards	Reservations	SPECIAL FEATURES
CONTINENTAL (Con't)	**Le Bistro** / *FALLBROOK - 119 North Main St* / In Jackson Square	723-3559	-- / -- / D (X:Su/M)				$		MC V AE	Rec	Intimate atmosphere, elegant but California casual / French accent, daily specials / Catering, B&W only
DELI	**Deer Park Winery** / *ESCONDIDO - 29103 Champagne Blvd* / North of Mountain Meadow Rd	749-1666	-- / L / --			$			MC V	None / 250	Gourmet deli, vineyard, orchard, park picnic / Auto museums (weekends) / Wine tasting
FRENCH	**Mille Fleurs** / *RANCHO SANTA FE - 6009 Paseo Delicias*	756-3085	-- / L (M-F) / D					$	all	Must / 20	Comfortable atmosphere with blazing fireplace / Small romantic atmosphere with outstanding food / Large Wine list, cooking by Martin Woesle
	Seafare / *RANCHO BERNARDO - 15721E Bernardo Hts Pkw* / West of Pomerado Rd (Rt 55)	451-2026	-- / L (X:S/S) / D (X:Su)				$		MC V AE	Rec	Small, intimate country French setting, elegant / Daily menu offering a variety of seafood, veal, chicken / Good selection of wines, B&W only
INTERNAT'L	**La Estancia Inn** / *FALLBROOK - 3135 Hwy 395 South* / Intersection of Hwy 76 & I-15	723-2888	-- / L(X:Su) / D		✓		$		MC V AE	Rec / 100	Tropical villa atmosphere with view of the mountains / Classic American & international cuisine / Banquet facilities & catering
ITALIAN	**Bruno's** / *SAN MARCOS - 1020 W. San Marcos Blvd* / West of Via Vera Cruz	744-7700	-- / L (X:Su) / D		✓	$			MC V	Rec / 10p+	Casual, typical Italian, family oriented, / Homemade pizza and pasta / Carry-out deli
	Ristorante Galileo / *POWAY - 12440 Poway Rd* / East of Pomerado Rd	748-2900	-- / L (X:S/S) / D				$		MC V AE DC	Rec	Tavern-style atmosphere, bakery & deli / Continental dishes, catering / B&W only
	Romano's Dodge House / *JULIAN - 2718 B St* / West of Main St	765-1003	-- / L (X:S/S) / D (X:Su)				$		NONE	Yes	Converted mansion, homey, right on the main street / Family oriented, menu features pizzas, pastas / and full entrees
	Valentino's / *RANCHO BERNARDO-11828 Rancho Bernardo Rd*	451-3200	-- / - / D				$		MC V AE	Yes	Elegant, classic romantic setting gourmet Italian / Patio seating, Harp music(W-Sa) / Catering
JAPANESE	**Katsu** Seafood & Steak House / *SAN MARCOS - 1020 San Marcos Blvd* / West of Twin Oaks Valley Rd	744-7156	-- / L (X:Sa-M / D (X:M)		$				MC V	Yes / 30	A north county favorite, sushi bar, teppan steak, / stir fry, tempura, traditional favorites also
	Restaurant Yae / *RANCHO BERNARDO - 11616 Iberia Pl* / East of Bernardo Center Dr	485-0390	-- / L (X-Sa-M) / D (X-Sa-M)					$	MC V AE DC	Rec / 64	Oriental atmosphere features teak wood & shoji screens / Indoor garden & pond, elegant & comfortable, sushi bar / Tatami room along with Japanese favorites
	Shien Of Osaka / *RANCHO BERNARDO-16769 Bernardo Center Dr* / At Lomica Dr	451-0074	-- / L (X:S/S) / D (X:Su)				$		MC V AE	Rec / 18	Modern but cozy Japanese setting to enjoy sushi, / tempura, yakitori & soft-shell crab / B&W only
MEXICAN	**El Establo** / *BONSALL - Hwy 76* / At West Lilac	758-0310	-- / L (X:S/S) / D			$			MC V AE	No	Rustic Mexican setting, outdoor seating / For lunch only, traditional menu
(FOOD-TO-GO)	**Rubio's Deli-Mex** / *SAN MARCOS - Nordhal at Hwy 78*	745-2062	-- / L / D			$					FOOD-TO-GO Carry-out only, limited seating, family run / Home of the famous San Felipe-style fish taco & other / Mexican favorites, multiple locations, catering
POLISH	**Stella's Hideaway** / *RANCHO PENASQUITOS-14323 Penasquitos Dr* / West of Carmel Mountain Rd	672-3604	-- / L (X:S/S) / D				$		MC V AE	Yes / 6p+	Homey, casual, old pictures of Poland on the walls / Everything is homemade, sausage, stuffed cabbage, / Recipes handed down through families,B&W only
SEAFOOD	**Anthony's II** / *RANCHO BERNARDO - 11666 Avena Pl* / West of Bernardo Center Dr	451-2070	-- / L / D				$		MC V AE	Rec	Park view in comfortable, contemporary setting / House specials include seafood, chicken & steak / Fish market offers carry-out
	Brigantine, The / *ESCONDIDO - 421 West Felicita Ave* / West of Centre City Pkwy	743-4718	-- / L (X:S/S) / D	F / Sa	✓		$		MC V AE DC CB	Rec	Nautical theme, Ship's mast & sails inside the dining / Room, Relaxed atmosphere, Seafood emphasis / Multiple locations
	Fish House Vera Cruz / *SAN MARCOS - 1020 W. San Marcos Blvd* / Old California Restaurant Row	744-8000	-- / L / D				$		MC V AE	No	Rustic and casual atmosphere, aquarium in the bar / Emphasis is seafood / Fish market, carry-out
	Rancho Vera Cruz / *SAN MARCOS - 1020 San Marcos Blvd*	744-8000	-- / L (X:S) / D		$				MC V AE	No	Casual fish house setting featuring a variety of / seafood, Cajun catfish, chicken & Mexican dishes / Carry-out, Fish market, B&W only

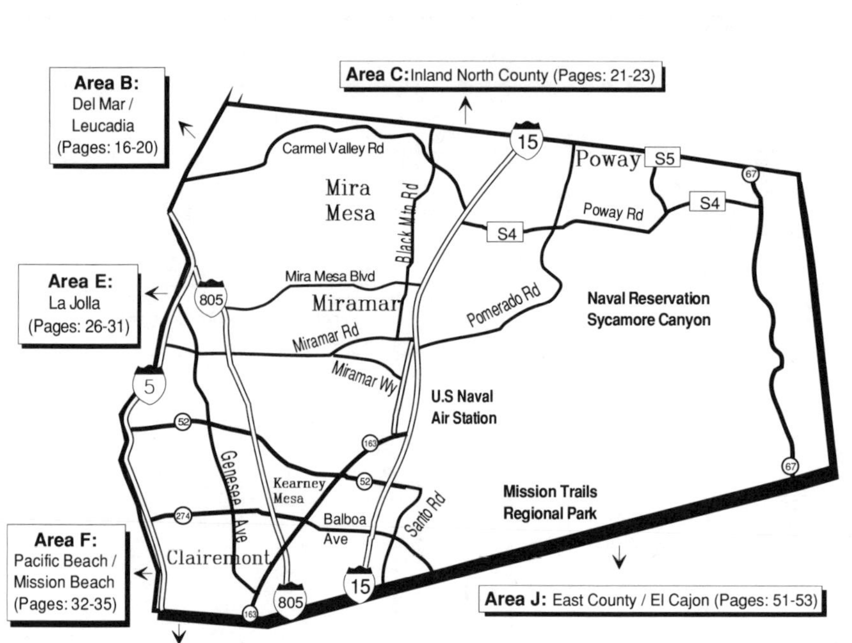

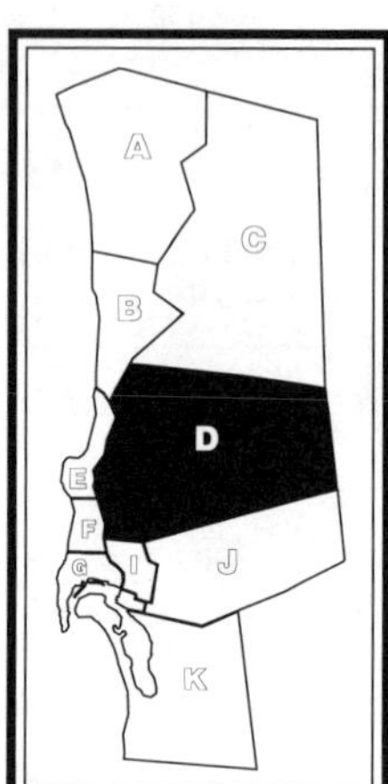

ALPHABETIC LISTINGS

RESTAURANT (CUISINE Category)	RESTAURANT (CUISINE Category)	RESTAURANT (CUISINE Category)
Butcher Shop (AMERICAN)	Hindquarter, The (AMERICAN)	Mandarin Garden (CHINESE)
Callahan's Pub & Brewery (IRISH)	Imperial Mandarin (CHINESE)	Mr. Noodle (JAPANESE)
Casa Machado (MEXICAN)	Katzra (JAPANESE)	Pho Pasteur (VIETNAMESE)
French Cafe (FRENCH)	Khyber Pass (AFGHAN)	Tawana Siamese Cuisine (THAI)
Godfather, The (ITALIAN)	Kooky's Diner (AMERICAN)	Tengu (JAPANESE)
Good Egg, The (AMERICAN)	Korea House (KOREAN)	Wei's Potsticker (CHINESE)

Cuisine (NOTES)	Restaurant / COMMUNITY - Street / Located Near	PHONE (619)	Serving: Brkfst / Lunch / Dinner / X=Closed	Late Night Din.	Sunday Brunch	Under $10	$10 to $20	$20 to $30+	Credit Cards	Reservations	SPECIAL FEATURES
AFGHAN	**Khyber Pass** / KEARNY MESA - 4647 Convoy St / North of Balboa Av	571-3749	-- / L (X:Su) / D				$		MC V	Yes / F/Sa / 25	Cave decor, dark, cozy, authentic setting / Vegetarian dishes / B&W only
AMERICAN	**Butcher Shop** / CLAIREMONT MESA-5255 Kearney Villa Rd / Hwy 163 & Clairemont Mesa	565-2272	-- / L / D	Y			$		MC V	Yes	Dark, comfortable, relaxed, dinner house atmosphere / Nebraska prime rib, steaks, seafood & Italian / specialties, large portions, late night dining
	Good Egg, The / CLAIREMONT MESA - 7947 Balboa Av	565-4244	B / L / --			$			MC V	Yes	Casual, cafe atmosphere / Menu features omelets, fritata, gourmet pancakes / burgers & salads, Sa/Su it's a non-smoking restaurant
	Hindquarter, The / MIRAMAR - 7040 Miramar Rd.	566-4292	-- / -- / D		✓	$			MC V	Yes	Steak & Seafood House, generous portions, good value / Family-oriented, family-run
	Kooky's Diner / MIRAMAR - 9449 Kearny Mesa Rd / At Miramar Rd	271-4670	B / L / D			$			MC V	Rec	1950's style diner open 24 hours, traditional menu / Memorabilia for the era on the walls, jukebox / 3 locations
CHINESE	**Imperial Mandarin** / KEARNY MESA - 3904 Convoy St / South of Balboa Av	292-1222	-- / L / D	Y	✓	$			MC V	Yes	Traditional Chinese setting & decor, feature Dim Sum / Traditional dishes / B&W only
	Mandarin Garden / MIRA MESA - 8242 Mira Mesa Blvd / In Mira Mesa Mall	566-4720	-- / L / D			$			MC V / AE DC	Rec	Mandarin & Szechuan cuisine / Dim Sum Lunch(Sa-Su)
	Wei's Potsticker / KEARNY MESA - 3860 Convoy St / In The Sunrise Town Center	560-5333	-- / L / D		✓	$			MC V / AE	Rec	Szechuan and Hunan style, San Diego Union said ``Good / interesting food very reasonably priced'' / Dumplings, full menu, Carry-out, B&W Only
FRENCH	**French Cafe** / MIRAMAR - 9823 Carroll Canyon Rd / In Eucalyptus Square	566-4000	-- / L / D		✓		$		MC V / AE / 45	Rec	Casual, Indoor & outdoor dining, Lunch offers salads / Hot specials, dinner features duck, 3 types of filet / mignon, desserts, Live music(M-Sa)
	Winesellar & Brasserie / MIRA MESA - 9550 Waples St, Suite 115 / Off Steadman 1 Blk S of Mira Mesa Bl	450-9557	-- / L (X:Su) / D (X:Su)				$		MC V / 50	Rec	Eclectic menu using French techniques and California / product, open kitchen, Wine Spectator Award Winner / Connected to wine shop and wine bar, B&W only
IRISH	**Callahan's Pub & Brewery** / MIRAMAR-8280 Mira Mesa Blvd	578-7892	-- / L / D			$			MC V / AE	Rec	Authentic Irish pub feeling, mircobrewery, hardwood floors / Beams, ceiling fans, lantern lighting / Menu offers stews, pot pies, burgers, sandwiches
ITALIAN	**Godfather, The** / KEARNY MESA - 7878 Clairemont Mesa Bl / West of Fwy 163	560-1747	-- / L (X:Sa/Su) / D	F / / Sa		$			MC V / AE / 35	Rec	Casual dining, spaghetti, lasagna, / Both booths and tables, 14 year old family restaurant / Piano(F-Su), Silver Award/SCRW
JAPANESE	**Katzra** / KEARNY MESA - 4229 Convoy St / South of Balboa Av	279-3430	-- / L (X:Sa/Su) / D			$			MC V / AE	5p+	Casual, traditional setting featuring Japanese / favorites, Sushi bar, Sampler Platter, Shabu Shabu / Cooked tableside
	Mr. Noodle / CLAIREMONT MESA - 4681 Convoy	576-7244	-- / L / D			$			MC V / AE	Rec	Unique dishes, Japanese noodles used to make chicken / fettucine, seafood spaghetti, 4 to 5 different kinds of / rice, Owned by Mr. Sushi, B&W only
	Tengu / CLAIREMONT MESA -8690 Aero Dr / At Montgomery Field	292-0141	-- / L (X:Sa/Su) / D	Fa / / Sa		$			MC V / AE D	Yes	Exotic Japanese decor, a wide variety of dishes with / Traditional preparation, extensive Sushi bar / Banquet Facilities, Catering
KOREAN	**Korea House** / KEARNY MESA - 4620 Convoy St / North of Balboa Av	560-0080	L / D	Y	✓	$			MC V / AE DC	Must / 40	Korean BBQ & kal bi / Private room; electric organ(F/Sa)
MEXICAN	**Casa Machado** / CLAIREMONT MESA -3750 J.Montgomery Dr.	292-4716	-- / L (X:Su) / D		✓	$			MC V / AE	Yes / 100	Watch planes takeoff and land at Montgomery Field / Traditional Mexican menu / Catering, Banquet facilities
THAI	**Tawana Siamese Cuisine** / CLAIREMONT- 5535 Clairemont Mesa Bl / West of I-805	541-1155	-- / L (X:Sa/Su) / D			$			MC V / AE DC	Rec	Traditional menu, family owned small intimate / Everything is cooked to order / B&W only
VIETNAMESE	**Pho Pasteur** / LINDA VISTA - 7612 Linda Vista Rd / South of Mesa College Rd	569-7515	B / L / D		✓	$			MC V	Yes	Vietnamese and Chinese / American family dinners from $6.95 / B&W only

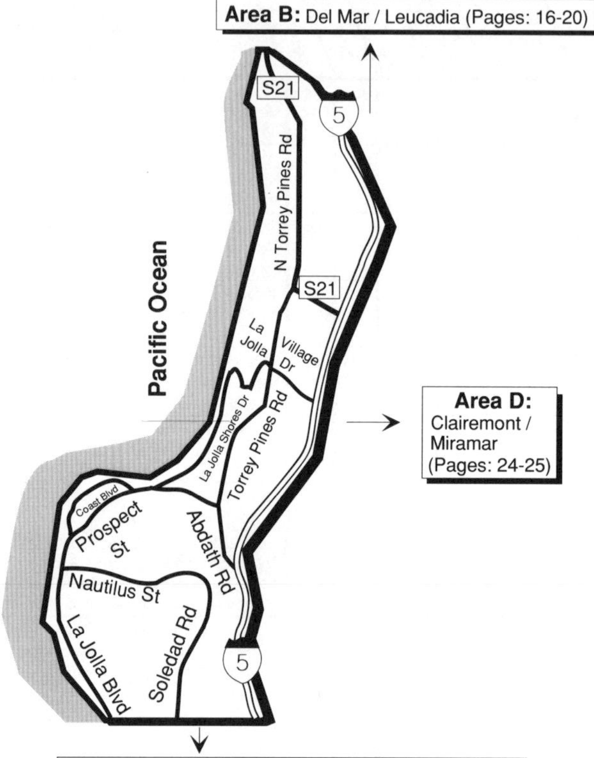

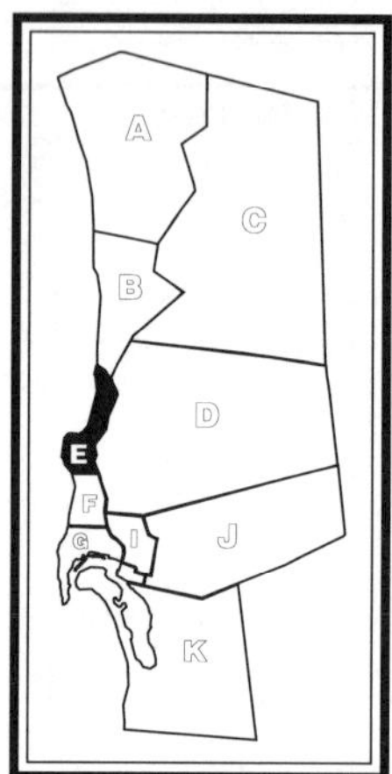

ALPHABETIC LISTINGS

RESTAURANT (CUISINE Category)	RESTAURANT (CUISINE Category)	RESTAURANT (CUISINE Category)
Aesop's Tables (GREEK)	Humphrey's La Jolla Grill (SEAFOOD)	Piret's (CALIFORNIA)
Alfonso's (MEXICAN)	Issimo (ITALIAN)	Pollo La Jolla (FOOD-TO-GO)
Aloha Louie's (SEAFOOD)	Jose's Court Room (MEXICAN)	Presto (ITALIAN)
Anthony's La Jolla (SEAFOOD)	Kiva Grill (SOUTHWEST)	Putnam's (AMERICAN)
Ashoka (INDIAN)	L'Auberge (FRENCH)	Rusty Pelican (SEAFOOD)
Avanti (ITALIAN)	La Playa Grill (MEXICAN)	Sammy's Cal. Woodfired Pizza (CALIFORNIA)
Barcino (MEDITERRANEAN)	La Terrace (FRENCH)	Samsons Deli-Restaurant (DELI)
Boll Weevil (AMERICAN)	Le Corbier (CONTINENTAL)	Sante (ITALIAN)
Bully's (AMERICAN)	Lemon Grass (THAI)	Shogun (JAPANESE)
Cafe Japengo (JAPANESE)	Magic Pan (FRENCH)	Shores at the Sea Lodge, The (SEAFOOD)
Cafe Roma (ITALIAN)	Maitre D' (FRENCH)	Sky Room (CONTINENTAL)
Chart House (AMERICAN)	Mandarin Cove (CHINESE)	Sluggo's (FOOD-TO-GO)
Chuck's Steak House (AMERICAN)	Mandarin House (CHINESE)	Spot, The (AMERICAN)
Cindy Black (FRENCH)	Manhattan (ITALIAN)	St. James Bar (FRENCH)
Clay's Texas Pit Bar-B-Q (AMERICAN)	Marine Room (SEAFOOD)	Star of India (INDIAN)
Desmond's Cuisine Of India (INDIAN)	Mediterranean Room (CONTINENTAL)	Su Casa (MEXICAN)
El Crab Catcher (ECLECTIC)	Miss China Restaurant (CHINESE)	Sushi On The Rocks (JAPANESE)
Elario's (FRENCH)	Nancaro's Elephant Bar (ECLECTIC)	Szechuan House (CHINESE)
Falcone's (ITALIAN)	Orchids (CONTINENTAL)	T. G. I. Friday's (ECLECTIC)
Fisherman's Grill (SEAFOOD)	Other Place of Dale Anderson (AMERICAN)	Top O' The Cove (CONTINENTAL)
French Gourmet Too, The (FRENCH)	P. J. Wolf's (AMERICAN)	Torrey Pines Inn (AMERICAN)
French Pastry Shop, The (FRENCH)	Papachinos (ITALIAN)	Torreyana Grille (AMERICAN)
George E. Wong (CHINESE)	Paparazzi (ITALIAN)	Tropical Patio, The (CONTINENTAL)
George's at the Cove (CALIFORNIA)	Pasha (AFGHAN)	Upstairs Cafe at the Cove (FRENCH)
Hard Rock Cafe (AMERICAN)	Pei's of La Jolla (CHINESE)	Vic's Restaurant (AMERICAN)
Harry's Cafe Gallery (AMERICAN)	Peking Palace (CHINESE)	Whaling Bar/Cafe La Rue (AMERICAN)

Cuisine (NOTES)	Restaurant / COMMUNITY - Street / Located Near	PHONE (619)	Serving: Brkfst / Lunch / Dinner / X=Closed	Late Night Din.	Sunday Brunch	Under $10	$10 to $20	$20 to $30+	Credit Cards	Reservations	SPECIAL FEATURES
AFGHAN	**Pasha** *LA JOLLA* - 1110 Torrey Pines Road	454-9229	-- L (X:Su) D (X:Su)			$			MC V AE	Yes	Diners have a choice of sitting at tables or on floor pillows in the traditional Afghan style, menu offers curry dishes, shish kabobs, rice dishes, B&W only
AMERICAN	**Boll Weevil** *LA JOLLA* - 1000 Prospect St North of La Jolla Blvd	454-2666	-- L D (Y)		$				MC V	Yes 10p+	Casual, family oriented, pool tables, burgers Locations throughout San Diego
	Bully's *LA JOLLA* - 5755 La Jolla Blvd North of Bird Rock Av	459-2768	B L D (Y)			$			MC V AE DC	No	Popular with the locals, prime rib, seafood, burgers Locations throughout San Diego
	Chart House *LA JOLLA* - 1270 Prospect St North of Girard Av	459-820	-- -- D	F / Sa				$	MC V AE DC D	Rec	Relaxed atmosphere with breathtaking view of La Jolla Cove, large salad bar, fresh catches of the day Grilled beef and chicken entrees, multiple locations
	Chuck's Steak House *LA JOLLA* - 1250 Prospect St In Pacific Plaza	454-5325	-- L (X:Sa/Su) D (Y)			$			MC V AE DC D	Rec	Dark and cozy setting, intimate atmosphere, fireplace Small dinner house menu Jazz(W-Su), Three awards for ``Best Steak''
	Clay's Texas Pit Bar-B-Q *LA JOLLA* - 5752 La Jolla Blvd North of Bird Rock Av	454-2388	-- L (X:Su/M D (X:M)			$			MC V AE DC	Rec Wkn	Very rustic, casual Old Southern family recipes for chicken, ribs, steak Catering
	Hard Rock Cafe *LA JOLLA* - 909 Prospect St North of La Jolla Blvd	454-5101	-- L D (Y)		$				MC V AE	No	World famous rock & roll museum, Rock memorabilia Outdoor dining, located in downtown La Jolla Cafe menu, large portions, Silver Award/SCRW
	Harry's Cafe Gallery *LA JOLLA* - 7545 Girard Av North of Pearl St	454-7381	B (X:Su) L (X:Su) --			$			NONE 16	No	Open 29 years, artists works on the walls ``the'' coffee shop in La Jolla for breakfast
	Other Place of Dale Anderson *LA JOLLA* - 4550 La Jolla Village Dr In the Embassy Suites Hotel	453-1418	-- L D (Y)			$			MC V AE	Yes	Contemporary, soft, subtle, low-light setting with a Southwestern accent, Lunch menu - sandwiches, burgers Dinner, filet mignon, seafood, banquets, Catering
	P. J. Wolf's *LA JOLLA* - 3787 La Jolla Village Drive IN THE AVENTINE COMPLEX	425-WOLF	-- L (X:Sa/Su) D (Y)				$		MC V AE	Yes	Elegant, china, crystal, silver, very dressy Steak house, daily specials
	Putnam's *LA JOLLA* - 910 Prospect St In The Colonial Inn	454-2181	B L D			$			MC V AE	Rec 50	Intimate restaurant, elegantly decorated with cherry wood paneling and deep forest green Cajun & Pacific Northwest Specialties
	Spot, The *LA JOLLA* - 1005 Prospect St North of La Jolla Blvd	459-0809	-- L D (Y)			$			MC V AE DC D	Rec 6p+ 25	Casual, lively & active spot, popular with locals and visitors, windows open to street, Gourmet specials BBQ ribs, chicken, pizzas
	Torrey Pines Inn *LA JOLLA* - 11480 Torrey Pines Rd North of Genesee Av	453-4420	-- L D			$			MC V AE DC	Rec	Outdoor seating available, view of the golfcourse Lobster dinners, Seafood buffet on Friday nights Sunday champagne brunch
	Torreyana Grille *LA JOLLA* - 10959 Torrey Pines Road In the Sheraton Grand Torrey Pines Hotel	450-4571	B L D		✓	$			MC V AE DC	Rec	Setting over looks the Torrey Pines golfcourse Elegant environment of marble and glass, Alfresco on ``The Terrace'' steaks, seafood & American cuisine
	Vic's Restaurant *LA JOLLA* - 7825 Fay Av In The Merrill Lynch Bldg.	456-3789	-- L (X:Su) D	F / Sa	✓			$	MC V AE DC	Rec 81	Comfortable, contemporary, unpretentious setting for seafood, prime rib, rotisserie specials Piano(W-Sa)
	Whaling Bar/Cafe La Rue *LA JOLLA* - 1132 Prospect St In La Valencia Hotel	454-0771	-- L (X:Su) D					+	MC V AE DC	Rec 12	Busy, active spot, popular with La Jollans Booths, seafood, prime rib, Jeanne Jones special menus Jacket suggested
CALIFORNIA	**George's at the Cove** *LA JOLLA* - 1250 Prospect St Cave St	454-4244	-- L (X:Su) D	F / Sa				+	MC V AE DC	Rec	Elegantly casual, Ocean view, classic California decor Innovative dishes, upstairs outdoor patio features lighter menu, Gold Medal/SCRW
	Piret's *LA JOLLA* - 8697 Villa La Jolla Dr In La Jolla Village Square	455-7955	-- L D				$		MC V AE	Yes 75	Bistro type atmosphere, daily specials, weekend brunch California/French fare, regular winemaker dinners Carry-out, catering, B&W only
	Sammy's California Woodfired Pizza *LA JOLLA* - 702 Pearl St At Draper St	456-5222	-- L D	F / Sa	✓	$			MC V AE DC	No	Easy, comfortable, ideal for families, outdoor patio Great portions, gourmet pizza, pasta, salads Carry-out, B&W only
CHINESE	**George E. Wong** *LA JOLLA* - 1250 Prospect St.	454-9664	-- L D			$			MC V AE	Rec	Modern black & white tiled dining room, very large Alfresco deck overlooking Prospect St., Outdoor seating Dim Sum specialties, pot stickers, traditional dishes

Cuisine (NOTES)	Restaurant / COMMUNITY - Street / Located Near	PHONE	SERVING: Brkfst/Lunch/Dinner X=Closed	Late Night Din.	Sunday Brunch	Under $10	$10 to $20	$20 to $30+	Credit Cards	Reservations	SPECIAL FEATURES
CHINESE (Con't)	Mandarin Cove LA JOLLA - 1299 Prospect St West of Coast Blvd	456-9500	-- L D				$		MC V AE	Yes	Art deco decor, stylish colors with accent of neon House specials include Peking Duck, Crispy Hunan Beef B&W only
	Mandarin House LA JOLLA - 6765 La Jolla Blvd North of Gravilla St	454-2555	-- L (X:Su) D	F / Sa		$			MC V AE	Rec	Traditional Chinese decor San Diego's oldest chinese restaurant Carry-out
	Miss China Restaurant LA JOLLA - 2240 Avenida de la Playa North of La Jolla Shores Dr	454-2311	-- L (X:Sa/Su) D				$		NONE	Rec	Traditional Chinese setting Very small, casual Carry-out, Silver medal/SCRW, No bar
	Pei's of La Jolla LA JOLLA -7660 Fay Av	456-6666	-- L (X:Sa/Su) D				$		MC V	Rec	Upscale Mandarin cuisine, contemporary setting, Family owned, entrees prepared using the freshest ingredients, Carry-out & Catering
	Peking Palace LA JOLLA - 4405 La Jolla Village Dr In University Towne Center	452-7500	-- L D				$		MC V AE	Rec 60	Intimate dining room decorated with authentic handcrafted pieces from China Mandarin & Szechuan dishes, daily specials
	Szechuan House LA JOLLA - 5771 La Jolla Blvd North of Bird Rock Av	454-8625	-- L (X:Su) D			$			MC V AE DC	Rec 4p+	Cozy, elegant surroundings, traditional Chinese setting No MSG used in its dishes
CONTINENTAL	Le Corbier LA JOLLA - 6941 La Jolla Blvd South of Westbourne St	456-8088	-- -- D (X:Su/M)					+	MC V DC	Rec	Art gallery with an art deco theme Cosmopolitan cuisine with a California accent
	Mediterranean Room LA JOLLA - 1132 Prospect St In La Valencia Hotel	454-0771	B L D				$		MC V AE DC	Rec 14	Elegant dining, outdoor seating, ocean view Mediterranean cuisine, daily specials Lavish Sunday Buffet Brunch
	Orchids LA JOLLA - 4240 La Jolla Village Dr In Marriott Hotel	587-1414	-- L (X:Sa/Su) D (X:Su/M)	✓			$		MC V AE DC D	Rec	Elegant fine dining atmosphere Seafood, pastas, veal
	Sky Room LA JOLLA - 1132 Prospect St Top of The La Valencia Hotel	454-0771	-- L (X:Sa/Su) D (X:Su)					+	MC V AE DC	Must	Splendid view of the ocean, elegant, quaint, intimate A San Diego institution, prix-fixe menu Jacket required
	Top O' The Cove LA JOLLA - 1216 Prospect St North of Girard Av	454-7779	-- L (X:Sa/Su) D					+	MC V AE	Must	Intimate cottage, romantic atmosphere, veal, chicken pastas, fabulous desserts, Extensive wine list Piano(W-Su), Jacket required
	Tropical Patio, The LA JOLLA - 1132 Prospect St In The La Valencia Hotel	454-0771	B L D	✓		$			MC V	Rec	Outdoor garden setting with cafe atmosphere, casual Menu features daily specials, sandwiches, soups, salads Hours vary depending on weather
DELI	Samsons Deli-Restaurant LA JOLLA - 8861 Villa La Jolla Dr In La Jolla Village Square	455-1461	B L D			$			MC V AE DC		Walls are covered with movie memorabilia Casual, New York-style deli, kosher food, bakery Carry-out, catering
ECLECTIC	El Crab Catcher LA JOLLA - 1298 Prospect St In Coast Walk	454-9587	-- L (X:Su) D	✓			$		MC V AE	Rec	View of the cove, patio, oyster bar Hawaiian import features fresh fish & Mexican specials Champagne Brunch
	Nancaro's Elephant Bar & Rest. LA JOLLA - 8980 Villa La Jolla Dr.	587-1993	-- L (X:Su) D	F / Sa	✓	$			MC V	Yes 130	Open feeling, comfortable, casual Salads, sandwiches, omelettes, beef & seafood Popular with the college crowd, Happy Hour daily
	T. G. I. Friday's LA JOLLA - 8801 Villa La Jolla Dr In La Jolla Village Square	455-0880	-- L D	Y			$		MC V AE DC	Yes 6p+	Fun atmosphere, loud, suitable for children Eclectic decor, Wide variety of menu items Multiple locations
FOOD-TO-GO	Pollo La Jolla LA JOLLA - 6875 La Jolla Blvd	456-9014	L D			$			None	No	Healthy, low cholesterol broiled chicken in fresh herbs Comes with salsa & tortillas, side dishes include beans, Spanish rice, salads, catering & delivery in LJ
	Sluggo's LA JOLLA -6980 La Jolla Blvd.		-- L D			$			--	--	Some seating, sports games on monitors Informal, Chicago-style hot dogs, burgers, fries New location in Hillcrest
FRENCH	Cindy Black LA JOLLA - 5721 La Jolla Blvd At Bird Rock Av	456-6299	-- -- D (X:Su)				$		MC V AE	Must 80	Award winning chef unpretentious, small intimate dining Country French menu, seasonal changes using lamb, duck chicken, Private luncheons available
	Elario's LA JOLLA - 7955 La Jolla Shores Dr Top of the Summer House Inn	459-0541	-- L (X:Sa/Su) D	✓			$		MC V AE DC D	Rec 100	Incredible view of the ocean, romantic, booths are very private, elegant dining, Awards for best view, romantic spot & desserts, Live jazz

Cuisine (NOTES)	Restaurant / COMMUNITY - Street / Located Near	PHONE	Serving (Brkfst / Lunch / Dinner, X=Closed)	Late Night Din.	Sunday Brunch	Under $10	$10 to $20	$20 to $30+	Credit Cards	Reservations	SPECIAL FEATURES
FRENCH (Con't)	**French Gourmet Too, The** *LA JOLLA* - 713 Pearl St East of La Jolla Blvd	454-6736	B / L / D	F / Sa					MC V AE DC	Rec	Very small, intimate bistro setting, outdoor patio Fresh breads, croissants, desserts Carry-out, catering
	French Pastry Shop, The *LA JOLLA* - 5550 La Jolla Blvd North of Midway St	454-9094	B / L / D (X:M)	Y		$			MC V	No	Casual bistro setting featuring daily specials, seafood Sandwiches, quiches and fresh baked pastries
	L'Auberge *LA JOLLA* - 1237 Prospect St In The International Shops Ctr	454-2524	L (X:Su) / D (X:Su)					$	MC V AE	Rec	Small country French setting with outdoor dining Intimate romantic setting Daily specials
	La Terrace *LA JOLLA* - 1295 Prospect St North of Girard Av	456-2661	L (X:Sa/Su) / D		✓		$		MC V AE	Rec	Elegant, yet informal, ocean view & terrace dining Traditional southern French menu, daily specials
	Magic Pan *LA JOLLA* - 4353 La Jolla Village Drive In University Towne Center	453-6616	L / D			$			MC V	Yes	Contemporary French countryside theme, relaxed, casual Crepes are the specialty
	Maitre D' *LA JOLLA* - 5523 La Jolla Blvd North of Midway St	456-2111	D (X:Su/M)	Y				+	MC V AE DC	Rec 80	Romantic, elegant, & classy atmosphere Classic French cuisine, specialties are flambeou meats pheasant and lamb, Piano, Jackets preferred
	St. James Bar *LA JOLLA* - 4370 La Jolla Village Dr West of I-805	453-6650	L (X:Sa/Su) / D (X:Su)	F / Sa				$	MC V AE	Rec	Country French setting, antique bar Owned by Paul Dobson, locally known bullfighter French cuisine with California accent, daily menu
	Upstairs Cafe at the Cove *LA JOLLA* - 8008 Girard Av North of Prospect St	454-8884	B / L / D	F / Sa			$		MC V AE DC	Rec 100	Multilevel patio with a great view, alfresco dining Dinner entrees are prepared with special sauces Banquet facilities
GREEK	**Aesop's Tables** *LA JOLLA* - 8867 Villa La Jolla Dr In La Jolla Village Square	455-1535	L (X:Su) / D			$			MC V AE DC	No 12	Lively taverna specializing in Greek street food Gyros sandwiches, fresh baked pastries Carry-out, B&W only
INDIAN	**Ashoka** *LA JOLLA* - 8008 Girard Av At Prospect St	454-6263	L / D					$	MC V AE DC	Rec 50	Beautiful La Jolla Cove view Buffet lunch, Tandoori Specials B&W only
	Desmond's Cuisine Of India *LA JOLLA* - 613 Pearl St East of La Jolla Blvd	454-8022	D (X:M)	F / Sa			$		MC V AE DC	Rec	Elegant dining, authentic curries, Spicy Lamb Vindaloo Paratha, Samosas, Eastern Indian cuisine
	Star of India *LA JOLLA* - 1025 Prospect St, Suite 100 Near Girard Av	459-3355	L (X:Sa/Su) / D	F / Sa	✓			$	MC V DC D	Rec 25	Patio dining, tables, booths, northern Indian, tandoori vegetarian dishes, lunch buffet Location also in Encinitas, B&W only
ITALIAN	**Avanti** *LA JOLLA* - 875 Prospect St North of La Jolla Blvd	454-4288	L / D	Y				+	MC V AE	Rec	Art deco interior, great spot to people watch Northern Italian Cuisine, open kitchen, fabulous homemade desserts, Dancing(W-Sa), Piano Bar
	Cafe Roma *LA JOLLA* - 7514 Girard Ave	454-4495	L (X:Su/M) / D (X:Su/M)	F / Sa			$		MC V	Yes	Ultra modern, lively bar, younger crowd Simple Italian pastas with a flair Gourmet pizza
	Falcone's *LA JOLLA* - 5518 La Jolla Blvd North of Midway St	454-6421	D				$		MC V AE	Rec	Family atmosphere, casual, cozy spot for pizza and Italian dishes, fresh fish of the day
	Issimo *LA JOLLA* - 5634 La Jolla Blvd South of Bird Rock Av	454-7004	L (X:Su) / D (X:Su)					+	MC V	Must 80	Sophisticated decor, French & Northern Italian specialties, weekly menu Jacket req'd, Gold Medal/SCRW
	Manhattan *LA JOLLA* - 7766 Fay Av In The Empress Hotel	454-1182	L (X:Sa/Su) / D		✓			$	MC V AE	Rec	Swank and upbeat, New York style dining Exotic salt water aquariums, singing waiters Classic Italian Cuisine, Silver Medal/SCRW
	Papachinos *LA JOLLA* - 7748 Regents Rd South of La Jolla Village Dr	546-7666	L / D	Y		$			MC V	No (L) 60	Family style dining with outrageous portions at moderate prices Carry-out
	Paparazzi *LA JOLLA* - 8990 University Center Lane Across from La Jolla Hyatt Regency Hotel	455-PAPA	L / D		✓		$		AE MC V DC	Yes	Relaxed, comfortable, American version of the famous Italian trattorias, village atmosphere, outdoor dining pizza, pasta, authentic dishes
	Presto *LA JOLLA* - 1025 Prospect St North of La Jolla Blvd	454-9711	L (X:Sa/Su) / D	F / Sa			$		MC V AE	Yes 75	Contemporary, slick, popular with the under 30 crowd Cove view, Pptio dining, pizza, pasta and nouvelle dishes, buffet appetizers, Reggae entertainment(F/Sa)

Cuisine (NOTES)	Restaurant / COMMUNITY - Street / Located Near	PHONE	Serving: Brkfst / Lunch / Dinner / X=Closed	Late Night Din.	Sunday Brunch	Under $10	$10 to $20	$20 to $30+	Credit Cards	Reservations	SPECIAL FEATURES
ITALIAN (Con't)	**Sante** / LA JOLLA - 7811 Hershel Av / South of Prospect St	454-1315	-- / L (X:Sa/Su) / D (X:Su)					$	MC V AE DC	Must	Elegant European surroundings, patio dining / Intimate & romantic, Northern Italian menu, fresh pasta / Jacket preferred
JAPANESE	**Cafe Japengo** / LA JOLLA - 8960 University Center Lane / In the Aventine Complex	450-3355	-- / L (X:Sa/Su) / D				$		MC V AE	Yes	Modern Japanese decor, Pacific Rim dinners, Sushi bar / Traditional Japanese dishes such as stir-fry & tempura / Voted ``Best Sushi Bar'' by SD Magazine
	Shogun / LA JOLLA - 4405 La Jolla Village Dr / In University Towne Center	453-8197	-- / L / D			$			MC V AE	Rec 60	Traditional Japanese decor, booths, favorites from / sushi to teriyaki chicken & tempura / Carry-out, banquet facilities, B&W only
	Sushi On The Rocks / LA JOLLA - 1277 Prospect	456-1138	-- / L (X:Su) / D		F / Sa		$		MC V	No	Modern Japanese setting, Popular with the locals / Unique sushi with clever names, / Located in the heart of La Jolla, B&W only
Mediteranean	**Barcino** / LA JOLLA - 377 La Jolla Village Dr. / La Jolla Village Dr & I-5	552-1234	-- / L / D				$		MC V AE	Yes	Very elegant, Roman feeling with the marble statues & / columns, menu offers: seafood, poultry and beef
MEXICAN	**Alfonso's** / LA JOLLA - 1251 Prospect St / North of Girard Av	454-2232	-- / L / D		F / Sa		$		MC V AE	Rec 6p+	Sidewalk cafe & cantina, fun, casual surroundings / Inside is dark & cozy, with big comfortable booths / Bar is popular with 40+ crowd, catering and carry-out
	Jose's Court Room / LA JOLLA - 1037 Prospect St / North of Girard Av	454-7655	-- / L / D		F / Sa	$			MC V AE DC		Loud, noisy, lively atmosphere, popular with the locals / A younger crowd, traditional Mexican menu, daily / specials
	La Playa Grill / LA JOLLA - 1298 Prospect St / In Coast Walk	454-9033	-- / L / D				$		MC V AE	Rec	Colonial Mexican atmosphere with palapa umbrellas / View of the cove & patio dining / Mesquite grill & traditional Mexican dishes
	Su Casa / LA JOLLA - 6738 La Jolla Blvd / North of Gravilla St	454-0369	-- / L (X:Su) / D (X:Su)		✓		$		MC V AE DC	Rec 55	Charming, casual, mesquite broiled fish and seafood, / Mexican emphasis, received 8 California gold medals for / Food Excellence, Food recognized by the Heart Assn.
SEAFOOD	**Aloha Louie's** / LA JOLLA - 1111 Prospect St / North of Girard Av	454-1166	-- / -- / D				$		MC V AE	Rec	Polynesian decor & ocean view create casual feeling / Fresh seafood & steaks, Hawaiian broiler specialties / Imported beer & wine
	Anthony's La Jolla / LA JOLLA - 4120 La Jolla Village Dr / West of Genesee Av	457-5008	-- / L (X:Sa/Su) / D				$		MC V AE	Rec 30	Open, warm & attractive atmosphere, plants in atrium / Four separate dining areas, one private dining room / Multiple locations
	Fisherman's Grill / LA JOLLA - 7825 Fay Av / In The Merrill Lynch Bldg.	456-3733	-- / L (X-Su) / D		F / Sa		$		MC V AE DC	Rec 173	Simple, fishhouse feeling, pine tables & booths, Casual / Regular specials, cooking classes / Silver Award/SCRW
	Humphrey's La Jolla Grill / LA JOLLA - 3299 Holiday Ct / East of Villa La Jolla Dr	587-0056	B / L / D					$	MC V AE DC D	Rec 12	View of the canyon, booths, shellfish specialties / Atmosphere is casual & comfortable, emphasis on / California cuisine
	Marine Room / LA JOLLA - 2000 Spindrift Dr / At Princess St	459-7222	-- / L (X:Su) / D		✓			+	MC V AE DC	Rec 60	A La Jolla institution located on the beach / Aquariums, very elegant dining / Jacket preferred, entertainment
	Rusty Pelican / LA JOLLA - 4340 La Jolla Village Dr / Across from University Towne Center	587-1886	-- / L (X:Su) / D		F / Sa		$		MC V AE DC	Rec 40	Tropical atmosphere,lush, greens & lots of glass / Young professionals after work spot, Caribbean dishes / Daily seafood specials, entertainment(W-Sa)
	Shores at the Sea Lodge / LA JOLLA - 8110 Camino del Oro / 2nd Block East of La Jolla Shores Beach	456-0600	B / L / D				$		MC V AE DC	Rec	Elegant restaurant sits right on the beach, relaxed & / Comfortable, seafood salad bar for dinner / Seafood, chicken & steak
SOUTHWEST	**Kiva Grill** / UNIVERSITY TOWNE CTR - 8790 University Ctr	558-8600	L (X-Sa/Su) / D		F / Sa		$		MC V AE DC	Yes	Slick, chic southwestern theme, trendy clientele / Traditional Southwest/Mexican dishes
THAI	**Lemon Grass** / LA JOLLA - 737 Pearl St.	456-2063	-- / L (X:Sa/Su) / D				$		MC V AE	yes	Upscale setting, stylish contemporary / Waterfall in restaurant / Traditional and New Style Thai Cuisine, B&W only

Cuisine
(NOTES)

Restaurant
COMMUNITY - Street
Located Near

PHONE

SERVING:
Brkfst
Lunch
Dinner
X=Closed

Late Night Din.
Sunday Brunch

Dinner /Person
Under $10
$10 to $20
$20 to $30+

Credit Cards

Reservations

SPECIAL FEATURES

A D D I T I O N S

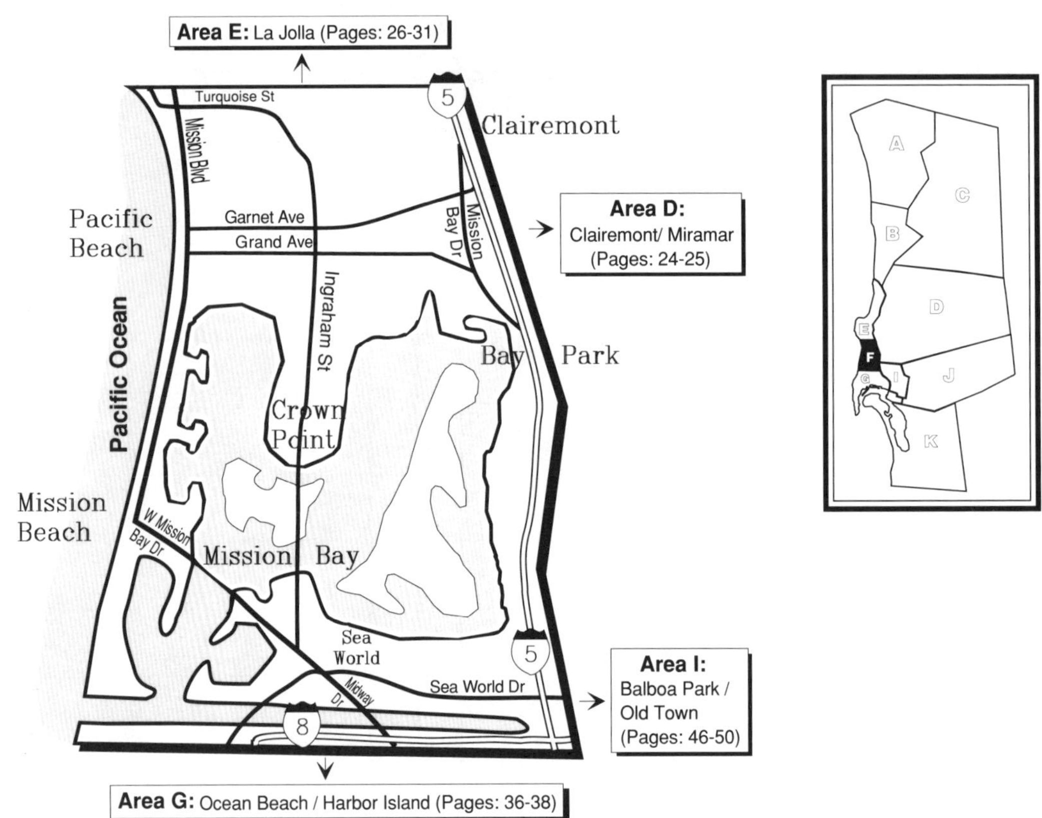

ALPHABETIC LISTINGS

RESTAURANT (CUISINE Category)

Alley Oops (AMERICAN)
Andres Cuban Restaurant (CUBAN)
Atoll, The (CALIFORNIA)
Baci (ITALIAN)
Bangkok Thai Cuisine (THAI)
Beach House, The (CALIFORNIA)
Boathouse, The (SEAFOOD)
Cafe Broken Yolk (AMERICAN)
Cafe Toulouse (FRENCH)
Cass Street Bar & Grill (AMERICAN)
Chateau Orleans (CAJUN/CREOLE)
Chez Beat & Rolf (CALIFORNIA)
Chicago Brothers (ITALIAN)
China Inn (CHINESE)
Daily Planet, The (AMERICAN)
Diego's Cafe Y Cantina (MEXICAN)
Dockside Broiler (SEAFOOD)
Eggery, Etc., The (AMERICAN)
El Chalan (PERUVIAN)
Esperanto (INTERNAT'L)

RESTAURANT (CUISINE Category)

Ethiopia (ETHIOPIAN)
Filippi's Pizza Grotto (ITALIAN)
French Gourmet (FRENCH)
Good Time Charlies (AMERICAN)
Green Flash, The (AMERICAN)
Hennessey's Tavern & Pub (AMERICAN)
Improvisation Comedy Club, (AMERICAN)
Islandia Bar & Grill, The (SEAFOOD)
Karinya Thai Cuisine (THAI)
Lamont Street Grill (CALIFORNIA)
Luigi's (ITALIAN)
McCormick & Schmick's (SEAFOOD)
Mercedes Room/Comedy Isle (AMERICAN)
Moose McGillycuddy's (AMERICAN)
Mr. Sushi (JAPANESE)
Newport Annie's (MEXICAN)
Old Ox (AMERICAN)
Old Pacific Beach Cafe (AMERICAN)
Old Trieste (ITALIAN)
Pacific Princess (POLYNESIAN)

RESTAURANT (CUISINE Category)

Palenque (MEXICAN)
Paradise Bay (SEAFOOD)
Pennant, The (AMERICAN)
Pizzeria Uno (ITALIAN)
Red Onion, The (MEXICAN)
Ricci's Ristorante Italiano (ITALIAN)
Rubio's Deli-Mex (MEXICAN)
Salmon House (SEAFOOD)
Saska's (AMERICAN)
Shanghai Restaurant (CHINESE)
Sheldon's Cafe (AMERICAN)
Sorrentino's (ITALIAN)
Spice Rack (AMERICAN)
Szechuan (CHINESE)
T. D. Hays Restaurant (AMERICAN)
Tablao Flamenco (SPANISH)
Tep's Villa Roma (ITALIAN)
Tony Roma's (AMERICAN)
Tradewinds (CONTINENTAL)
Yiurio's (ITALIAN)

Cuisine (NOTES)	Restaurant / COMMUNITY - Street / Located Near	PHONE	Serving (B/L/D, X=Closed)	Late Night Din.	Sunday Brunch	Under $10	$10 to $20	$20 to $30 +	Credit Cards	Reservations	SPECIAL FEATURES
AMERICAN	**Alley Oops** / PACIFIC BEACH - 4475 MISSION BLVD / In Seacoast Square	272-OOPS	B, L, D	Y		$			MC V	No	Old fashion diner, memorabilia on the walls, mini jukeboxes at each table, family-oriented, informal, fun. Typical diner menu, burgers, sandwiches, shakes, sodas
	Cafe Broken Yolk / PACIFIC BEACH - 1851 Garnet Ave	270-0045	B, L, --		✓	$			MC V AE DC D		Casual, cafe setting, booths & tables, large omelettes good portions, sandwiches seafood. Multiple Locations
	Cass Street Bar & Grill / PACIFIC BEACH - 4612 CASS STREET	270-1320	--, L, D	Y		$			NONE	No	Pub-like atmosphere where the beach crowd gathers. Informal, pool tables, limited menu offering seafood sandwiches, salads, appetizers
	Daily Planet, The / PACIFIC BEACH - 1200 Garnet Av	272-6066	--, L (X:Su), D	Y		$			NONE	No	Local hangout, pub-like atmosphere, pool tables. Informal, limited menu offers sandwiches, salads. Daily Specials
	Eggery, Etc., The / PACIFIC BEACH - 4130 Mission Blvd / In the Promenade Shopping Center	274-3122	B, L, D			$			MC V	No	Homey country setting, outdoor seating. Variety of omelets, pancakes and muffins. Daily seafood specials, B&W only
	Good Time Charlies / PACIFIC BEACH - 910 Grand Av	274-3834	B (Sa/Su), L, D			$			MC V AE	Yes 8p+	Old-time feeling, casual, beachy crowd doors open to street, long oak bar, menu offers burgers, sandwiches, pastas, salads
	Green Flash, The / PACIFIC BEACH - 701 Thomas Av / West of Mission Blvd	483-6630	B, L, D	F / Sa			$		MC V AE	Yes 7p+	Sits on the boardwalk, ocean & sunset views, outdoor seating available, casual, popular with the beach crowd. Daily specials and catch of the night
	Hennessey's / PACIFIC BEACH - 4650 Mission Blvd	483-8847	B, L, D	Y		$			MC V AE	No	Casual, beach tavern atmosphere, popular with the locals, fun, lively, burgers, sandwiches & salads
	Improvisation Comedy Club / PACIFIC BEACH - 832 Garnet Ave	488-4520	--, --, D	F / Sa			$		MC V AE	Yes (D)	Reservations for dinner show only, 3 comics nightly. Black & white theme, intimate feeling. Prime rib, chicken, seafood, desserts, 2 item minimum
	Mercedes Room/Comedy Isle / MISSION BAY - 998 West Mission Bay Dr / In The Bahia Hotel	488-0551	--, --, D	F / Sa			$		MC V AE DC D	Rec	View of Mission Bay. Dinner/comedy show nightly with three different acts
	Moose McGillycuddy's / PACIFIC BEACH - 1165 Garnet Av	274-2323	L (X:Su), D	Y	✓	$			MC V	No / 50	Great food value, family oriented, fun, lively. DJ entertainment nightly from 8p, burgers, sandwiches salads, Popular with the younger crowd, banquet facility
	Old Ox / PACIFIC BEACH - 4474 Mission Blvd / North of Grand Av	275-3790	L (X:Sa/Su), D	F / Sa			$		MC V AE	Rec	Patio dining, garden room. Bar scene, Sunday Mimosa Brunch, Beef & Seafood. Popular with the beach crowd
	Old Pacific Beach Cafe / PACIFIC BEACH - 4287 Mission Blvd / North of Pacific Beach Dr	270-7522	B (Sa-Su), --, D	Y		$			MC V AE	Yes	Casual, lots of greenery & neon art, beers from around the world, menu offers soups, salads, sandwiches omelettes, live entertainment & dancing nightly
	Pennant, The / MISSION BEACH - 2843 Mission Blvd / South of San Jose Pl	488-1671	B, L, D	Y		$			NO	No	Rooftop deck, ocean view, hangout for locals. Adults only, lively & rowdy on the weekends. Menu is very limited
	Saska's / MISSION BEACH - 3768 Mission Blvd / South of Zanzibar Ct	488-7311	--, L (X:Sa/Su), D	Y				$	MC V AE DC	Yes	Dark, cozy, intimate atmosphere. Upper deck & patio, popular beach spot, seafood, steaks chicken, fish market, Silver Medal/SCRW
	Sheldon's Cafe / PACIFIC BEACH - 4711 Mission Bay Dr / North of Clairemont Dr	273-3833	B, L, D	Y		$			MC V	No	All night, 24 hour coffee shop, one of the first in PB. Home-style cooking, daily lunch & dinner specials. All you can eat breakfast bar, B&W only
	Spice Rack / PACIFIC BEACH - 4315 Mission Blvd / South of Grand Av	483-7666	B, L, --				$		MC V AE	No / 30	Garden setting, beachy casual, outdoor patio dining. Fresh baked pastries daily, omelettes, sandwiches, salads, popular beach eatery especially for breakfast
	T. D. Hays Restaurant / PACIFIC BEACH - 4713 Ocean Blvd	270-6850	--, D	F / Sa	✓			$	MC V AE	Yes	Rustic atmosphere with lots of wood & plants. Ocean view dining, comfortable & cozy. Seafood, chicken, prime rib, homebaked breads
	Tony Roma's / PACIFIC BEACH - 4110 Mission Blvd / North of Pacific Beach Dr	272-7427	--, L (X:Sa/Su), D	F / Sa			$		MC V AE	Rec	Family oriented, fun atmosphere, neon art, booths. Specialty is BBQ ribs & loaves of onion rings, burgers. Chicken dishes & burgers, multiple locations
CAJUN/CREOLE	**Chateau Orleans** / PACIFIC BEACH - 926 Turquoise St / West of Cass St	488-6744	--, D					$	MC V AE DC	Rec / 45	Soft understated decor in the romantic Louisiana style French Cajun cuisine, Innovative dishes like alligator soft shell crab, seafood & prime rib, B&W only

Cuisine (NOTES)	Restaurant / COMMUNITY - Street / Located Near	PHONE	SERVING: Brkfst / Lunch / Dinner (X=Closed)	Late Night Din.	Sunday Brunch	Under $10	$10 to $20	$20 to $30+	Credit Cards	Reservations	SPECIAL FEATURES
CALIFORNIA	**Atoll, The** — PACIFIC BEACH - 3999 Mission Blvd — In The Catamaran Resort Hotel	488-1081	B / L / D	F / Sa	✓			$	MC V / AE DC / D	Rec	Richly appointed restaurant with relaxing bay view Accented with lush tropical foliage California cuisine
	Beach House, The — MISSION BEACH - 3750 Ocean Front Walk	488-6706	B / L / D					$	MC V / AE	Rec	Indoor dining warm and intimate, upstairs patio Outdoor dining is right on the boardwalk Daily specials, emphasis seafood, B&W only
	Chez Beat & Rolf — PACIFIC BEACH - 1762 Garnet Av — West of Lamont St	483-2600	B (X-Su-M) / L (X:Su-M) / D (X:Su-M)	Y			$		MC V	Rec	California cuisine with Swiss accent, daily specials Open kitchen allows you to watch chefs Fabulous desserts, catering, B&W only
	Lamont Street Grill — PACIFIC BEACH - 4445 Lamont St — South of Garnet Av	270-3060	-- / -- / D	F / Sa			$		MC V / AE	Rec	Intimate bungalow, warm, cozy feeling Outdoor courtyard dining, family run, pasta specials Innovative cuisine, fabulous desserts, Gold medal/SCRW
CHINESE	**China Inn** — PACIFIC BEACH - 877 Hornblend St — West of Cass St	483-6680	-- / L / D			$			MC V	Yes	Traditional Chinese decor, lanterns, booths Low lights, casual Banquet room, Carry-out
	Shanghai Restaurant — MISSION BAY - 1930 Quivira Way — In Marina Village	226-6200	-- / L / D	F / Sa		$			MC V / AE	Yes	On the waterfront with a marina view, traditional oriental decor, Mandarin, Szechuan & Mongolian BBQ
	Szechuan — CLAIREMONT - 4577 Clairemont Dr — In Wilson Plaza	270-0251	-- / L (X:Su) / D	F / Sa		$			MC V	Rec / 150	Szechuan & mandarin dishes authentically prepared handmade noodles, nightly demonstration Banquet facilities, catering, carry-out, B&W only
CONTINENTAL	**Tradewinds** — BAY PARK - 1775 East Mission Bay Dr — in the San Diego Hilton Hotel	276-4010	-- / -- / D	Y			$		MC V / AE DC / D	Rec	Bay view, nautical theme & decor, rustic Fresh seafood, live entertainment & dancing(W-Sa) Jazz entertainment(Su-Tu)
CUBAN	**Andres** Cuban Restaurant — BAY PARK - 1235 Morena Blvd — South of Tecolote Rd	275-4114	-- / L (X-Su/M) / D (X-Su/M)				$		MC V	Rec	Enchanting & cozy tropical setting, featuring Caribbean dishes, favorites are the pork & seafood dishes black beans and plateneaus
ETHIOPIAN	**Ethiopia** — PACIFIC BEACH - 2710 Garnet Av — West of Mission Bay Dr	270-6453	-- / L / D			$			MC V	Rec	Ethiopian antiques, hanging beads, African posters menu features spicy chicken & lamb, vegetarian dishes Catering, (formerly the Blue Nile) B&W only
FRENCH	**Cafe Toulouse** — PACIFIC BEACH - 4475-F Mission Blvd. — Corner of Garnet Ave & Mission Blvd	483-3988	B (Sa-Su) / L / D			$			MC V	No	Informal, casual, European cafe feeling, small tables Homemade quiches, soups, sandwiches, Variety of coffees and teas, ideal for late night desserts at the beach
	French Gourmet — PACIFIC BEACH - 940 Turquoise St	488-1725	-- / L (X:Su) / D (X:Su)				$		MC V	Yes	Sister to La Jolla location, casual bistro setting Menu features everything from omelettes to seafood specials, Carry-out counter with fabulous desserts
INTERNAT'L	**Esperanto** — PACIFIC BEACH - 4462 Mission Blvd — North of Grand Av	273-9030	B / L / D	Y			$		MC V	12	French & Italian fare, fresh pastas & croissants made on the premises, sandwiches, very casual, indoor & patio dining, carry-out & catering
ITALIAN	**Baci** — BAY PARK - 1955 Morena Blvd — North of Ashton St	275-2094	-- / L (X:Sa-M) / D (X:Su)				$		MC V / AE DC	Must Wknd	Intimate atmosphere, Tuxedo clad waiters Homemade pastas, seafood and veal specials Silver award/SCRW
	Chicago Brothers — BAY PARK - 4605 East Mission Bay Dr — South of Clairemont Dr	270-2244	-- / L (X:Sa/Su) / D			$			MC V	Rec 6p+	Quick & easy, deep-dish pizzas, salads Made to order sandwiches, BBQ baby back ribs, spare ribs & chicken, carry-out and catering
	Filippi's Pizza Grotto — PACIFIC BEACH - 962 Garnet Av	483-6222	-- / L / D			$			MC V	10+	Dark cozy, red & white table clothes, family oriented Casual, pizza, spaghetti, ravioli & linguini Carry-out, B&W only
	Luigi's — MISSION BEACH - 3210 Mission Blvd — South of Yarmouth Ct	488-2818	-- / L / D	Y		$			MC V	No / 20	Outdoor patio dining, very relaxed, casual Daily specials, giant slices of pizza available B&W only
	Old Trieste — BAY PARK - 2335 Morena Blvd — North of Lister St	276-1841	L (X-Sa-M) / D (X-Su/M)					+	MC V / AE DC	Rec	Intimate, comfortable booths, in elegant setting Northern Italian cuisine, Jacket required
	Pizzeria Uno — PACIFIC BEACH - 4465 Mission Blvd — North of Grand Av	483-4143	-- / L / D	Y			$		MC V / AE	Yes 6p+	Home of the original Chicago deep dish pizza, lively 1930's style eatery, upstairs bar, outdoor seating, Family oriented, a variety of deep dish pizzas
	Ricci's Ristorante Italiano — PACIFIC BEACH - 1203 Garnet Av — Corner of Everts St	272-6632	-- / L (X:Sa/Su) / D	F / Sa		$			MC V	Yes / 40	Patio dining, trellises with greenery, quaint Popular neighborhood spot, pastas & seafood specials Pizzas, Catering, B&W only

Cuisine (NOTES)	Restaurant / COMMUNITY - Street / Located Near	PHONE	Serving: Brkfst Lunch Dinner X=Closed	Late Night Din.	Sunday Brunch	Under $10	$10 to $20	$20 to $30+	Credit Cards	Reservations	SPECIAL FEATURES
ITALIAN (Con't)	Sorrentino's BAY PARK - 4724 Clairemont	483-1811	-- L (X:Sa/Su) D			$			MC V	No	Casual Italian setting, one side is a restaurant, the other is a deli with carry-out, homemade Italian specialties, lasagne, veal, chicken, sandwiches
	Tep's Villa Roma CLAIREMONT - 3010 Clairemont Dr South of Iroquois Av	276-3462	-- -- D (X:M/T)		F / Sa		$		MC V AE	No	Bay view, subtle ambience, candlelight, open fireplace Homemade soups, veal, seafood & pastas dishes antipasto bar, neighborhood favorite
	Giulos PACIFIC BEACH - 809 Thomas Av	483-7726	-- L (X:Sa/Su) D				$		MC V AEDC	Yes	Dark and cozy spot, traditional Italian decor, tuxedo clad waiters, Northern Italian cuisine, homemade pastas, veal, poultry, scampi
JAPANESE	Mr. Sushi PACIFIC BEACH - 1535 Garnet Ave West of Ingraham St	581-2664	-- L (X:Sa/Su) D				$		MC V AE	Rec	Contemporary atmosphere, small & casual Sushi bar, stir fry & tempura, emphasis on presentation Carry-out, B&W only
MEXICAN	Diego's Cafe Y Cantina PACIFIC BEACH - 860 Garnet Av East of Mission Blvd	272-1241	-- L D		Y	✓$			MC V AE	No 8p+	Garden patio dining, fun, lively, casual, popular with locals & tourists, large platters of food Traditional menu, Dancing nightly, Jazz in the loft
	Newport Annie's MISSION BEACH - 3714 Mission Blvd North of Santa Clara Place	270-5550	-- -- D		Y		$		MC V	Rec 6p+	Casual, fun, South of the border decor, neighborhood hangout, specialty is Puerto Nuevo style lobster served with all you can eat rice & beans, fajitas & seafood
	Palenque PACIFIC BEACH - 1653 Garnet Av	272-7816	-- L(X:M) D (X:M)			$			MC V	Yes	Family run, small and quaint, colorful Mexican artifacts, authentic Mexican regional dishes from Oaxaca & Puebla, B&W only
	Red Onion, The MISSION BEACH - 3125 Ocean Front Walk In Belmont Park	488-9040	-- L (X:Su) D		F / Sa	✓$			MC V AE	Yes (D)	Ocean view, festive, tropical, jungle-like setting Traditional Mexican fare & dishes from Yucatan area DJ entertainment & nightly, Younger crowd
(FOOD-TO-GO)	Rubio's Deli-Mex PACIFIC BEACH - 4505 Mission Bay Dr	272-4800	-- L D			$					Carry-out only, limited patio seating, family run Famous for the San Felipe-style fish tacos, burritos & combo plates, multiple locations, catering
PERUVIAN	El Chalan PACIFIC BEACH - 1050 Garnet Av West of Cass St	459-7707	-- -- D		F / Sa		$		MC V AE	Rec	In San Diego for over 15 years, patio dining Harp/guitar background music, elegant surroundings Authentic dishes
POLYNESIAN	Pacific Princess MISSION BAY - 1404 West Vacation Rd In The San Diego Princess Resort	274-4630	-- -- D				$		MC V AE DC	Rec	Bay view, patio dining, seasonal outdoor entertainment South seas setting
SEAFOOD	Boathouse, The PACIFIC BEACH - 4325 Ocean Blvd On The Boardwalk	274-3474	-- -- D		F / Sa		$		MC V AE DC D	Rec	On the boardwalk overlooking the ocean Wood, brass, lighted umbrellas & greenery are the decor Locations throughout San Diego
	Dockside Broiler MISSION BAY - 1404 West Vacation Rd In The San Diego Princess Resort	274-4630	-- -- D (X:Su)		✓	$			MC V AE DC	Rec 30	Overlooks Mission Bay, romantic setting with candlelight, casual but elegant Seafood, prime rib & beef
	Islandia Bar & Grill, The MISSION BAY - 1441 Quivra Rd In The Hyatt Islandia Hotel	221-4810	-- L D		F / Sa		$		MC V	Rec	Tropical setting, wicker furniture, relaxed Relaxed and comfortable
	McCormick & Schmick's PACIFIC BEACH - 4190 Mission Blvd In The Promenade	581-3938	-- L (X:Su) D		✓		$		MC V AE DC D	Rec	Ocean view & outdoor courtyard dining, elegant but casual atmosphere with rich woods, beveled glass Fabulous oyster selection, Silver medal/SCRW
	Paradise Bay MISSION BAY - 1935 Quivra Rd In Marina Village	223-2335	-- L (X:Su) D		✓		$		MC V AE	Rec	Over the water setting with a bay view Daily menu specialties Dancing(W-Sa)
	Salmon House MISSION BEACH - 1970 Quivira Rd In Marina Village	223-2234	-- L (X:Sa/Su) D		✓			$	MC V AE DC	Rec	On the water, rustic, early American Indian decor Totem poles, menu features salmon, seafood, Chicken, prime rib, dancing to live music(F-Su)
SPANISH	Tablao Flamenco PACIFIC BEACH - 3567 Del Rey St South of Bunker Hill St	483-2703	-- -- D (F/Sa)		F / Sa		$		MC V	Rec 100	17 century decor, flamenco dancers, lively Authentic Spanish dishes
THAI	Bangkok Thai Cuisine PACIFIC BEACH - 4656 Mission Blvd	581-1401	-- -- D			$			MC V AE	No	Colorful, unique atmosphere, casual Seafood, curries, chicken, beef & vegetarian dishes
	Karinya Thai Cuisine PACIFIC BEACH - 4475 Mission Blvd In SeaCrest Square	270-5050	-- L (X:Sa-M) D (X:M)				$		MC V AE	Rec 60	Contemporary oriental decor, relaxed comfortable setting, authentic Thai recipes, chef specials, catering & carry-out, Gold Medal/SCRW)

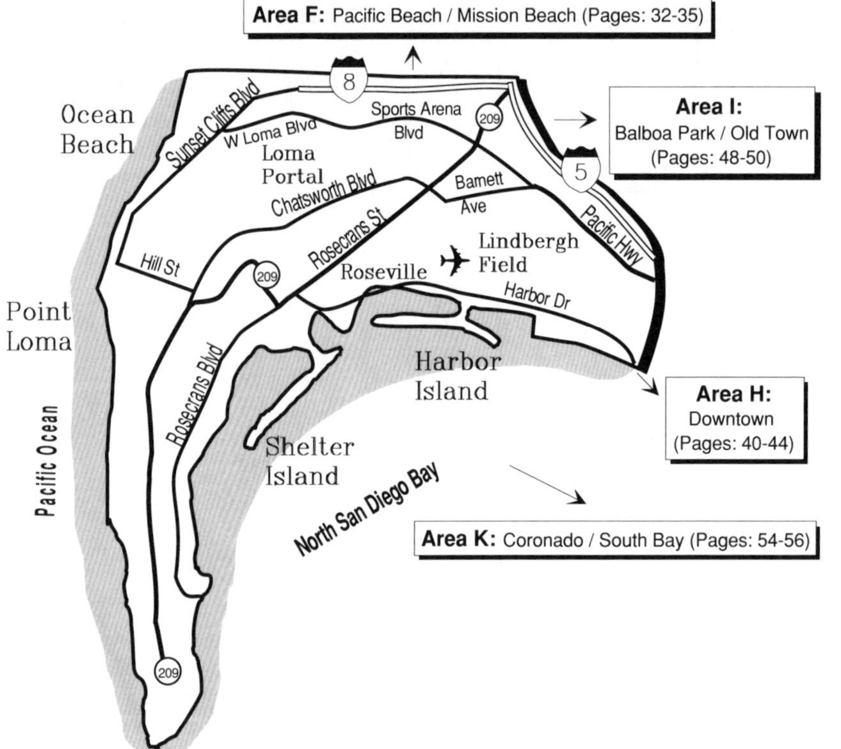

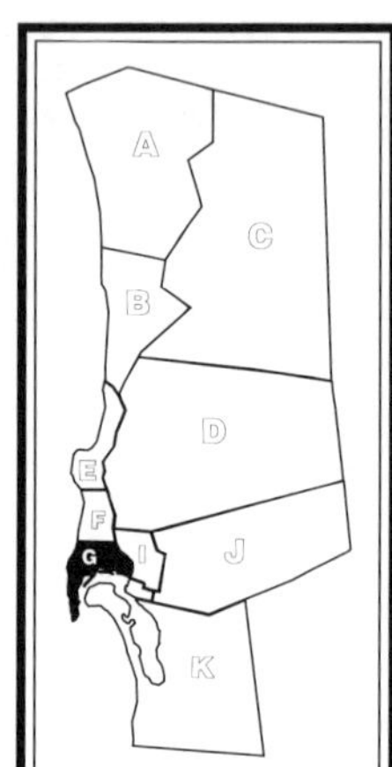

ALPHABETIC LISTINGS

RESTAURANT (CUISINE Category)	RESTAURANT (CUISINE Category)	RESTAURANT (CUISINE Category)
19th Buoy, The (SEAFOOD)	John Tarantino's (ITALIAN)	Pizza Nova (ITALIAN)
A La Francaise (FRENCH)	La Scala (ITALIAN)	Point Loma Seafoods (SEAFOOD)
Bali Hai (POLYNESIAN)	Little Italy Pizza (ITALIAN)	Qwiig's Bar & Grill (AMERICAN)
Barnacle Bill's (SEAFOOD)	Mandarin China (CHINESE)	Red Sails Inn (SEAFOOD)
Belgian Lion (BELGIAN)	Merlano's (ITALIAN)	Reuben E. Lee (SEAFOOD)
Blue Crab Restaurant (SEAFOOD)	Michelangelo Ristorante Italiano (ITALIAN)	Rubio's Deli-Mex (FOOD-TO-GO)
Boathouse, The (SEAFOOD)	Miguel's Cocina (MEXICAN)	Spencer's (AMERICAN)
Brigantine, The (SEAFOOD)	Mug-n-Mallet (SEAFOOD)	Sunset Bar & Grill (AMERICAN)
Cecil's Cafe & Fish Market (SEAFOOD)	Nati's Mexican Restaurant (MEXICAN)	Thee Bungalow (CONTINENTAL)
China Land Restaurant (CHINESE)	Nordic Inn (SWEDISH)	Tom Ham's Lighthouse (SEAFOOD)
Cotton Patch (AMERICAN)	North China (CHINESE)	Yakitori II (JAPANESE)
Fairouz Cafe (MIDDLE EAST)	Old Ocean Beach Cafe (AMERICAN)	Yet Wah Restaurant (CHINESE)
Garcia's (MEXICAN)	Old Venice (ITALIAN)	
Humphrey's (SEAFOOD)	Palm Grill, The (CONTINENTAL)	

Cuisine (NOTES)	Restaurant / COMMUNITY - Street / Located Near	PHONE	SERVING: Brkfst Lunch Dinner X=Closed	Late Night Din.	Sunday Brunch	Under $10	$10 to $20	$20 to $30 + (Dinner /Person)	Credit Cards	Reservations	SPECIAL FEATURES
AMERICAN	**Cotton Patch** / *LOMA PORTAL* - 2720 Midway Dr / East of Rosecrans St	223-7179	-- / L (X:Sa/Su) / D				$		MC V	Rec	Replica of an old Bayou hunting lodge, animal trophies, guns on the wall, booths & tables, a San Diego institution, prime rib, seafood, Piano bar(T-Sa)
	Old Ocean Beach Cafe / *OCEAN BEACH* - 4969 Newport Av / East of Bacon St	223-2521	-- / L / D	Y	✓	$			MC V AE	Yes / 60	Beer drinkers hall of fame, casual dress, favorite of beach crowd, cafe menu ranging from omelets, sandwiches soups, salads, seafood & crepes
	Qwiig's Bar & Grill / *OCEAN BEACH* - 5083 Santa Monica Av / West of Bacon St	222-1101	L / D	Y			$		MC V AE	Rec / 125	Ocean view of 180 degrees, spacious, intimate, booths Lush greenery, oyster bar, seafood emphasis Catering & banquet facilities
	Spencer's / *HARBOR ISLAND* - 1590 Harbor Island Dr / In The Sheraton Grand Hotel	692-2777	B / L / D		✓			$	MC V AE DC D	Rec / 30	Steakhouse, featuring mesquite grilled entrees Harborview, patio dining, casual Private dining area
	Sunset Bar & Grill / *SHELTER ISLAND* - 2051 Shelter Island Dr / In Shelter Island Marina Inn	223-2572	B / L / D		✓	$			MC V AE DC D	Rec	Marina view, romantic bayside dining Daily specials, bar features big screen TV & happy hour Catering
BELGIAN	**Belgian Lion** / *OCEAN BEACH* - 2265 Bacon St / North of Voltaire St	223-2700	-- / -- / D (X:Su/M)				$		MC V AE DC	Rec / 10	Country decor, outdoor dining French nouvelle & traditional Belgian cuisine
CHINESE	**China Land Restaurant** / *LOMA PORTAL* - 3135 Midway Dr / West of Rosecrans St	224-2861	-- / L (X:Sa/Su) / D	F / / Sa			$		MC V AE	Yes	Served San Diegans since 1950, family-owned Traditional Chinese decor Carry-out, delivery
	Mandarin China / *OCEAN BEACH* - 4110 W. Point Loma Bl / West of Midway Dr	222-6688	L (X:Sa/Su) / D	F / / Sa			$		MC V AE DC D	Rec 6p+	Traditional setting for Hong Kong style dim sum Mandarin, Szechuan & Cantonese dishes Private dining room, carry-out, catering, B&W only
	North China / *POINT LOMA* - 5043 North Harbor Dr	224-3568	L / D	F / / Sa		$			MC/V	YES	Traditional oriental decor, Mandarin & Szechuan cuisine Combination luncheon plates available M-F Must order from dinner menu for Sa-Su lunch
	Yet Wah Restaurant / *LOMA PORTAL* - 3146 Sports Arena Blvd / In the Glasshouse Square center	295-2232	L / D				$		MC V AE	Yes	San Diego branch of the San Francisco group Mandarin cuisine, pot stickers & vegetarian dishes
CONTINENTAL	**Palm Grill, The** / *HARBOR ISLAND* - 1960 Harbor Island Dr / In The Travelodge Hotel	291-6700	B / L / D				$		MC V AE DC D	Rec	Panoramic view of the bay Seafood and Prime ribs Daily breakfast buffet
	Thee Bungalow / *OCEAN BEACH* - 4996 W. Point Loma Bl / West of Sunset Cliffs Blvd	224-2884	D (X:M)				$		MC V	Rec / 40	Small, intimate, dining is leisurely in this country inn atmosphere, weekly menu, fresh baked goods Silver award/SCRW
FRENCH	**A La Francaise** / *LOMA PORTAL* - 4030 Sports Arena Blvd	223-5957	B / L / D (X:Su)			$			MC V	No	European bakery atmosphere, casual Croissants, omelets, quiches, fresh breads & pastries Other locations in San Diego
ITALIAN	**John Tarantino's** / *POINT LOMA* - 5150 North Harbor Dr / At Scott St	224-3555	-- / L (X:Su) / D (X:Su)	F / / Sa			$		MC V AE	Rec / 70	Bay view, casual, booths, candlelight & romantic Seafood, pasta specials
	La Scala / *POINT LOMA* - 1101 Scott St / at Cannon St.	224-2274	-- / L / D	Y			$		MC V	Yes	Popular with local community Menu offers wide choice of tradional Italian dishes Pizza & pasta, Carry-out
	Little Italy Pizza / *OCEAN BEACH* - 4204 Voltaire / West of Catalina Blvd	225-9900	-- / L / D	Y			$		MC V AE	No	One of the 10 best independent operations according to USA Today, Red & white decor with Chianti bottles 18 pizza combinations, B&W only, carry out, delivery
	Merlano's / *HARBOR ISLAND* - 1380 Harbor Island Dr / In Sheraton Harbor Island Hotel	291-2900	-- / -- / D (X:M)					+	MC V AE DC	Rec	Country-Italian atmosphere, accordion music Split level dining, Prix-fixe menu available Regional dishes, veals, pastas, chicken, seafood
	Michelangelo 's / *POINT LOMA* - 1878 Rosecrans St / North of Nimitz Blvd	224-9478	-- / L / D	F / / Sa			$		MC V AE DC	Rec	Homey, Italian folk art on the walls, small, quaint, Casual, cozy, homemade pizzas, & pastas Private room, Catering, B&W only
	Old Venice / *POINT LOMA* - 2910 Canon St / Between Scott & Rosencrans	222-5888	-- / L (X:Sa/Su) / D			$			MC V AE	Rec 10p+	Intimate eatery, simple & classic, neighborhood spot Gourmet pizza, pasta & seafood entrees Enclosed patio dining, carry-out, B&W only
	Pizza Nova / *POINT LOMA* – 5120 North Harbor Dr / Near Lindbergh Field	226-0268	-- / L / D			$			MC V AE	Yes / 32	Lively, harborside dining, booths, a counter and outdoor seating, gourmet, woodfired pizzas, pasta salads, carry-out, B&W only

Cuisine (NOTES)	Restaurant / COMMUNITY - Street Located Near / PHONE	SERVING: Brkfst Lunch Dinner (X=Closed)	Late Night Din.	Sunday Brunch	Under $10	$10 to $20	$20 to $30+	Credit Cards	Reservations	SPECIAL FEATURES
JAPANESE	**Yakitori II** 223-2641 *LOMA PORTAL* - 3740 Sports Arena Blvd In Sports Arena Village Shop Ctr	-- L (X:Sa/Su) D	F / Sa			$		MC V	Rec 6p+ 45	Sushi & Robata bars Japanese stir fry, tempura & BBQ Carry-out & Catering, Silver Medal/SCRW
MEXICAN	**Garcia's** 223-5441 *LOMA PORTAL* - 3106 Sports Arena Blvd Next to the Glasshouse Square Center	-- L D	F / Sa		$			MC V AE DC	Rec	Lively, colorful atmosphere, painted murals on walls Casual, traditional Mexican menu Banquet room and carry-out
	Miguel's Cocina 224-2401 *POINT LOMA* - 2912 Shelter Island Dr At Scott Street	L (X:Sa/Su) D			$			MC V AE	Rec 6p+	Outdoor dining, comfortable setting indoors Hefty portions, traditional Mexican & seafood specials Catering, carry-out
	Nati's Mexican Restaurant 224-3369 *OCEAN BEACH* - 1852 Bacon St At Niagara Av	B (Sa-Su) L D	F / Sa		$			MC V		Indoor & outdoor patio dining, small, very casual Daily Mexican specials Served San Diego for 30 years
(FOOD-TO-GO)	**Rubio's Deli-Mex** 223-2641 *POINT LOMA* - 3555 Rosecrans	-- L D			$					Carry-out only, some seating available, family run Home of the San Felipe-style fish taco & other Mexican favorites, multiple locations, catering
MIDDLE EAST	**Fairouz Cafe** 225-0308 *LOMA PORTAL* - 3166 Midway Dr West of Rosecrans St	-- L (X:Su) D		✓	$			MC V AE	Rec Wknd	Combo art gallery & eatery, casual atmosphere Greek & Lebanese specialties Artist owned
POLYNESIAN	**Bali Hai** 222-1181 *SHELTER ISLAND* - 2230 Shelter Island Dr On Shelter Island	-- L D		✓		$		MC V AE DC	Rec	Harbor/city view, Cantonese & American dishes Luau lunches, floor show(W-Su) Tropical setting with rattan furniture & screens
SEAFOOD	**19th Buoy, The** 224-8888 *SHELTER ISLAND* - 2131 Shelter Island Dr In The Bay Club Hotel & Marina	B L D	Sa / Su			$		MC V AE DC		Marina view in this classic California casual eatery Daily seafood specials, Wine by the glass Patio entertainment(F/Sa), Breakfast buffet daily
	Barnacle Bill's 297-1673 *HARBOR ISLAND* - 1880 Harbor Island Dr On Harbor Island	-- L (X:Sa/Su) D	F / Sa			$		MC V AE	Rec	Fresh seafood specialties, outdoor dining Harbor, marina & downtown view, enclosed patio
	Blue Crab Restaurant 224-3000 *POINT LOMA* - 4922 North Harbor Dr In Fisherman's Village	-- L D	F / Sa	✓		$		MC V	Rec 6p+	Bay view, fish house feeling Express lunch, mesquite grill, wine by the glass
	Boathouse, The 291-8010 *HARBOR ISLAND* - 2040 Harbor Island Dr On Harbor Island	-- L (X:Su) D	F / Sa	✓		$		MC V AE DC D	Rec	Harbor view, elegant atmosphere, casual & comfortable Daily specials, poultry, prime rib, pastas Locations throughout San Diego
	Brigantine, The 224-2871 *SHELTER ISLAND* - 2725 Shelter Island Dr On Shelter Island	-- L (X:S/S) D	F / Sa			$		MC V AE	Rec	Oyster bar, seafood specialties Plus Mexican dishes Locations throughout San Diego
	Cecil's Cafe & Fish Market 222-0501 *OCEAN BEACH* - 5083 Santa Monica Av West of Bacon St	B L D		✓	$			MC V AE	No	View of ocean & pier, atmosphere is cozy with the wood and granite & neon accents, casual Seafood, pizzas, pastas, sandwiches
	Humphrey's 224-3577 *SHELTER ISLAND* - 2241 Shelter Island Dr In The Half Moon Inn	-- L (X:Su) D	F / Sa				$	MC V AE DC D	Rec 180	Setting by the yacht club, Casablanca feeling Romantic atmosphere with ceiling fans and rattan Emphasis is seafood, fabulous Sunday brunch
	Mug-n-Mallet 224-2777 *POINT LOMA* - 2830 Cannon St	-- L D				$		MC V AE	Rec 6P+	Fun, very casual, when you order the crab you crack it yourself right on the table, similar to East Coast Crab Houses, Catering, Banquets, Carry-out
	Point Loma Seafoods 223-1109 *POINT LOMA* - 2805 Emerson St West of Rosecrans St	-- L D			$			None	No	Harborside fish market with seating, enclosed patio Informal, seafood, sandwiches, family-owned Carry-out, B&W only
	Red Sails Inn 223-3030 *SHELTER ISLAND* - 2614 Shelter Island Dr On Shelter Island	B L D	Y	✓		$		MC V AE DC	Yes 6p+ 30	Bayside dining, relaxed seafaring atmosphere Nautical decor, seafood, beef & chicken
	Reuben E. Lee 291-1880 *HARBOR ISLAND* - 880 E. Harbor Island Dr On Harbor Island	-- L (X:Su) D		✓		$		MC V AE DC D	Rec 100	Wheelhouse has view of the bay and turn of the century riverboat, beef and seafood specials Dancing and entertainment, banquet facilities
	Tom Ham's Lighthouse 291-9110 *HARBOR ISLAND* - 2150 Harbor Island Dr On Harbor Island	-- L (X:S/S) D	F / Sa				$	MC V AE DC D	Rec 225	On Harbor Island, beautiful view of San Diego harbor and skyline, coast guard certified lighthouse Seafood, chicken, beef, late night dining
SWEDISH	**Nordic Inn** 223-7721 *LOMA PORTAL* - 3577 Midway Dr South of Sports Arena Blvd	-- L (X:Su) D			$			v/mc	No	Swedish smorgasbord, daily specials Children's prices available B&W only

Cuisine	Restaurant	PHONE	SERVING:			Dinner /Person			Credit Cards	Reservations	SPECIAL FEATURES
(NOTES)	COMMUNITY - Street Located Near		Brkfst Lunch Dinner X=Closed	Late Night Din.	Sunday Brunch	Under $10	$10 to $20	$20 to $30 +			

ADDITIONS

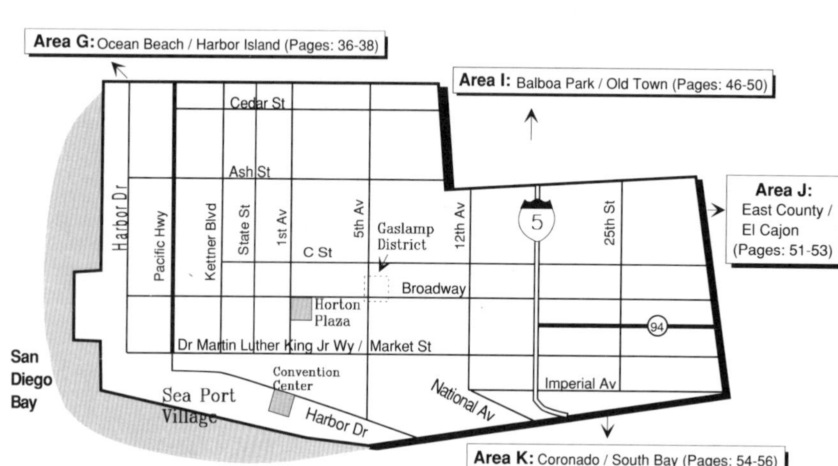

ALPHABETIC LISTINGS

RESTAURANT (CUISINE Category)

515 Fifth Avenue (CALIFORNIA)
Alfonso's (MEXICAN)
Anthony's Fish Grotto (SEAFOOD)
Anthony's Harborside (SEAFOOD)
Anthony's Star Of The Sea (SEAFOOD)
Asaggio Pizza, Pasta, Plus (FOOD-TO-GO)
Athens Market (GREEK)
B Street Cafe (AMERICAN)
Barnett's Grand Cafe (AMERICAN)
Barry's Cafe (AMERICAN)
Bayou Bar & Grill (CAJUN/CREOLE)
Blarney Stone Pub (IRISH)
Cabo Cabo Grill (MEXICAN)
Cafe 6th & K (AMERICAN)
Cafe Bon Appetit (CONTINENTAL)
Cafe San Diego (INTERNAT'L)
Cafe' Sevilla (SPANISH)
California Cafe (CALIFORNIA)
Chart House/SD Rowing Club (AMERICAN)
China Camp (CHINESE)
City Rock Cafe (AMERICAN)
Croce's (INTERNAT'L)
Dobson's (AMERICAN)
Falco (CALIFORNIA)
Fat City (ECLECTIC)
Fifth & Hawthorn (SEAFOOD)

RESTAURANT (CUISINE Category)

Filippi's Pizza Grotto (ITALIAN)
Fio's (ITALIAN)
Fish Market, The (SEAFOOD)
Five Star Thai Cuisine (THAI)
Flamingo's Bistro (AMERICAN)
Fontainebleau Restaurant (FRENCH)
Frenchy Marseilles (CONTINENTAL)
Frogg Lane Bar And Grill (AMERICAN)
Galaxy Grill (AMERICAN)
Gellerosa Ranch Barbecue (AMERICAN)
Golden Lion Tavern (AMERICAN)
Grant Grill & Lounge,(CONTINENTAL)
Greek Town Restaurant (GREEK)
Grill on The Park (ECLECTIC)
Harbor House (SEAFOOD)
Harbor House's Top of the Plaza SEAFOOD)
Homeport Cafe (CALIFORNIA)
Ida Bailey (AMERICAN)
Imperial House (CONTINENTAL)
Jerry G. Bishop's Greek Islands Cafe (GREEK)
Kansas City Barbeque (AMERICAN)
Kansas City Steakhouse (AMERICAN)
Karl Strauss' Old Columbia Brewery (AMERICAN)
La Gran Tapa (SPANISH)
Las Cascadas (AMERICAN)
Little Joe's (ITALIAN)

RESTAURANT (CUISINE Category)

Lubach's (CONTINENTAL)
Malcolm's First Avenue (CALIFORNIA)
Marina Sea Grill (SEAFOOD)
McDougal's (AMERICAN)
Molly's (AMERICAN)
Mystery Cafe (AMERICAN)
Overlook Restaurant (AMERICAN)
Pacifica Grill (AMERICAN)
Panda Inn (CHINESE)
Panda Inn (CHINESE)
Papagayo (SEAFOOD)
Pepper's Cafe (AMERICAN)
Rainwater's Chop House (AMERICAN)
Reidy O'Neil's (IRISH)
Renditions Restaurant (AMERICAN)
Restaurant Festival (SOUTHWEST)
Reuben's (SEAFOOD)
Salvatore's Cucina Italiana (ITALIAN)
Samsons Deli Restaurant (DELI)
San Diego Pier Cafe (SEAFOOD)
Sibyl's Down Under (AUSTRALIAN)
Sushi Bar Nippon (JAPANESE)
Tambo D'oro (CALIFORNIA)
Tango Grill (ARGENTINE)
Westgate Dining Room (CONTINENTAL)
Yacht Club (AMERICAN)

Cuisine (NOTES)	Restaurant / COMMUNITY - Street / Located Near	PHONE (619)	Serving: Brkfst / Lunch / Dinner / X=Closed	Late Night Din.	Sunday Brunch	Under $10	$10 to $20	$20 to $30+	Credit Cards	Reservations	SPECIAL FEATURES
AMERICAN	**B Street Cafe** / DOWNTOWN - 425 West B St / West of Fourth Av	236-1707	-- / L (M-F) / D	Y			$		MC V AE	Rec 35	Loud and noisy tiled bar, outdoor patio East Room offer quieter seating Live jazz nightly
	Barnett's Grand Cafe / DOWNTOWN - 601 Pacific Hwy / In Embassy Suites Hotel	544-1122	-- / L (X:Sa/Su) / D	Y			$		MC V AE DC	Rec	Indoor outdoor dining, gourmet pizza bar Northwest seafood specialties and Nebraska beef Walking distance to Convention Center
	Barry's Cafe / DOWNTOWN-1435 Sixth Ave	696-5314	B / L / D				$		MC V		Cafe setting, quaint & casual Menu offers a variety of dishes, beef, chicken, seafood, B&W only
	Cafe 6th & K / DOWNTOWN - 660 K St / In The Ramada Hotel	696-0234	B / L / D		✓		$		MC V AE DC D	Rec	Traditional cuisine with California accents Seafood specials, lunch buffet(M-F), seafood specials Sunday brunch with piano
	Chart House /SD Rowing Club / DOWNTOWN - 525 E. Harbor Dr / South of Market St	233-7391	-- / -- / D	Sa				$	MC V AE DC D	Rec 170	Historic renovated boathouse at new Convention Center Oyster bar, Prime rib and seafood Restaurant may be booked for private parties at lunch
	City Rock Cafe / DOWNTOWN - 895 Fourth Av / At E St	234-2040	-- / L / D	Y		$			MC V AE DC	Rec 10p+	Old movie memorabilia, cars on walls, high tech decor Hot colors, hamburgers, steaks, chicken, sundaes Live bands(W-Sa)
	Dobson's / DOWNTOWN - 956 Broadway Circle / 2nd Av	231-6771	-- / L (X:Sa/Su) / D (X:Su)	M - Sa				+	MC V AE	Must	Balcony dining overlooking the social scene Special bar menu from 4 pm, before or after theater Extensive wine list, Gold Medal/SCRW
	Flamingo's Bistro / DOWNTOWN - 1765 Union St / At I-5 (Front St) Offramp	234-6787	B / L / D	Y	✓	$			MC V AE DC	No	Bistro/Key West Caribbean atmosphere, Buffet jazz brunch, late night, burgers & diner fare Piano entertainment nightly, Carry-out
	Frogg Lane Bar And Grill / DOWNTOWN - The Top of Horton Plaza	235-0110	-- / L / D	Y		$			MC V AE D	Yes 75	Boston style eating and drinking establishment TV for sports, Happy hour Appetizers, sandwiches, full dinner entrees
	Galaxy Grill / DOWNTOWN - 522 Horton Plaza / In The Horton Plaza	234-7211	-- / L / D			$			MC V	Yes 8p+	David Cohn of Corvette diner, retro space age eatery Patio dining, 50's style soda fountain Great place for movie goers and shoppers
	Gellerosa Ranch Barbecue / DOWNTOWN - 120 Ash St / At Second Av	232-2838	-- / L (X:Su) / D (X:Su)			$			NONE	No	Oklahoma style ribs and combination plates, barbecued hot links, homemade barbecue sauce Weekday specials, carry-out, B&W only
	Golden Lion Tavern / DOWNTOWN - 801 Fourth Av / South of I-5	233-1131	-- / L (X:Su) / D				$		MC V AE	Rec	Stained glass ceiling, daily catch, steak special sandwich menu all day, live entertainment and dancing(Th-Sa 8:30p-1a), Happy Hour Duet(M-Th)
	Ida Bailey / DOWNTOWN - 311 Island Av / In The Horton Grand Hotel	544-1886	B / L / D	F / / Sa	✓			$	MC V AE DC D	Rec	Traditional American fare from Yankee pot roast to apple brown betty, Courtyard dining June-Oct Champagne brunch
	Kansas City Barbeque / DOWNTOWN - 610 West Market St / West of Sixth Av	231-9680	-- / L / D		✓	$			MC V	Rec 8p+	Rustic style, site of Top Gun movie filming chicken & ribs combo is superb Jukebox, catering
	Kansas City Steakhouse / DOWNTOWN - 535 Fifth Av / North of Market St	557-0525	-- / L (X:Sa/Su) / D (X:Su)		✓		$		MC V AE	Yes	Large exhibition kitchen, turn-of-the-century decor Downstairs bistro/coffehouse Ragtime and jazz
	Karl Strauss' Old Columbia Brew. / DOWNTOWN - 1157 Columbia St / West of B St	234-2739	-- / L / D	Y	✓	$			MC V	Rec 165	Downtown's first pub-brewery, brick walls give rustic feeling, working brewery can be seen through a glass wall behind the bar, snack foods
	Las Cascadas / DOWNTOWN - 333 West Harbor Dr / In The Marriott Hotel & Marina	234-1500	B / L / D				$		MC V AE DC		Health oriented menu using fiber, reduced fat, low cholesterol, low sodium and low sugar Dinner buffet(F-Sa), Lunch Buffet(Sa-Su)
	McDougal's / DOWNTOWN - 1125 Fifth Av / At C St	239-4194	B (X:Su) / L (X:Sa/Su) / D				$		MC V	Rec 75	Newly remodeled neighborhood pub on trolley line Steaks, seafood, oyster bar Banquet facilities, catering
	Molly's / DOWNTOWN - 333 West Harbor Dr / In the San Diego Marriott & Marina	230-8909	-- / -- / D					$	MC V AE DC	Rec	Elegant dining and service by tuxedoed waiters Covered platters, wines by the glass Daily gourmet specials, piano music nightly
	Mystery Cafe / DOWNTOWN - 505 Kalmia (Imperial Tower) / Attached to Imperial House Restaurant	544-1600	-- / -- / D (F/Sa)					$	MC V AE	Yes	A mystery play while you eat, "Murder at Cafe Noir" Described as "a 1940's movie come to life", audience participation, price includes dinner & show, F/Sa only

The "SERVING:" columns are Brkfst / Lunch / Dinner (X=Closed), Late Night Din., and Sunday Brunch. The three price columns (Under $10, $10 to $20, $20 to $30+) fall under the heading "Dinner /Person".

Cuisine (NOTES)	Restaurant / COMMUNITY - Street / Located Near	PHONE	Serving (B/L/D, X=Closed)	Late Night Din.	Sunday Brunch	Under $10	$10 to $20	$20 to $30+	Credit Cards	Reservations	Special Features
AMERICAN (Con't)	Overlook Restaurant DOWNTOWN - 1617 First Avenue On top floor of Holiday Inn	239-6171	B L D		✓		$		MC V AE D	Yes	Great harbor and airport view Variety of American and seafood specialties
	Pacifica Grill DOWNTOWN - 1202 Kettner Blvd In McClintock Plaza	696-9226	-- L (X:Sa/S)u D	F / Sa				$	MC V AE DC	Rec	Subdued decor in soft colors, atrium and patio dining Seafood specialties from regional southwest Great desserts, Chef Neil Stuart creates daily specials
	Pepper's Cafe DOWNTOWN- 905 Fourth Ave. In the Gaslamp Quarter	235-9902	B L --			$			MC V	No	Cafe setting in the historic Gaslamp Quarter, popular with business people & shoppers, menu offers a variety of sandwiches, salads, soups, B&W only, Carry-out
	Rainwater's Chop House DOWNTOWN - 1202 Kettner Blvd (2nd Fl) In McClintock Plaza	233-5757	-- L (X:Sa/Su) D	F / Sa				+	MC V AE DC	Rec 40	Large wooden booths and outdoor dining Maine Lobster, prime eastern beef & fresh seafood Wine Spectator Award Winner, private wine room
	Renditions Restaurant DOWNTOWN - 701 A STREET In the Marriott Suites	696-9800	B L D		✓		$		MC V AE	Yes 0	Express lunch buffet, soup and salad bar Happy hour (4-7p) Live entertainment and hors d'oeuvres Breakfast buffet
	Yacht Club DOWNTOWN - 333 W. Harbor Drive In the Marriott Hotel	234-1500	-- L D			$			MC V AE	Yes	Dine indoors or out Light dining, Live entertainment(Tu-Sa) Jazz on Monday with Fattburger
ARGENTINE	Tango Grill DOWNTOWN - 335 Market St East of Third Av	696-9171	-- L (X:Sa-M) D (X:M)	F - Su		$			MC V	Rec	Cafe atmosphere, some dinners served on parilla stone Feature empenadas, extensive selection of South American desserts, B&W only
AUSTRALIAN	Sibyl's Down Under DOWNTOWN - 500 Fourth Av South of Market St	239-9117	-- -- D (X:Su/M)			$			MC V AE	Rec 650	Fresh seafood Live entertainment nightly Dancing on large dance floor
CAJUN/CREOLE	Bayou Bar & Grill DOWNTOWN - 329 MARKET	696-8747	-- L (X:F-T) D (X:F-T)	W - Su			$		MC V AE	Limit	White linen casual but not pretentious Louisiana creole pizzas, New Orleans po-boy sandwiches Twelve years in New Orleans and Atlanta
CALIFORNIA	515 Fifth Avenue DOWNTOWN - 515 Fifth Ave South of Market St	232-3352	-- L (X:Sa/Su) D (X:Su)				$		MC V DC	Rec 30	Rotating art show in art deco bistro Wide range of flavors from Mexican to Oriental Innovative seasonly changing menu, Award/SCRW
	California Cafe DOWNTOWN - 502 Horton Plaza In The Horton Plaza	238-5440	-- L D	F / Sa	✓		$		MC V AE	Rec 14	Fabulous views, large sunken bar with outdoor seats Daily changing menu, hot rock cooking Wines by the glass, Piano player
	Falco DOWNTOWN - 835 Fifth Av In the Gaslamp Quarter	233-5687	-- L (X:Su/M) D (X:M)				$		MC V	Yes	Elegant atmosphere, crystal chandeliers, original artwork, Sidewalk dining, Serve a high tea, Menu offers seafood, duck, chicken & beef, B&W only
	Homeport Cafe DOWNTOWN - 1355 North Harbor Drive In the Holiday Inn	232-3861	B L D		✓	$			MC V AE D	Yes 18	California continental cuisine, salad bar buffet Sunday brunch Prime rib, seafood, pasta, NY steak
	Malcolm's First Avenue DOWNTOWN - 1055 First Ave In The Kingston Hotel (1st & Broadway)	232-6141	B L D	F / Sa	✓			$	MC V AE DC	Yes 12	Continental menu, high tea in the afternoon Before and after theater dining Newly renovated downtown location
	Tambo D'oro DOWNTOWN - 530 B St. In the Union Bank Building	231-0801	B (X:Sa/Su) L (X:Sa/Su) D(X:Su)					$	AE V MC V	Rec	On the 11th floor, has a beautiful view of downtown & the waterfront, menu offers international cuisine with California accent, Jackets required
CHINESE	China Camp DOWNTOWN - 2137 Pacific Hwy In Fat City Bldg.	232-1367	-- L (X:Sa/Su) D	F / Sa			$		MC V AE	Rec	Old time memorabilia, 1840's railroading atmosphere Old California-Chinese recipes like Beggar Chicken Owned by Fat family of Sacramento, Entertainment(Th-Sa)
	Panda Inn DOWNTOWN - 506 Horton Plaza In The Horton Plaza	233-7800	-- L D	F / Sa	✓		$		MC V AE	Rec 50	contemporary Chinese decor Mandarin & Szechuan menu, Silver Medal/SCRW Banquet facilities, catering & carry-out
CONTINENTAL	Cafe Bon Appetit DOWNTOWN - 701 B St In The Imperial Bank Bldg.	696-0225	-- L (X:Sa/Su) --			$			MC V AE	Yes	Atrium cafe caters to business crowd, informal lunch Pianist plays daily, Deli to go in the early morning
	Frenchy Marseilles DOWNTOWN - 801 C St Corner of 8th & C St.	233-3413	-- L D	F / Sa				$	MC V AE DC	Yes	Patio and sidewalk cafe, favorite for theater goers Tableside cooking Piano(F-Sa)
	Grant Grill & Lounge, The DOWNTOWN - 326 Broadway In U. S. Grant Hotel	239-6806	B L D	Y	✓			+	MC V AE	Rec	S.D.'s Premier historic hostelry, mahogany & brass Lunch buffet(M-F), Extensive wine/port list Entertainment(T-Sa), Silver Medal/SCRW

Cuisine (NOTES)	Restaurant / COMMUNITY - Street / Located Near	PHONE	SERVING: Brkfst / Lunch / Dinner / X=Closed	Late Night Din.	Sunday Brunch	Under $10	$10 to $20	$20 to $30+	Credit Cards	Reservations	SPECIAL FEATURES
CONTINENTAL (Con't)	**Imperial House** DOWNTOWN - 505 Kalmia In The Imperial Tower	234-3525	-- L (X:Sa/Su) D (X:Su/M)	Tu - Sa				$	MC V AE DC	Rec	Elegant European charm with a park view 21 years a San Diego favorite Entertainment at the piano bar, banquet and catering
	Lubach's DOWNTOWN - 2101 North Harbor Dr South of Laurel St	232-5129	-- L (X:Sa/Su) D (X:Su)	M - Sa				+	MC V AE	Rec 150	One of San Diego's oldest restaurants, waterfront view Power lunch location, dessert cart Banquet facilities, Jacket required
	Westgate Dining Room DOWNTOWN - 1055 Second Av In The Westgate Hotel	238-1818	B L D	Y	✓			$	MC V AE DC D	Rec	Small intimate dining room on the first floor of the Westgate hotel serving all day from breakfast to dinner
DELI	**Samsons Deli Restaurant** DOWNTOWN - 501 W Broadway In the Koll Building	232-2340	B (X:Su) L (X:Su) D (X:Su)			$			MC V AE D	No	Dining area in built around an aviary filled with birds and tropical foliage, Traditional New York deli items, homemade desserts, sandwiches, catering
ECLECTIC	**Fat City** DOWNTOWN - 2137 Pacific Hwy In Tops Bldg.	232-0686	-- L D	F / Sa	✓	$			MC V AE	Rec	Outdoor cafe/courtyard, famous art deco pink building Neon art includes 1958 pink Cadillac, winged victory Banquet facilities, Art nouveau bar, Entertainment Th-S
	Grill on The Park DOWNTOWN - 901 Fifth Av In Horton Park Plaza Hotel	231-0055	-- L D				$		MC V AE	Yes	American grill, blond wood, black lacquer, plants, fun Contemporary & casual atmosphere, seafood, beef, pizza, pasta
FOOD-TO-GO	**Asaggio Pizza, Pasta, Plus** DOWNTOWN - 879 West Harbor Dr In Seaport Village	234-2407	-- L D			$			NONE	No 20	Casual bayside dining with outdoor seating Homemade deep dish pizza, and special pastas B&W only
FRENCH	**Fontainebleau** DOWNTOWN - 1055 Second Av In The Westgate Hotel	238-1818	-- L (X:Sa/Su) D (X:Su)		✓			+	MC V AE DC D	Must	Elegant dining atmosphere, authentic antiques White gloved waiters, Travel Holiday Award Winner Harpist at lunch/piano at dinner, champagne brunch
GREEK	**Athens Market** DOWNTOWN - 109 West F St In The Senator Hotel	234-1955	-- L (X:Su) D	Y			$		MC V AE DC	Rec	Lively atmosphere, before theater and after shopping Fixed price menu available, Special late menu 11-1am Greek and belly dancers(F-Sa), Catering
	Greek Town Restaurant DOWNTOWN - 431 East E St East of Fourth Av	232-0461	-- L D	Th - Sa			$		MC V AE	Yes F/Sa	Over 300 seats, 30 years experience in the restaurant business, family-owned, traditional dishes Belly dancers and live bands
	Jerry G. Bishop's DOWNTOWN - 879 West Harbor Dr In Seaport Village	239-5216	-- L D			$			--	No 20	FOOD TO GO, Some seating with view of the harbor & marina, Greek specialties, B&W only
INTERNAT'L	**Cafe San Diego** DOWNTOWN - 910 Broadway Circle In The Omni San Diego Hotel	239-2200	B L D		✓	$			MC V AE DC D	Rec	Three ways for lunch, Rotisserie Club All you can eat taco bar Deli Counter, carry-out
	Croce's DOWNTOWN - 802 Fifth Av At F St	233-4355	B L D	F / Sa	✓		$		MC V AE	Rec 6p+	Restored turn of the century pub Owned by the wife of the late Jim Croce Live jazz, Rhythm and Blues nightly
IRISH	**Blarney Stone Pub** GASLAMP - 501 Fifth	2338519	-- L D	Y		$			MC V	Yes	Home of the famous baseball museum Genuine Irish cuisine, great Irish breakfast Live Irish entertainment(W-Sa)
	Reidy O'Neil's DOWNTOWN - 939 Fifth	231-8500	-- L (X:Su) D (X:Su)	F / Sa		$			MC V AE	Yes	Irish/American food in an Irish bar Monday night corned beef and cabbage Piano player, sometimes sing-a-long
ITALIAN	**Filippi's Pizza Grotto** DOWNTOWN - 1747 India St South of Laurel St	232-5095	-- L D	Y		$			MC V	Yes	In little Italy district on India Street Noisy Italian restaurant, family atmosphere Gourmet pizza, full Italian menu, carry-out counter
	Fio's GASLAMP - 801 Fifth	234-3467	-- L (X:Su) D	Y			$		MC V AE	Yes	Northern Italian cuisine in a contemporary setting Gourmet pizza bar, happy hour 5-7p Extensive wine list and wines by the glass
	Little Joe's DOWNTOWN - 750 Fifth Av In the Gaslamp	234-1320	-- L D			$				No	Served San Diegans since 1950, informal casual setting Menu offers pizzas, pastas, sandwiches & ribs B&W only
	Salvatore's Cucina Italiana DOWNTOWN - 750 Front St In The Meridian Tower	544-1865	-- L (X:Sa/Su) D					$	MC V AE	Rec 100	Elegant dining with very attentive service Northern Italian specialties Gold medal/SCRW, Best Restaurant 1989
JAPANESE	**Sushi Bar Nippon** DOWNTOWN - 532 Fourth Av North of Market St	544-9779	-- L (X:Su) D (X:Su)				$		MC V AE DC	Rec	Gaslamp quarter, owner chef Akira

Cuisine (NOTES)	Restaurant / COMMUNITY - Street / Located Near	PHONE	Serving: Brkfst / Lunch / Dinner (X=Closed)	Late Night Din.	Sunday Brunch	Under $10	$10 to $20	$20 to $30+	Credit Cards	Reservations	SPECIAL FEATURES
MEXICAN	**Alfonso's** DOWNTOWN - 135 Broadway East of First Av	234-7300	-- -- D (X:Su)	F / Sa			$		MC V AE	Rec 6p+	Location also in La Jolla Extensive menu of Mexican classics using family recipes Daily specials, catering and carry-out
	Cabo Cabo Grill DOWNTOWN - 203 Fifth Av 5th Ave. at L St. in the Gaslamp Qtr.	232-2272	-- L D	F / Sa	✓	$			MC V AE DC	Yes 300	Mexican cantina featuring Baja coastal seafood and Mexican regional cooking using a mesquite grill Happy hour with free hors d'oeuvres(M-F)
SEAFOOD	**Anthony's Fish Grotto** DOWNTOWN - 1360 North Harbor Dr North of Broadway	232-5103	-- L D		✓	$			MC V AE	No	Built over the bay, one of the Ghio Family restaurants Fish & chips, seafood salads Daily fresh fish specials
	Anthony's Harborside DOWNTOWN - 1355 North Harbor Dr North of Broadway	232-6358	-- L (X:Sa/Su) D	Y			$		MC V AE	Rec	Harbor view, second story picture windows Seafood salad bar Band and dancing(Tu-Sa), Jazz(Tu), Jacket required
	Anthony's Star Of The Sea DOWNTOWN - 1360 North Harbor Dr Ash St	232-7408	-- -- D	Y				+	MC V AE	Must	Formal dining room with large windows overlooking the harbor, tableside service, Mama Catherine Ghio created the original recipes, Coat & Tie required
	Fifth & Hawthorn DOWNTOWN - 515 Hawthorn St At Fifth Av	544-0940	-- L (M-F) D				$		MC V AE	Rec 40	Latin American chef who studied in Japan ''Pacific Rim Restaurant'' intimate fresh seafood & pasta ''Most Promising Newcomer''/SCRW
	Fish Market, The DOWNTOWN - 750 Harbor Dr South of Hawthorn St	232-FISH	-- L D		✓		$		MC V AE	Yes 45	Brand new, mesquite grill, bay view, fish market Oyster and sushi bar, downstairs dining is very casual upstairs is fine dining room, own fishing fleet
	Harbor House DOWNTOWN - 831 West Harbor Dr In Seaport Village	232-1141	-- L D	F / Sa	✓		$		MC V AE DC D	Rec 400	Harbor and bridge view, oyster bar Mesquite grilled fresh seafood and fresh shellfish Dancing and entertainment(F-Sa)
	Harbor House's Top of the Plaza DOWNTOWN - 510 Horton Plaza In Horton Plaza Restaurant Row	233-5923	-- L (X:Su) D	F / Sa				$	MC V AE D	Rec	Fresh seafood featuring New England clam chowder Dancing on weekends, 3 distinct rooms, patio dining Downtown and bay view
	Marina Sea Grill DOWNTOWN - 333 West Harbor Dr In the San Diego Marriott Hotel & Marina	230-8990	-- L D	Y	✓		$		MC V AE DC D	Rec 40	Windows are floor to ceiling to view yachts in marina Early bird dinner 5-7p, Sunday champagne brunch Live jazz(Tu-Sa)
	Papagayo DOWNTOWN - 861 West Harbor Dr In Seaport Village	232-7581	-- L D	F / Sa	✓			$	MC V	Yes 70	Bay view, mesquite grill used for grilling seafood South America shellfish specialties Entertainment(Th-Sa)
	Reuben's DOWNTOWN - 880 East Harbor Dr South of Fifth Av	291-5030	---- L (X:Sa/Su) D		✓		$		MC V AE DC D	Rec	On the Water with a Downtown view Specializing in Seafood Multiple locations
	San Diego Pier Cafe DOWNTOWN - 885 West Harbor Dr In Seaport Village	239-3968	B L D	F / Sa	✓		$		MC V AE DC	No 50	Outdoor dining on deck over the water Seafood, lobster, crab, salads Fresh seafood mesquite grilled
SOUTHWEST	**Restaurant Festival** DOWNTOWN - 910 Broadway Circle In The Omni San Diego Hotel	239-2200	-- L (X:Sa-M) D (X:Su/M)					$	MC V AE DC D	Rec	Wide choice of beef, chicken or seafood
SPANISH	**Cafe' Sevilla** GASLAMP DISTRICT - 555 Fourth Av South of Market St	233-5979	-- L (Sa-Su) D				$		MC V DC D	Rec 20	Rustic tapa bar decor, tables close together, lively Assorted tapas on menu, menu features Spanish wine Guitarist(Tu-Sa)
	La Gran Tapa DOWNTOWN - 611 B St West of Sixth Av	234-8272	-- L (X:Sa/Su) D	Y			$		MC V AE	Rec	Spanish tapas bar decor featuring wines by the glass Imported wines and sherry, Paella, Spanish favorites Daily empanada specials, owned by Paul Dobson
THAI	**Five Star Thai Cuisine** DOWNTOWN - 816 Broadway	231-4408	-- L (X:Su) D			$			MC V AE D	No	Very chic, lots of neon and other types of art More than 100 Thai entrees & traditional specialties B&W only

GOING TO TIJUANA?
Here's a handy reference map of the San Diego Trolley System showing the location of stations in the Downtown area. →

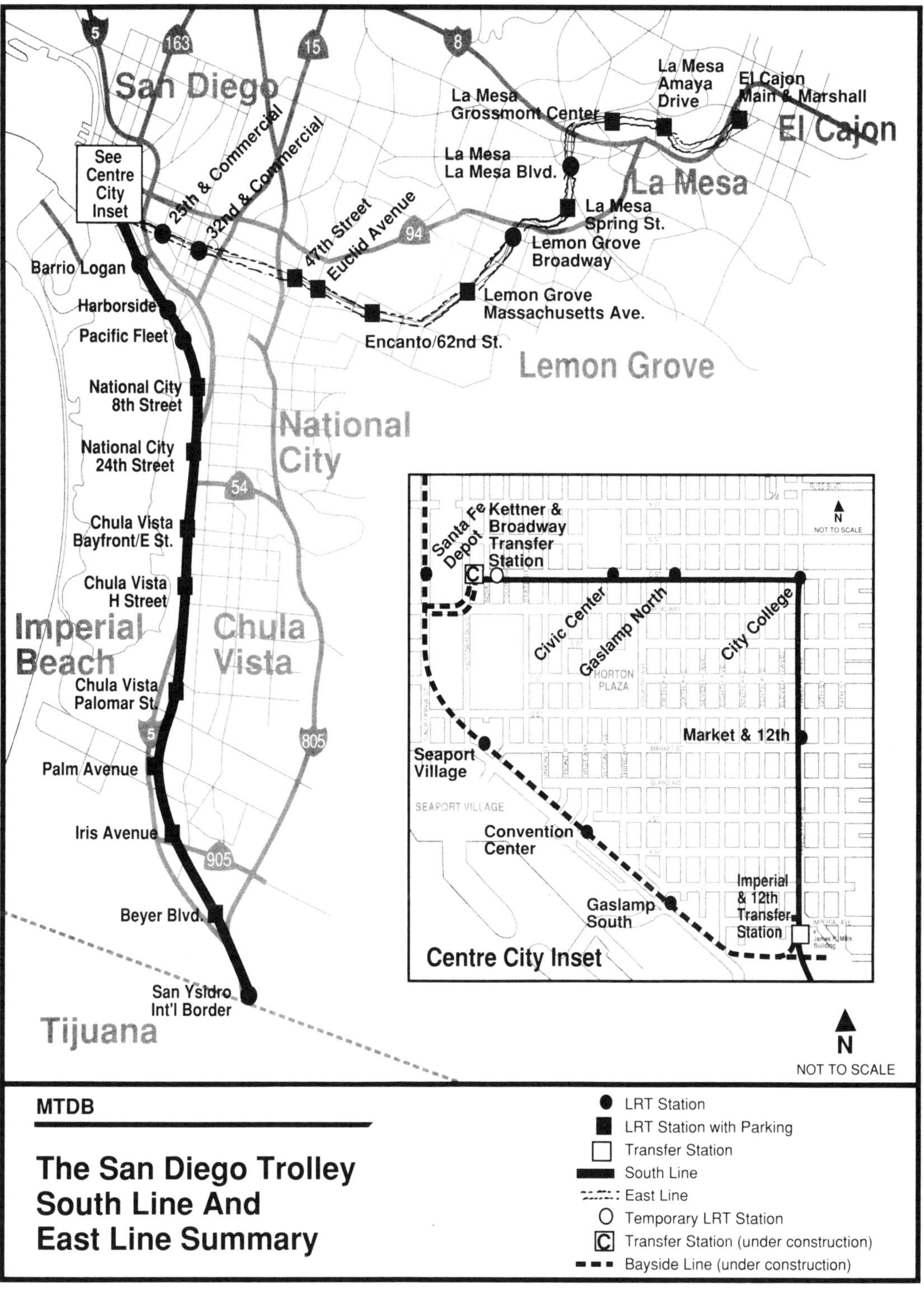

The San Diego Trolley South Line And East Line Summary

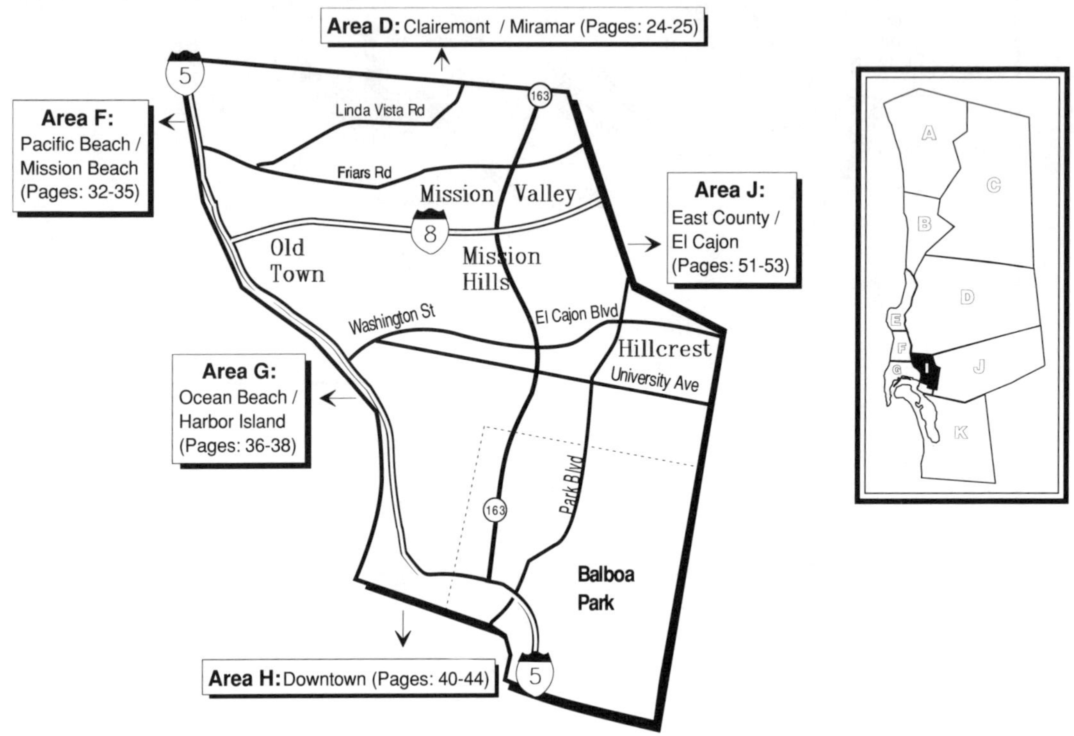

ALPHABETIC LISTINGS

RESTAURANT (CUISINE Category)

Abbey, The (CONTINENTAL)
Adam 'n' Albie's Beef Inn (AMERICAN)
Alta Vista Mexican Restaurant (MEXICAN)
Athenian Gardens (GREEK)
Aztec (MEXICAN)
Belgian Garden, The (BELGIAN)
Benihana of Tokyo (JAPANESE)
Bennigan's (AMERICAN)
Bonacci's Pizza & Pasta (ITALIAN)
Brigantine, The (SEAFOOD)
Bully's East (AMERICAN)
Busalacchi's Ristorante (ITALIAN)
Cafe Coyote (SOUTHWEST)
Cafe De Paris (FRENCH)
Cafe Del Rey Moro (CALIFORNIA)
Cafe Eleven (FRENCH)
Cafe Pacifica (SEAFOOD)
California Cuisine (CALIFORNIA)
California Earthquake Cafe (AMERICAN)
Calliope's (GREEK)
Canes (CALIFORNIA)
Casa De Bandini (MEXICAN)
Casa De Pico (MEXICAN)
Celadon (THAI)
Chicken Pie Shop (AMERICAN)
Chu Dynasty (CHINESE)
City Deli (DELI)

RESTAURANT (CUISINE Category)

Cornucopia (VEGETARIAN)
Corvette Diner (AMERICAN)
Crest Cafe (AMERICAN)
Drowsy Maggie's (NATURAL FOOD)
El Indio (FOOD-TO-GO)
El Tecolote (MEXICAN)
Emil's (CONTINENTAL)
Figaro (ITALIAN)
French Side of The West, The (FRENCH)
Fung Lin (CHINESE)
Gathering, The (AMERICAN)
Georgia's Greek Cuisine (GREEK)
Gourmet Room (CONTINENTAL)
Gratzi (AMERICAN)
Guadalajara Grill (MEXICAN)
Hamburguesa (MEXICAN)
Hob Nob Hill (AMERICAN)
Ironwoods, The (CONTINENTAL)
Islands Restaurant, The (POLYNESIAN)
JR's (AMERICAN)
Kelly's Steak House (AMERICAN)
King's Grille (ENGLISH)
Kung Food (VEGETARIAN)
La Boheme (CALIFORNIA)
La Hacienda (MEXICAN)
La Pinata (MEXICAN)
Le Pavillon (FRENCH)

RESTAURANT (CUISINE Category)

Lino's Italian Restaurant (ITALIAN)
Ly's Garden #1 (CAMBODIAN)
Mandarin House (CHINESE)
Mister A's (CONTINENTAL)
Montana's American Grill (AMERICAN)
Monterey Whaling Company (SEAFOOD)
Old Town Mexican Cafe (MEXICAN)
Palmier Bistro (FRENCH)
Phoung Nam (VIETNAMESE)
Piccadilly Line, The (ENGLISH)
Ristorante Pasta Al Dente (ITALIAN)
Rusty Pelican (SEAFOOD)
Saffron (THAI)
Sculpture Garden Cafe (CONTINENTAL)
Sheik Cafe (MIDDLE EAST)
Stephen Zolezzi's Stefano's (ITALIAN)
T. G. I. Friday's (ECLECTIC)
Taste of Thai (THAI)
Thai Chada (THAI)
Tickled Trout, The (SEAFOOD)
Twelve Stars European Cafe (FRENCH)
Villanis (ITALIAN)
Willy's American Bistro (AMERICAN)
Yoshino Japanese Restaurant (JAPANESE)
Yumi (JAPANESE)
Zodiac Restaurant, The (CALIFORNIA)

Cuisine (NOTES)	Restaurant / COMMUNITY - Street / Located Near	PHONE	SERVING: Brkfst / Lunch / Dinner / X=Closed	Late Night Din.	Sunday Brunch	Under $10	$10 to $20	$20 to $30+	Credit Cards	Reservations	SPECIAL FEATURES
AMERICAN	**Adam 'n' Albie's** MISSION VALLEY - 1201 Hotel Circle South In The Mission Valley Travelodge	291-1103	B L (X:Su) D (X:Su)	F / Sa			$		MC V AE DC D	Rec	Old fashion setting, lots of wood & glass, chandeliers Intimate, cozy, menu offers prime rib, fillet, lamb, seafood, Piano bar(Tu-Sa)
	Bennigan's MISSION VALLEY-1760 Camino del Rio North Mission Valley Center	291-8853	-- L D		✓		$		MC V AE	Rec	Eclectic surroundings, busy, fun, lively, Irish bar Warm, friendly, menu offers a variety of appetizers, burgers, sandwiches, entrees
	Bully's East MISSION VALLEY-2401 Camino del Rio South East of Fwy 163	291-2665	-- L D	Y	✓		$		MC V AE DC	No	Casual, relaxed atmosphere, patio seating Known for its prime rib & burgers, seafood as well Multiple locations
	California Earthquake Cafe MISSION VALLEY - 7919 Mission Center Ct South of Friars Rd	297-3603	-- L D	W - Sa		$			MC V	Yes 200	Lively diner, fun for families, nostalgic decor giant colorful billboards, burgers, sandwiches, shakes Unusual daily specials, Dancing to oldies(W-Sa)
	Chicken Pie Shop HILLCREST - 3801 Fifth Av 1 Block South of University Av	295-0156	-- L D			$			NONE	No	San Diego's oldest diner 1938 Casual, known for its chicken pie Carry-out
	Corvette Diner HILLCREST - 3946 Fifth Av North of University Av	542-1001	-- L D	Y		$			MC V	No 75	Fun, soda fountain, memorabilia everywhere Blue plate specials, DJ entertainment nightly, menu items have nostalgic names, Silver Award/SCRW
	Crest Cafe HILLCREST - 425 Robinson Av West of Fourth Av	295-2510	B L D	Y			$		MC V AE	Rec 5p+	Art deco style cafe, soda fountain with homemade desserts, small, casual known for its Crest burgers & onion loaves, seafood, chicken pastas & sandwiches
	Gathering, The MISSION HILLS - 4015 Goldfinch St At Washington Av	260-0400	B L D	M - Sa			$		MC V AE	Rec 5p+ 25	American style, casual eatery with its wooden bar, and lots of plants, omelets, seafood, salads, and specialty sandwiches, Magic shows(Th-Su)
	Gratzi MISSION VALLEY - 8757 Rio San Diego Dr In The Marriott Mission Valley	692-3800	B (X:Sa/Su) L (X:Sa/Su) D				$		MC V AE DC	Yes	Tropical setting, open casual, ceiling fans Breakfast & lunch buffet Grilled seafood, pastas, sandwiches
	Hob Nob Hill BALBOA PARK - 2271 First Av South of Laurel St	239-8176	B (X:Sa) L (X:Sa) D (X:Sa)			$			MC V AE DC	Rec 4p+	Owners have served since 1946, breakfast served all day long, homemade rolls and breads, coffee cakes Dinner entrees include chicken fried steak & prime rib
	JR's BAY PARK - 5021 Linda Vista Road Near USD	299-2055	B L --			$			MC V	No	Older diner setting, casual, family oriented, homemade American favorites, hot & cold sandwiches, breakfast with homemade biscuits & home fried potatoes
	Kelly's Steak House MISSION VALLEY - 248 Hotel Circle North In The Town & Country Hotel	291-7131	-- L (X:Sa/Su) D	Y			$		MC V AE DC	Rec 6p+	Relaxed setting with a waterfall view, specialty is Chateaubriand for two, seafood & chicken dishes Piano bar, early bird specials
	Montana's American Grill HILLCREST - 1421 University Av	297-0722	-- L D				$		MC V AE	Rec 25	Contemporary, unique with sophisticated decor, menu is ''Western regional Cuisine'' blending Pacific Northwest, Cal. & Southwest cooking, Banquet facilities, B&W only
	Willy's American Bistro MISSION VALLEY-911 Camino del Rio South East of Fwy 163	692-0094	B (X:Sa/Su) L (X:Sa/Su) D	Y			$		MC V AE	Rec 45	Fun California cuisine in this unpretentious bistro Salads, omelettes, fresh baked breads, pastas
BELGIAN	**Belgian Garden, The** MISSION HILLS - 808 Washington St	296-8010	-- L (X:Sa/Su) D				$		AE DC CB	Yes	Bright, cheery cafe setting featuring Belgian entrees, lamb, chicken, fish & pork, imported chocolates, waffles & crepes, wine only
CALIFORNIA	**Cafe Del Rey Moro** BALBOA PARK - 1549 El Prado At Sixth Av	234-8511	-- L (X:Sa/Su) D (X:Sa-M)		✓		$		MC V AE	Rec 14	Located in Balboa Park, sits in the beautifully landscaped patio, dine in the garden terrace before the theater; box lunches to go
	California Cuisine HILLCREST - 1027 University Av West of Hwy 163	543-0790	-- L (X:Sa/Su) D					$	MC V AE DC	Rec	Contemporary cuisine and setting Patio dining, daily menu, homemade desserts Catering, Gold Medal/SCRW
	Canes HILLCREST - 1270 Cleveland St. In the Uptown District	299-3551	B L D	Y	✓		$		MC V AE	Yes	Contemporary bistro atmosphere, outside seating California cuisine, pizzas, pastas, dishes prepared fresh daily
	La Boheme HILLCREST - 3167 Fifth Av In the Park Manor Hotel	296-0057	-- L (X:Sa/Su) D				$		MC V AE	Rec	Intimate setting, cozy with the old fashioned high back booths, grand, elegant, menu offers Innovative cuisine B&W only
	Zodiac Restaurant, The MISSION VALLEY - 280 Fashion Valley Rd In Neiman Marcus	692-9100	-- L (X:Su) --				$		AE	Rec	Department store fine dining, elegant, private room Soups, salads, sandwiches and daily specials B&W only

Cuisine (NOTES)	Restaurant / COMMUNITY - Street / Located Near	PHONE	SERVING: Brkfst / Lunch / Dinner (X=Closed)	Late Night Din.	Sunday Brunch	Under $10	$10 to $20	$20 to $30+	Credit Cards	Reservations	SPECIAL FEATURES
CAMBODIAN	Ly's Garden #1 CITY HEIGHTS - 3645 University Av East of I-805	265-1885	-- / L (X-W) / D (X-W)					$	MC V	Rec	Traditional Oriental setting, very casual Carry-out
CHINESE	Chu Dynasty MISSION VALLEY-1400 Camino de la Reina East of Fwy 163	298-4680	-- / L (X:Sa/Su) / D				$		MC V AE	Rec	Traditional Chinese atmosphere with screens, lanterns Warm & subdued, Mandarin & Szechuan cuisine Carry-out
	Fung Lin MISSION VALLEY-10467 San Diego Mission Rd East of I-15	283-9883	-- / L (X:Sa/Su) / D			$			MC V AE	Yes 68	Everything is served family style, comfortable Mandarin & Szechuan specialties Catering
	Mandarin House BALBOA PARK - 2604 Fifth Av North of Laurel St	232-1101	-- / L (X:Sa/Su) / D	F / Sa		$			MC V AE	Rec 50	Decor is traditional Chinese Mandarin, Peking duck, Hunan scallops Banquet, catering, Carry-out
CONTINENTAL	Abbey, The BALBOA PARK - 2825 Fifth Ave At Olive St	291-4779	-- / L(X:Sa/Su) / D					$	MC V AE DC	Rec 500	1910 church turned restaurant, after theater dining in the wine cellar, very grand feeling, seafood specials Live entertainment, Jacket required
	Emil's OLD TOWN - 3928 Twiggs St At Congress St	295-2343	-- / -- / D (X:Su)					$	MC V AE DC	Rec	European country setting with tile floors Planters and lace curtains, quiet intimate Menu offers veal and seafood
	Gourmet Room MISSION VALLEY - 500 Hotel Circle North In The Town & Country Hotel	291-7131	B (X:Su) / L (X:Su) / D				$		MC V AE DC D	Rec	Patio setting, popular with the business crowd Terrific sandwiches, seafood, steaks, piano bar
	Ironwoods, The MISSION VALLEY - 950 Hotel Circle North In The Handlery Stardust Hotel	298-0511	-- / -- / D				$		MC V AE DC D	Yes	Newly remodeled, elegant, comfortable, seafood specials Entertainment(Tu-Sa)
	Mister A's BALBOA PARK - 2550 Fifth Av In The Fifth Avenue Financial Ctr	239-1377	-- / L (X:Sa/Su) / D					+	MC V AE	Rec 75	San Diego Institution with an incredible view Watch the planes take off and land European service in elegant surroundings
	Sculpture Garden Cafe BALBOA PARK - 1450 El Prado In San Diego Museum of Art	232-7931	L (X:Sa-M) / D					$	MC V AE	Must (D)	Garden seating, light lunches Open befor the Old Globe Theater Piano bar(Sa/Su), B&W only
DELI	City Deli HILLCREST - 535 University Av West of Fwy 163 at 6th Ave	295-2747	B / L / D			$			MC V	No 15	New York style deli, black & white art deco theme Traditional deli food, fresh baked goods Carry-out
ECLECTIC	T. G. I. Friday's MISSION VALLEY-403 Camino del Rio South East of Fwy 163	297-8443	- / L / D		Y		$		MC V AE DC	Rec 10p+ 100	Live, loud, fun, suitable for families Location is an after work gathering spot for young professionals, Menu offers sandwiches, salads, seafood
ENGLISH	King's Grille MISSION VALLEY - 1333 Hotel Circle South West of Fwy 163	297-2231	-- / L (X:Su) / D				$		MC V AE DC	Rec	English country atmosphere, plush intimate booths 18th century inn decor, hearty English fare
	Piccadilly Line, The HILLCREST - 3900 FIFTH AVE	574-7700	-- / L / D	F / Sa			$		MC V	Yes 6p+	English decor, plaster replicas of the Piccadilly Circus, English specialties include shepherd pie, fish & chips
FOOD-TO-GO	El Indio HILLCREST - 3695 India St South of Washington St	299-0333	-- / L (X:Su) / D (X:Su)			$			None	No	Carry-out only, some outdoor seating, fresh tortillas & chips made daily, Family run Catering
FRENCH	Cafe De Paris HILLCREST - 2468 Fifth Av North of Laurel St	234-2737	-- / L (X:Su) / D (X:Su)	F / Sa			$		MC V AE	Rec	Classic French Bistro menu, fabulous desserts Small & intimate Second location on Miramar Road offers patio dining
	Cafe Eleven HILLCREST - 1440 University Av At Normal St	543-0790	-- / L (X:Sa-M) / D (X:Sa-M)				$		MC V AE	Rec	Intimate cafe decorated by local artists Innovative Menu: country French cooking, salads, lamb, sandwiches, pastas, dinner-sweetbreads, filet mignon
	French Side of The West, The BALBOA PARK - 2202 Fourth Av South of Laurel St	234-5540	-- / -- / D				$		MC V AE	Must 24	Five course fixed price menu Entrees include generous charcuterie plate, soup or salad, choice of dessert, B&W only
	Le Pavillon MISSION VALLEY - 500 Hotel Circle North West of Fwy 163	291-7131	-- / -- / D (X-Su/M)					+	MC V AE DC	Must	View of Mission Valley, Nouvelle cuisine Extensive wine list, Champagne by the glass
	Palmier Bistro MISSION HILLS - 902 West Washington St West of Goldfinch St	297-2993	B (Sa-Su) / L (X:Sa/Su) / D				+	$	MC V AE	Rec	Outdoor dining and provencale menu California accent, daily specials Wine dessert bar, Carry-out, B&W only

Cuisine (NOTES)	Restaurant / PHONE / COMMUNITY - Street / Located Near	Serving: Brkfst / Lunch / Dinner / X=Closed	Late Night Din.	Sunday Brunch	Under $10	$10 to $20	$20 to $30+	Credit Cards	Reservations	SPECIAL FEATURES
FRENCH (Con't)	**Twelve Stars European Cafe** 298-3032 *OLD TOWN* - 2391 San Diego Av	-- L (X:Su/M) D				$		MC V AE	Yes	Romantic setting, candlelight, French music, outdoor dining, traditional French fare Summer Lobster Festival, B&W only
GREEK	**Athenian Gardens** 295-0812 *HILLCREST* - 3731 India St S. of Washington St; I-5 Wash. St. Exit	-- L (X:F-Su) D (X:Su)		F / Sa	$			MC V	Rec	Bay view, terrace, belly dancing Live international music(F/Sa) B&W only
	Calliope's 291-5588 *HILLCREST* - 3958 Fifth Av South of Washington Av	-- L D		F / Sa		$		MC V AE DC	Rec 6p+	Homey Greek atmosphere, authentic lamb sandwiches Innovative & creative Greek specialties, wine bar Deli, carry-out, B&W only
	Georgia's Greek Cuisine 284-1007 *NORMAL HEIGHTS* - 3641 Madison Av West of Ward Rd (Fwy 15)	-- L (X:Sa/Su) D (X:Su)			$			MC V	Rec Wknd	Tavern decor Homemade desserts, big portions Greek dancers (F/Sa)
ITALIAN	**Bonacci's Pizza & Pasta** 291-7131 *MISSION VALLEY* - 500 Hotel Circle North In The Town & Country Hotel	-- L (X:Sa/Su) D				$		MC V AE DC	Rec	Family style atmosphere, pastas, soup & salad bar Dancing in the adjacent bar(Tu-Sa)
	Busalacchi's Ristorante 298-0119 *HILLCREST* - 3683 Fifth Av 1/2 Block South of University Av	-- L (X:Sa/Su) D		F / Sa		$		MC V DC	Rec 60	Converted residence, intimate, comfortable decorated in subtle elegant colors Sicilian specialties, pasta made daily
	Figaro 296-4811 *HILLCREST* - 741 West Washington St West of Falcon St	-- L (X:M) D (X:M)			$			MC V AE DC	Rec 6p+ 20	Small family run restaurant using Milanese recipes Italian decor in red velvet drapes, opera music A favorite for 25 years, carry-out, B&W only
	Lino's Italian Restaurant 299-7124 *OLD TOWN* - 2754 Calhoun St In Bazaar del Mundo	-- L D			$			MC V AE DC D	Rec	Colorful, lively atmosphere, outdoor dining, casual Family oriented, fresh pasta specialties & pizzas
	Ristorante Pasta Al Dente 295-2727 *HILLCREST* - 420 Robinson Av West of 4th Av	-- L (X:Su) D (X:Su)		F / Sa	$			MC V	 20	Casual, comfortable, hardwood floors & etched windows A neighborhood favorite, outdoor dining, pizza & pasta Ideal for people watching, B&W only
	Stephen Zolezzi's Stefano's 296-0975 *HILLCREST* - 3671 Fifth Av 2 1/2 Blocks South of University Av	-- L (X:Sa/Su) D		F / Sa		$		MC V AE DC	Rec 50	Elegant, contemporary setting, romantic & comfortable Northern Italian cuisine, homemade pastas Great wine list, after theater menu, banquet facilities
	Villanis 293-0550 *SAN DIEGO* - 1515 Hotel Circle South In the Travelodge Plaza Hotel	B L D					$	AE MC V	Yes	Casual, but elegant setting overlooking Mission Valley Northern Italian dishes, veals, pastas, chicken seafood Piano(W-Sa)
JAPANESE	**Benihana of Tokyo** 298-4666 *MISSION VALLEY* - 477 Camino del Rio South East of Fwy 163	-- L(X-S/S) D		F / Sa	$			MC V AE DC	Rec	Sushi bar, table cooking, seafood, beef, chicken Oriental atmosphere with bridges & fountains
	Yoshino Japanese Restaurant 295-2232 *MISSION HILLS* - 1790 W. Washington St East of India St	L (X:Su/M) D (X:Su/M)			$			MC V	Yes	Cafe decor, casual, daily lunch menu Unusual interpretations of traditional Japanese food B&W only
	Yumi 281-6448 *MISSION VALLEY* - 10330 Friars Rd	-- L (X:TS/S) D(X:Su,T)			$			AE MC/V		Casual restaurant with very large menu Tempura, Sushi, Gyoza, Teriyaki B&W only
MEXICAN	**Alta Vista Mexican Restaurant** 543-1121 *OLD TOWN* - 2152 San Diego Av South of Old Town Av	B (X:Su/M) L (X:Su/M) D (X:Su/M)			$			MC V	Yes	Festive Mexican decor, patio dining with umbrellas Lots of foliage, casual, Menu offers regional dishes, Chicken mole, carnitas, fajitas, carne asada, carry-out
	Aztec 295-2965 *OLD TOWN* - 2811 San Diego Av South of Harney St	-- L (X:Su) D (X:Su)		✓	$			None	Rec 6p+	Quick service, live entertainment on weekends Breakfast on Sunday, glass enclosed patio Carry-out, very casual
	Casa De Bandini 297-8211 *OLD TOWN* - 2660 Calhoun St South of Bazaar del Mundo	-- L D		✓	$			MC V AE DC	8p+	Flower covered building, was the home of the Mexican Don, Juan Bandini, garden setting with fountains, lush greenery, historical landmark traditional Mexican menu
	Casa De Pico 296-3267 *OLD TOWN* - 2754 Calhoun St In The Bazaar del Mundo	-- L D			$			MC V AE DC D	8p+	Garden setting, lively, colorful, some indoor seating Traditional Mexican menu, mariachis(W-Su)
	El Tecolote 295-2087 *MISSION VALLEY* - 6110 Friars Road	-- L (X:Su) D			$			MC V AE	No	Truly traditional Mexican food, family run, decor is a simple Mexican theme, regional dishes and a good selection of vegetarian dishes
	Guadalajara Grill 295-5111 *OLD TOWN* - 4105 Taylor St North of Juan St	-- L D	Y		$			MC V AE DC D	Rec Wknd 160	Patio dining, warm, casual atmosphere, authentic Mexican dishes, offspring of the Tijuana Cantina Banquet facilities

Cuisine (NOTES)	Restaurant / COMMUNITY - Street / Located Near	PHONE	Serving: Brkfst / Lunch / Dinner / X=Closed	Late Night Din.	Sunday Brunch	Under $10	$10 to $20	$20 to $30+	Credit Cards	Reservations	SPECIAL FEATURES
MEXICAN (Con't)	Hamburguesa / OLD TOWN - 4016 Wallace St / Next to Bazaar del Mundo	295-0584	B (Sa-Su) / L (X:Su) / D			$			MC V AE DC	Rec Wknd	Great for families, colorful, fun, festive atmosphere / Garden setting, great hamburgers with Mexican emphasis / Entertainment(F/Sa), in the Bazaar del Mundo
	La Hacienda / MISSION VALLEY - 875 Hotel Circle South / West of Fwy 163	298-8281	-- / L (X:Sa/Su) / D (X:Su)	✓		$			MC V AE DC	Rec	Hacienda decor, rustic, relaxed, patio dining, all-you-can-eat soup & salad bar, Puerto Nuevo style lobster / Seafood specials, Entertainment(Th-Su)
	La Pinata / OLD TOWN - 2836 San Juan St / North of Harney St	297-1631	-- / L / D			$			MC V DC		Small, intimate setting, patio dining / Sits on a small golfcourse / House specialties
	Old Town Mexican Cafe / OLD TOWN - 2489 San Diego Av / North of Congress St	297-4330	-- / L (X:Su) / D	Y	✓	$			MC V AE DC	Rec 10p+	Fresh tortillas made on premises, loud, noisy, festive, fun for all ages, a San Diego favorite, selection of Mexican beer, catering
MIDDLE EAST	Sheik Cafe / HILLCREST - 2664 FIFTH AVE	234-5888	L (X:Sa/Su) / D (X:Su-M)			$			MC V AE	Rec	Casbah decor, ceiling fans, belly dancers / Lebanese cuisine / B&W only
NATURAL FOOD	Drowsy Maggie's / NORTH PARK - 3089 University Av / At 31st Av	298-8584	-- / L (X:Sa/Su) / D	Y		$			None	No 100	Folk music coffee house, country French theme / No smoking or alcohol, Vegetarian, American, / Italian, healthy menu, events calendar available
POLYNESIAN	Islands Restaurant, The / MISSION VALLEY - 2270 Hotel Circle North / In The Hanalei Hotel	297-1101	-- / L (X:Su) / D	F / Sa	✓	$			MC V AE DC	Rec	Polynesian decor and food, low lights, intimate / A la carte dinner, wok cooking / Entertainment(Tu-Sa), Sunday champagne brunch
SEAFOOD	Brigantine, The / OLD TOWN - 2444 San Diego Av / North of Congress St	298-9840	L (X:Sa/Su) / D	F / Sa		$			MC V AE	Rec	Nautical decor, outdoor dining / Seafood specialties with Mexican emphasis, oyster bar / Multiple locations
	Cafe Pacifica / OLD TOWN - 2414 San Diego Av / 2 1/2 Blocks N. of Old Town Ave.	291-6666	-- / L (X:Sa/Su) / D				$		MC V AE DC	Rec 90	Intimate setting, lots of lattice with mini lights, / Courtyard with patio, daily menu, Southwestern accent / An award winning restaurant
	Monterey Whaling Company / SAN DIEGO - 901 Camino del Rio South / In the Doubletree Hotel	543-9000	B / L / D	F / Sa			$		MC V AE	Yes	Casual atmosphere, lively bar, dancing nightly / Popular with the singles crowd / Seafood with a California accent beef & chicken
	Rusty Pelican / MISSION VALLEY - 5010 Mission Center Rd / South of Friars Rd	291-6974	L (X:Su) / D	F / Sa			$		MC V AE DC	Rec 30	Tropical greenery, rocks and fountains inside / Seafood steak & chicken, Caribbean dishes daily / specials, location also in La Jolla
	Tickled Trout, The / MISSION VALLEY - 2151 Hotel Circle South / In The Ramada Inn	291-6505	B (X:Sa/Su) / L (X:Sa/Su) / D	F / Sa		$			MC V AE DC	Rec 15	Stained glass and crystal decor, lace tablecloths / English pub atmosphere, catch of the day, trout, steaks / lobster, prime rib and pasta
SOUTHWEST	Cafe Coyote / OLD TOWN - 2461 San Diego Av / North of Conde St	291-HOWL	-- / L / D			$			MC V AE DC	Rec 65	Sante Fe decor, patio dining, espresso bar / Southwestern New Mexican specialties
THAI	Celadon / HILLCREST - 3628 Fifth Av / Brookes Av	295-8800	-- / L (X:Sa/Su) / D (X:Su)			$			MC V AE	Rec	Art deco decor, oriental accents with extensive use of / glass brick, soft subtle colors, elegant yet relaxed / Menu offers standard Thai dishes, B&W only
(FOOD-TO-GO)	Saffron / HILLCREST - 3731-B India St / South of Washington St	574-0177	-- / L (X:Su) / D (X:Su)			$			MC V		Carry-out only, some outdoor seating for quick lunches / Daily specials, grilled chicken with choice of 5 sauces / B&W only
	Taste of Thai / HILLCREST - 527 University Ave	291-7525	L (X:Su) / D			$			MC V	Yes	Contemporary western setting with many Thai accents / Traditional dishes prepared with a choice of sauces / B&W only
	Thai Chada / HILLCREST - 142 University Av / West of 1st Av	297-9548	L (X:Sa/Su) / D				$		MC V AE DC	Rec	Quiet, intimate atmosphere featuring authentic Thai / dishes, vegetarian, curry, duck, seafood, chicken
VEGETARIAN	Cornucopia / HILLCREST - 112 West Washington St / West of First Av	299-4174	-- / L (X:Sa/Su) / D		✓	$			NONE	No 20	Lots of greenery, ceiling fans, old movie posters on / the walls, eclectic decor, booths & tables, casual / Healthy vegetarian cuisine, Carry-out
	Kung Food / HILLCREST - 2949 Fifth Av / South of Quince St	298-7302	B (Sa-Su) / L (X:Sa/Su) / D			$			MC V AE	Rec 6p+	Eclectic decor, heated garden patio, contemporary / Mural of Japanese mountains on the wall, booths / No smoking, tofu specials, low oil/salt cooking
VIETNAMESE	Phoung Nam / HILLCREST - 540 University Av / West of Fwy 163	298-0810	L (X:Su) / D	Y		$			MC V AE	Rec 4p+	Modern, stylish oriental decor with green/peach theme / Southeastern specialties / Imported Vietnamese Beer & Wine

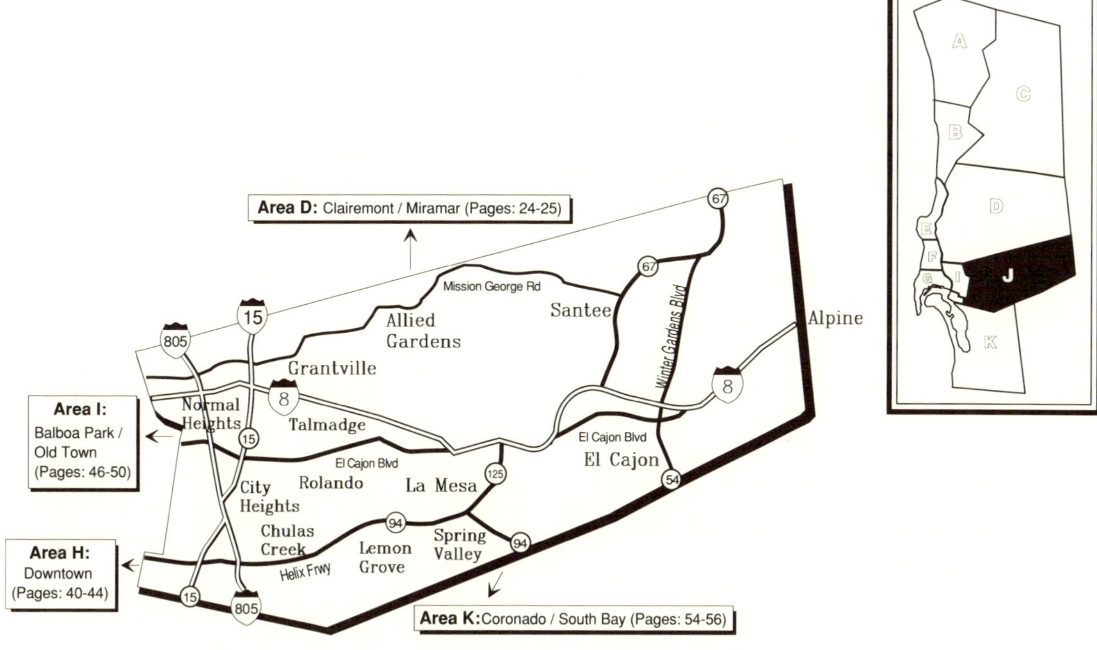

ALPHABETIC LISTINGS

RESTAURANT (CUISINE Category)	RESTAURANT (CUISINE Category)	RESTAURANT (CUISINE Category)
A-Dong (VIETNAMESE)	College Restaurant, The (AMERICAN)	Marrakesh (MOROCCAN)
Alpine Inn (AMERICAN)	D. Z. Akins (AMERICAN)	Mr. D's (CONTINENTAL)
Anthony's Fish Grotto (SEAFOOD)	Dansk Restaurant (SCANDINAVIAN)	Nicolosi's (ITALIAN)
Barrett Cafe (SEAFOOD)	Dookies (AMERICAN)	Panda Inn (CHINESE)
Blue Nile (ETHIOPIAN)	Jim's Hickory Wood Bar-B-Q (AMERI-CAN)	Red Ox (SEAFOOD)
Bobby McGee's (AMERICAN)	Jorg's Gourmet Cuisine (CONTINENTAL)	Rock Lobster (MEXICAN)
Boondocks, The (AMERICAN)	Julians (AMERICAN)	Rory's (AMERICAN)
Bread Basket, The (AMERICAN)	Kaiserhof (GERMAN)	Rubio's Deli-Mex (MEXICAN)
Brigantine, The (SEAFOOD)	Kozak's (AMERICAN)	Senor Frog's (MEXICAN)
Bull And Bear (AMERICAN)	Lido's Italian Foods (ITALIAN)	Shanghai Restaurant (CHINESE)
California Club Sushi Bar (JAPANESE)	Little Italy Pizza (ITALIAN)	Tony Roma's (AMERICAN)
Chang, Cuisine of China (CHINESE)		Woodstock's Pizza (ITALIAN)
Chateau Basque (BASQUE)		

Cuisine (NOTES)	Restaurant / COMMUNITY - Street / Located Near	PHONE	Serving (Brkfst/Lunch/Dinner, X=Closed)	Late Night Din.	Sunday Brunch	Under $10	$10 to $20	$20 to $30+	Credit Cards	Reservations	SPECIAL FEATURES
AMERICAN	**Alpine Inn** — ALPINE - 2225 Alpine Blvd, Off I-8; Tavern Rd.	445-5172	-- / L / D	Y	✓		$		MC V AE D	No	Looks and feels just like a log cabin, cozy, intimate / Large brick fireplace, antique pictures, romantic / Prime rib & seafood
	Bobby McGee's — LA MESA - 5500 Grossmont Ctr Dr, In Grossmont Ctr	589-0444	-- / L / D				$		MC V AE DC	Rec	Each room has a unique motif in this dinner house / Waitstaff dresses up in various costumes / Dancing nightly
	Boondocks, The — LA MESA - 8320 Parkway Dr, West of Jackson Dr	465-3660	-- / -- / D	F / Sa			$		MC V AE DC	Rec / 20	Two dining rooms, booths in front and tables in back / Beef and fresh seafood, Fresh fish of the day / Piano in lounge nightly, Happy hour with hors d'oeuvres
	Bread Basket, The — ALPINE - 1347 Tavern Road, In the Alpine Creek Shopping Center	445-0706	B / L / D			$			MC V	Yes	Comfortable, relaxed, rustic decor, down-home family-style cooking, great value, fried chicken, BBQ ribs, homemade gravy, soups, pies & cobblers
	Bull And Bear — EL CAJON - 690 North Second St, South of I-8	440-5757	L (M-F) / --		✓		$		MC V AE DC	Rec	Traditional steak house, comfortable, relaxed / Menu offers beef, chicken & seafood
	College Restaurant, The — ROLANDO - 6695 El Cajon Blvd, 67th & El Cajun Blvd. at Montezuma Rd.	469-1140	B / L / D		✓	$			MC V AE DC	No / 15	Home cooking, big portions / Home style breakfasts / Chicken fried steak, No Bar
	D. Z. Akins — ROLANDO - 6930 Alvarado Road, Near SDSU	265-0218	B / L / D			$			MC V	6p+	Informal, casual New York-style deli/restaurant/bakery / 104 different sandwiches, burgers, omelets, soda / fountain, cheesecakes & other desserts, carry-out
	Dookies — TALMADGE - 4125 El Cajon Blvd, East of Fwy 15	283-6581	B / L / D	Y	✓		$		MC V AE DC	Rec	Comfortable neighborhood steak house / Serving aged Kansas and Nebraska Beef and seafood / Piano Bar nightly
	Jim's Hickory Wood Bar-B-Q — ROLANDO - 5312 El Cajon Blvd, West of 54th St	286-8220	-- / L / D			$			MC V	Rec 5p+ / 35	10 Types of BBQ, Cajun Catfish / Weekly talent show 'hoot night' every Wednesday 7-10p / B&W only
	Julians — EL CAJON - 780 North Second	441-8181	-- / L / D			$			MC V	--	Family-oriented, BBQ Sandwiches & dinner / Home-style ribs chicken & beef
	Kozak's — EL CAJON - 401 West Main St, West of Magnolia	442-776	B / L / D				$		MC V AE	Rec	Front is 24 hour coffee shop, dining room and lounge in rear, garden atmosphere, big portions "never walk away hungry", Entertainment(W-Sa)
	Rory's — ALLIED GARDENS - 6069 Mission Gorge Rd, East of Jackson Dr	284-3617	-- / L / D			$			NONE	No	50'S diner, nostalgia music / "cruise" hot rod cars, juke box, 10 different burgers / hot dogs, flavored cokes, "side orders" outdoor patio
	Tony Roma's — LA MESA - 5500 Grossmont Center Dr, In Grossmont Ctr	466-8000	-- / L (X:Sa/Su) / D	F / Sa			$		MC V AE	Rec	Family oriented, fun atmosphere, neon art, booths / Specialty is BBQ ribs & loaves of onion rings, / also offers chicken & burgers, Multiple locations
BASQUE	**Chateau Basque** — BOULEVARD - 40080 Old Hwy 80, East of Hwy 94	766-4663	-- / L / D				$		MC V	Rec 6p+	Dine in old Spanish Style at long tables / Huge portions, dinners include salads, homemade soup / B&W only
CHINESE	**Chang, Cuisine of China** — LA MESA - 5500 Grossmont Ctr Dr, In Grossmont Ctr	464-2288	-- / L (X:Su) / D (X:Su)	F / Sa			$		MC V AE	Rec	Mandarin and Szechuan dishes in natural sauces / Traditional Chinese setting, warm & comfortable
	Panda Inn — SANTEE - 9643 Mission Gorge Rd, In The Santee Village	449-7061	-- / L / D	F / Sa			$		MC V AE	Rec	Mandarin and Cantonese cooking / 16 specials on the menu, Panda Beef
	Shanghai Restaurant — ROLANDO - 4055 54th St, North of University Av	286-2345	--			$			MC V AE		Mandarin, Szechuan, and Mongolian BBQ dishes / Carry-out
CONTINENTAL	**Jorg's Gourmet Cuisine** — LA MESA - 8235 University Av, East of Spring St	462-4800	-- / L(X:Su/M / D(X:Su-M					$	MC V AE	Rec / 50	Former chef to Swedish king / Scandinavian specialties, dinner menu changes every / 2 weeks, 5 course prix fixe menu, B&W only
	Mr. D's — EL CAJON - 596 Broadway, East of Rt. 67	442-9696	-- / L / D	Y	✓		$		MC V AE DC	Rec	Small Intimate, Dine by Candlelight, Tuxedo type servic / Tableside preparations, Beef, Seafood, Italian specials / 50's- 60's rock and roll to a live band(T-Sa)
ETHIOPIAN	**Blue Nile** — CHOLLAS CREEK - 4703 Federal Blvd, West of 47th Av	264-4724	-- / L (X:M) / D (X:M)	T - Su	✓	$			MC V	Rec	African motif / Chicken and lamb specialties / In business since 1983, catering, B&W only

Cuisine (NOTES)	Restaurant / COMMUNITY - Street / Located Near	PHONE	Serving: Brkfst Lunch Dinner X=Closed	Late Night Din.	Sunday Brunch	Under $10	$10 to $20	$20 to $30 +	Credit Cards	Reservations	SPECIAL FEATURES
GERMAN	Kaiserhof / GRANTVILLE - 5351 Adobe Falls Rd / East of Waring Rd	287-3075	-- / L (X:Su/M) / D (X:M)			$			AE DC	Rec / 50	Distinctive German American dining / Old world charm, private banquet room / Daily specials, patio
ITALIAN	Lido's Italian Foods / LEMON GROVE - 7252 Broadway / East of Massachusetts Av	469-9901	-- / L / D		Sa / / Su	$			MC V	Rec	Northern Italian, Pasta, Rigatoni, Lasagne, Ravioli / American Food, NY Steak, spare ribs, 3 kinds of chicken
	Little Italy Pizza / CITY HEIGHTS - 4367 University Av / At Fairmount	281-4949	-- / L / D		Y	$			MC V AE		Bargain dinner for two, Hearty portions, Late dining / pasta & pizza, lunch specials / Delivery
	Nicolosi's / CORRIDOR - 4009 El Cajon Blvd / East of Fwy 15	282-9919	-- / L / D	$	F / / SA				MC V AE	Rec 8p+	Large selection of vegetarian dishes including pizza / lasagna, pizzas, and pastas / B&W only
	Woodstock's Pizza / ROLANDO - 6548 El Cajon Blvd / Rolando Blvd	265-0999	-- / L / D		F	$			MC V	No / 25	Casual, fun rustic but very open & light, Menu is pizza / salads, popular with the college crowd, B&W only / Carry-out, Delivery
JAPANESE	California Club Sushi Bar / ROLANDO - 5522 El Cajon Blvd / East of 54th St	287-1593	-- / L / D		M - Sa	$			MC V AE	Rec / 100	Traditional sushi bar setting,Chinese, American cuisine / Special dessert plum wine and plum ice cream / Carry-out, catering, ``Let's all dine out''-Award ``89
MEXICAN	Rock Lobster / ALLIED GARDENS - 6690 Mission Gorge Rd / South of Friars Rd	562-7838	-- / L / D	✓	F / / Sa	$			MC V	No / 50	Puerto nuevo style includes all you can eat rice / beans and tortillas, Mexican seafood specialties / Enclosed patio, golf course view
(FOOD-TO-GO)	Rubio's Deli-Mex / UPTOWN - 5157 College Av / Near SDSU	286-3844	-- / L / D			$					Take out only, some seating available, family run / Home of the famous San Felipe-style fish taco & other / Mexican favorites, multiple locations, catering
	Senor Frog's / ROLANDO - 6390 El Cajon Blvd / East of College Av	583-0045	-- / L / D	✓	F Sa	$			MC V AE	Rec	Casual, fun & festive, Menu items are large from the / Quesadillas & carne asada tacos to the burritos / Cantina is popular with the college crowd
MOROCCAN	Marrakesh / LA MESA - 8240 Parkway Dr / West of Jackson Dr	462-3663	-- / -- / D		Th - Sa			$	MC V AE DC	Rec	Authentic Moroccan cuisine and rituals, Eat with your / Fingers, choice of entrees, 6,8,or 9 course meals, / Belly dancing, traditional Sahara decor and dress
SCANDINAVIAN	Dansk Restaurant / LA MESA - 8425 La Mesa Blvd / West of Jackson Dr	463--640	B (X:M) / L (X:M)					$	MC V AE DC	Rec / 50	Swedish and Danish Fare / Exciting choices for breakfast and lunch / Banquets and catering, B&W only
SEAFOOD	Anthony's Fish Grotto / LA MESA - 9530 Murray Dr / North of I-8	463-0368	-- / L / D	✓		$			MC V AE	No	Located on spring fed lake with outdoor patio / Seasonal fresh seafood specials / Multiple locations
	Barrett Cafe / DULZURA - 1029 Barrett Lake Road / Off Hwy 94 at Barrett Lake Rd	468-3416	-- / L (X:M) / D (X:M)			$			MC V	Yes / 200	Everyone sits at long tables on a first come first / First serve basis, Family Style Fish Fry at $7.95 & up / From hamburgers, shrimp & steak
	Brigantine, The / LA MESA - 9350 Fuerte Dr / East of I-8	465-1935	-- / L (M-F) / D	✓		$			MC V AE	Rec / 66	Casual dining, wooden tables and booths with / A nautical motif including lighthouses and boats / Specializing in seafood, Multiple locations
	Red Ox / EL CAJON - 722 Jamacha Rd / South of Main St	447-0183	-- / L (X:Su) / D	✓	Sa	$			MC V	Rec 6p	Cozy cocktail lounge, Meals include corn bread muffins / Homemade cheesecake,Barbeque baby back ribs, / Beef brisket, Deep fried tortillas with fruit sauce
VIETNAMESE	A-Dong / CITY HEIGHTS - 3874 Fairmount Ave / South of University Av	298-4420	B (Sa/Su) / L / D			$			MC V AE	Rec	Family owned, featuring over 120 items on menu / Lunch special 11a-3p, extensive vegetarian selections / Ancient hot pot cooking at table, B&W only

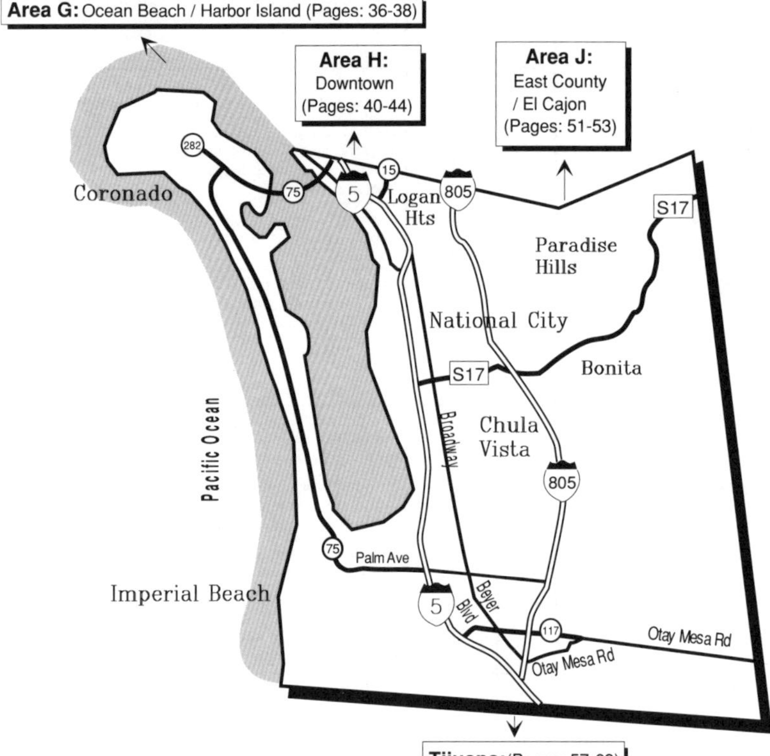

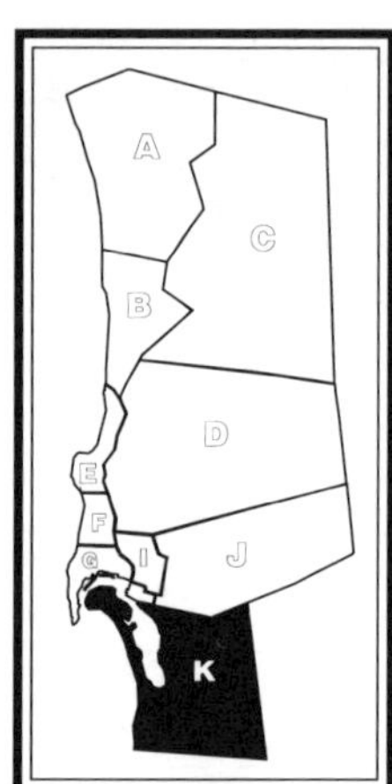

ALPHABETIC LISTINGS

RESTAURANT (CUISINE Category)	RESTAURANT (CUISINE Category)	RESTAURANT (CUISINE Category)
Adobe Rose (SOUTHWEST)	Chez Loma (CONTINENTAL)	La Salsa (MEXICAN)
Anthony's Fish Grotto (SEAFOOD)	Chu Dynasty (CHINESE)	Marius (FRENCH)
Bonita Store Rest. & Nite Club (AMERICAN)	Chuey's Cafe (MEXICAN)	Mexican Village (MEXICAN)
Brigantine, The (SEAFOOD)	Crown-Coronet Room (CONTINENTAL)	Miguel's Cocina (MEXICAN)
Butcher Shop (AMERICAN)	House of Munich (GERMAN)	Peohe's, The Landing (SEAFOOD)
Cafe La Maze (AMERICAN)	Jake's South Bay (SEAFOOD)	Primavera (ITALIAN)
Cafe Ole (MEXICAN)	Koto (JAPANESE)	Prince of Wales Room (CONTINENTAL)
Casa Martinez (MEXICAN)	L'Escale (FRENCH)	Rubio's Deli-Mex (MEXICAN)
Casa Salsa (MEXICAN)	La Fonda Roberto's (MEXICAN)	

Cuisine (NOTES)	Restaurant / COMMUNITY - Street / Located Near	PHONE	Serving: Brkfst / Lunch / Dinner / X=Closed	Late Night Din.	Sunday Brunch	Under $10	$10 to $20	$20 to $30+	Credit Cards	Reservations	SPECIAL FEATURES
AMERICAN	**Bonita Store Restaurant** BONITA - 4014 Bonita Road	479-3537	-- / L (X:Su) / D		✓		$		MC V	Yes	Comfortable, casual dinner house Menu features seafood, chicken, beef Entertainment/dancing nightly
	Butcher Shop CHULA VISTA - 556 Broadway Broadway at H St	42-944-	-- / L / D				$		MC V	Yes	Dark, comfortable, dinner house setting, Nebraska prime rib, steaks, seafood & Italian dishes Late night dining
	Cafe La Maze NATIONAL CITY - 1441 Highland Ave	474-3222	-- / -- / D				$		MC V AE	Yes	Dinner house setting, Old fashioned cooking, Large portions, steak, prime rib & seafood
CHINESE	**Chu Dynasty** CORONADO - 1033 B St South of 10th St	435-5300	-- / L (X:Sa/Su) / D	F / / Sa			$		MC V AE	Rec	Owned by Chester Chu family, Each dish is cooked to order, Mandarin and Szechuan Carry out
CONTINENTAL	**Chez Loma** CORONADO - 1132 Loma Blvd At Orange Av	435-0661	-- / L (X:Sa-M) / D (X:Su-M)		✓			$	MC V AE D	Rec	Landmark building from 1889, Indoor and outdoor dining Regional classic European cuisine, extensive wine list Sit down Sunday Brunch, B&W only
	Crown-Coronet Room CORONADO - 1500 Orange Av In The Hotel del Coronado	435-6611	B / L / D		✓		$		MC V AE D D	Must	Site of filming of Some Like It Hot/ Victorian Opulence Can seat up to 1100 people, Sunday dinner buffet, 33" domed ceiling, Piano(F-Su), Dancing, Jacket Sug'st.
	Prince of Wales Room CORONADO - 1500 Orange Av In The Hotel del Coronado	435-6611	-- / -- / D (X:Su)					+	MC V AE D D	Rec 20	Red leather booths, Stained glass windows Elegant understated atmosphere, Mobil 4 star winner Named for Edward, Prince of Wales who met his wife there
FRENCH	**L'Escale** CORONADO - 2000 Second St In Le Meridien Hotel	435-3000	B / L / D		✓		$		MC V AE D D	Rec	Bay, pool and downtown view, California accent Brazilian Barbeque/W seafood buffet(Thursdays) Lobster cook out(Sundays)
	Marius CORONADO - 2000 Second St In Le Meridien Hotel	435-3000	-- / -- / D(X:M)	T - Su				+	MC V AE D D	Rec	Provencale cooking in this elegantly appointed room Dinner begins with free hors d'oeuvres, 5 course meals Cocktails & music in La Provence Lounge, Jacket Required
GERMAN	**House of Munich** CHULA VISTA - 230 Third Av South of E St	426-5172	-- / L (X:Sa-M) / D (X:M)				$		MC V AE	Rec	Charming, downtown location, German specialties Favorites include sausage platter, potato pancakes Strudels, B&W only
ITALIAN	**Primavera** CORONADO - 932 Orange	435-0454	-- / L (X:Sa/Su) / D				$		MC V AE D	Must	Northern Italian Food specializing in homemade pastas veal, chicken, different types of seafood beef dishes, sometimes Ossobucco, Dinner a La Carte
JAPANESE	**Koto** CHULA VISTA - 651 Palomar St In Trolley Square	691-1418	-- / L (X:W) / D (X:W)				$		MC V AE	Yes	Large Sushi bar, New Japanese food,"Kamameshi" Tempura, Teriyaki, a dinner time there's live Koto music B&W only
MEXICAN	**Cafe Ole** CHULA VISTA - 833 Broadway	426-0323	B / L / D			$			--	--	A local favorite for 30 years, bright, noisy cafe Great portions at reasonable prices Soups made on the premises
	Casa Martinez PARADISE HILLS - 6086 1/2 Banbury Street Located in Shopping Center	475-4120	-- / L / D			$			MC V	No	Specializing in homemade Mexican food Specials, chile verde, chile colorado, carnitas Catering, Beer only
	Casa Salsa CHULA VISTA - 625 H St West of Broadway	422-0161	-- / L / D (X:Su)	F / Sa	✓	$			MC V	Yes 100	Mexican cantina atmosphere Old Mexican recipes, chile verde, colorado, menudo Catering and banquet, Champagne brunch
	Chuey's Cafe LOGAN HEIGHTS - 1894 Main St Corner of Crosby and Main	234-6937	-- / L / D (X:Su)		✓	$			MC V	Yes 300	For decades, a San Diego Institution for "The Most Authentic Mexican Food"
	La Fonda Roberto's CHULA VISTA - 300 3rd Av At F St	585-3017	-- / L / D		✓	$			MC V DC	Rec	Home cooking Lunch buffet(M-F-11a-3p) San Diego favorite for authentic Mexican food
	La Salsa CORONADO - 1360 Orange Av North of Dana Pl	435-7778	-- / L / D	F / Sa		$			NONE	No	Patio dining Taquerilla with salsa bar B&W only
	Mexican Village CORONADO - 120 Orange Ave South of 1st St	435-1822	-- / L / D	Y	✓	$			MC V AE D D	Yes 125	Converted 1898 landmark location popular for over 45 yr Original Sonora style recipes, Children's Menus Mobil Travel Award, Dancing
	Miguel's Cocina CORONADO - 1351 Orange Av North of Dana Point	437-4237	-- / L (X:Sa/Su) / D			$			MC V AE	Rec 6p+	Outdoor dining, Sunday brunch Special menu Saturday 10a-1p and Sunday 11a-1p Carry-out

Cuisine (NOTES)	Restaurant COMMUNITY - Street Located Near	PHONE	Brkfst Lunch Dinner X=Closed	Late Night Din.	Sunday Brunch	Under $10	$10 to $20	$20 to $30+	Credit Cards	Reservations	SPECIAL FEATURES
MEXICAN (Con't) (FOOD-TO-GO)	**Rubio's Deli-Mex** CHULA VISTA - 481 Broadway	427-3811	-- L D			$					Take out only, some seating available, family run Famous for the San Felipe-style fish taco & other Mexican favorites, multiple locations, catering
SEAFOOD	**Anthony's Fish Grotto** CHULA VISTA - 215 Bay Blvd South of E St	425-4200	-- L D		✓	$			MC V AE	No 46	Candlelight dinners available in the cocktail lounge Huge assortment of fresh seafoods Private room
	Brigantine, The CORONADO - 1333 Orange Av North of Dana Pl	435-4166	-- L (X:Sa/Su) D	F / Sa	✓	$			MC V AE	Rec 40	Nautical theme creates a comfortable relaxed atmosphere Seafood specials with a Mexican emphasis, oyster bar Multiple locations
	Jake's South Bay CHULA VISTA - 570 Marina Parkway	476-0400	-- L (X:Sa/Su) D			$			MC V AE	Yes 120	Waterfront restaurant, with a nautical atmosphere Patio dining, oyster bar, menu features fresh seafood daily specials, banquet facilities
	Peohe's, The Landing CORONADO - 1201 First St East of Orange St	437-4474	-- L D		✓			+	MC V AE D	Rec 100	Polynesian tropical decor, waterfall, downtown view Slips for boat owners, patio Sunday brunch, oyster bar
SOUTHWEST	**Adobe Rose** CHULA VISTA - 1396 Third Ave	426-3040	-- L D			$			MC V AE	Yes	Casual, Southwest motif, murals on the walls Photographs of old western movie stars Live entertainment(F/Sa)

ADDITIONS

TIJUANA
Mexico

Due to a general lack of information and the prevalence of misleading stereotypes such as "not drinking the water" (Tijuana's fine restarants serve bottled water) the majority of visitors to Tijuana come and go with little or no awareness of the number and variety of fine restaurants that are based in Tijuana. If you're thinking about a trip to Tijuana remember: 1) The majority of the better restaurants will accept either US currency or credit cards (You don't need to purchase pesos.);
 2) You don't have to drive into Mexico to get to Tijuana. (You can either drive to the San Ysidro Border Crossing and park or take the trolley (See page 45 for trolley stop map). Crossing the border is only a short walk. Once across, cabs are plentiful or you can even walk into town.

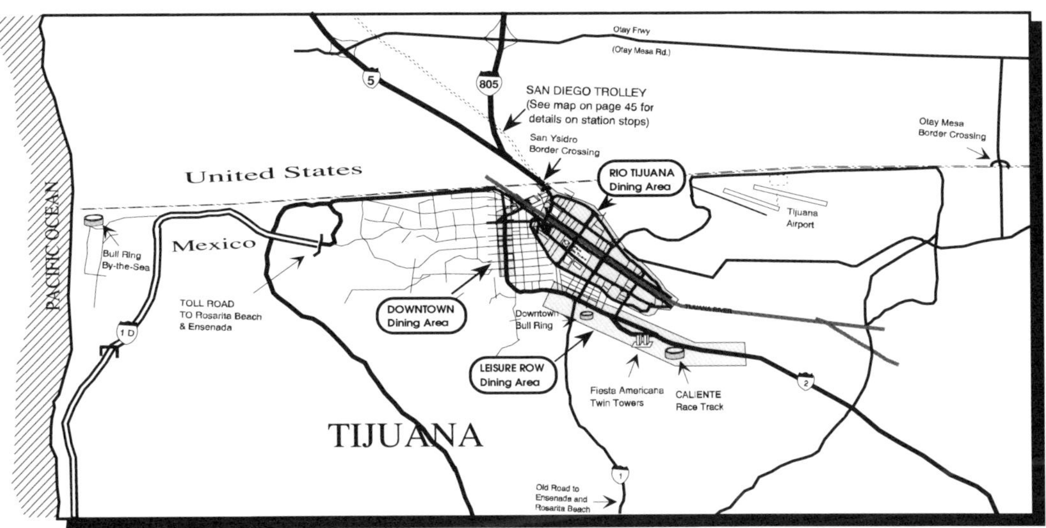

ALPHABETIC LISTINGS

RESTAURANT (DINING AREA)	RESTAURANT (DINING AREA)	RESTAURANT (DINING AREA)
Alcazar Del Rio (RIO TIJUANA)	El Rodeo (LEISURE ROW)	La Placita (DOWNTOWN)
Boccacio's (LEISURE ROW)	El Rodeo De La Mesa (LEISURE ROW)	La Taberna Espanola (RIO TIJUANA)
Bol Corona (DOWNTOWN)	Freeday (RIO TIJUANA)	Las Espuelas (RIO TIJUANA)
Caesar's Palace (DOWNTOWN)	Giragril (RIO TIJUANA)	Las Mananitas (DOWNTOWN)
Cafe La Especial (DOWNTOWN)	Giuseppi's (LEISURE ROW)	Le Chateau (DOWNTOWN)
Capistrano Grill (RIO TIJUANA)	Guadalajara Grill (RIO TIJUANA)	Los Arcos (LEISURE ROW)
Carnitas Uruapan (LEISURE ROW)	Hacienda Del Rio (RIO TIJUANA)	Margaritas Village (DOWNTOWN)
Carnitas Uruapan Rio (RIO TIJUANA)	Hacienda El Abajeno (RIO TIJUANA)	Mr Fish (LEISURE ROW)
Chiki-jai (DOWNTOWN)	Hacienda Las Torres (LEISURE ROW)	Ochoa's (RIO TIJUANA)
Cilantro's (DOWNTOWN)	Jacaranda (LEISURE ROW)	Paellas Tonico (LEISURE ROW)
Coronet (DOWNTOWN)	Komasa (RIO TIJUANA)	Palacio De Oro Cafe (LEISURE ROW)
Dionnysos (LEISURE ROW)	La Costa (DOWNTOWN)	Palacio Imperial Cage (DOWNTOWN)
Don Quijote (LEISURE ROW)	La Escondida (LEISURE ROW)	Pedrin's (DOWNTOWN)
Dragon De Oro (DOWNTOWN)	La Espadana (RIO TIJUANA)	Place De La Concorde (LEISURE ROW)
Dragon Plaza (RIO TIJUANA)	La Flamita (LEISURE ROW)	Popeye's Seafood (RIO TIJUANA)
El Capitan (LEISURE ROW)	La Fogata (DOWNTOWN)	Rinciocito Gaucho (LEISURE ROW)
El Faro De Mazatlan (RIO TIJUANA)	La Fonda Roberto's (LEISURE ROW)	Senor Frog's (RIO TIJUANA)
El Gaucho (RIO TIJUANA)	La Léna (DOWNTOWN)	Tequila Circo (DOWNTOWN)
El Mason Espanol (DOWNTOWN)	La Léna (LEISURE ROW)	Tia Juana Tilly's (DOWNTOWN)
El Puente (RIO TIJUANA)		

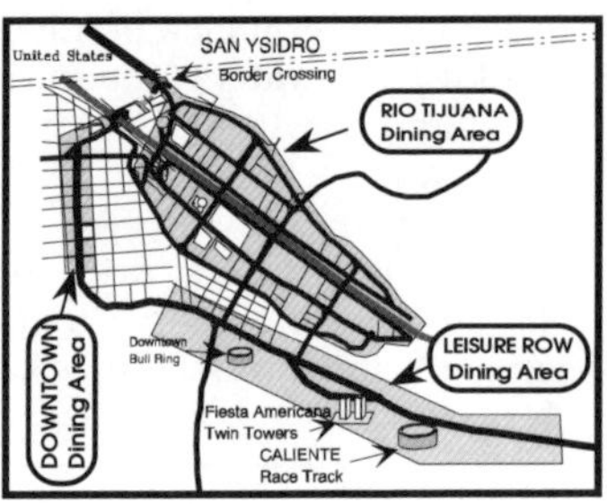

United States
SAN YSIDRO
Border Crossing
RIO TIJUANA
Dining Area
DOWNTOWN
Dining Area
LEISURE ROW
Dining Area
Downtown
Bull Ring
Fiesta Americana
Twin Towers
CALIENTE
Race Track

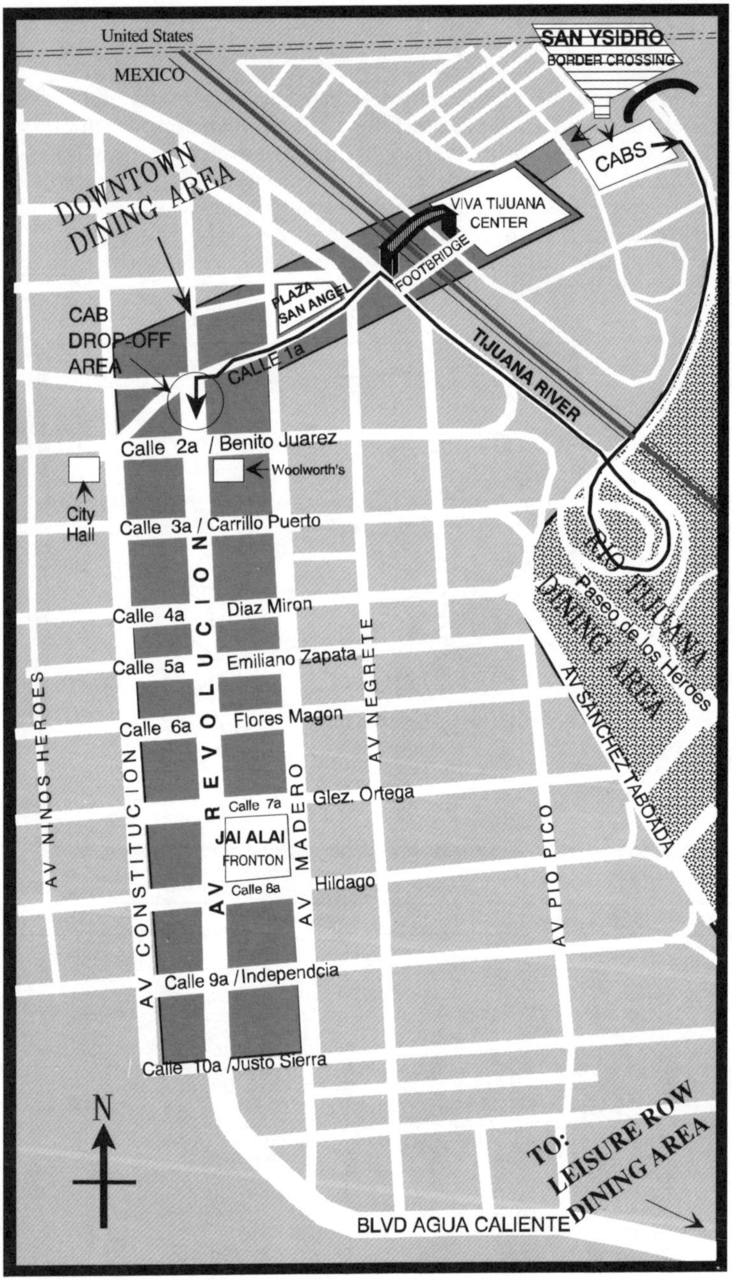

United States
MEXICO
SAN YSIDRO
BORDER CROSSING
CABS
VIVA TIJUANA
CENTER
DOWNTOWN DINING AREA
CAB DROP-OFF AREA
PLAZA SAN ANGEL
FOOTBRIDGE
CALLE 1a
TIJUANA RIVER
Calle 2a / Benito Juarez
Woolworth's
City Hall
Calle 3a / Carrillo Puerto
AV REVOLUCION
Calle 4a
Diaz Miron
Calle 5a
Emiliano Zapata
AV NEGRETE
RIO TIJUANA DINING AREA
Paseo de los Heroes
AV SANCHEZ TABOADA
Calle 6a
Flores Magon
AV NINOS HEROES
AV CONSTITUCION
Calle 7a
Glez. Ortega
JAI ALAI FRONTON
AV MADERO
AV PIO PICO
Calle 8a
Hildago
Calle 9a / Independcia
Calle 10a / Justo Sierra
N
TO: LEISURE ROW DINING AREA
BLVD AGUA CALIENTE

Cuisine (NOTES)	Restaurant / COMMUNITY - Street / Located Near	PHONE (Country Dialing Code 011 - 52 - 66)	SERVING (Brkfst / Lunch / Dinner / X=Closed)	Late Night Din.	Su. Brk/Brunch	Under $10	$5 to $15	$15-$25+	Credit Cards	SPECIAL FEATURES
CHINESE	**Dragon De Oro** 1835 Calle 7a - Glez Ortega (7th St) Off Av. Revolucion	85-85-77	— L D	Y			$		None	Comfortable atmosphere Cantonese-style cuisine
	Palacio Imperial Cage 1233 Av Revolucion Btwn Calle 8a (St) and Calle 9a (St)	85-35-60	— L D	Y			$			Cantonese style cuisine Mexican & American dishes are also featured
CONTINENTAL	**Coronet** 1939 Calle 7a - Glez. Ortega (7th St) Just east of Av. Revolucion	85-55-51	— L D	Y			$		MC V	This small bar and restaurant is a Tijuana institution Beef & Seafood specials Piano and guitarist play nightly
FRENCH	**Le Chateau** 1940 Calle 7a - Glez. Ortega (7th St) Just east of Av. Revolucion	85-07-44	— L D	Y				$		Ornate ambience on three levels Well known for its extensive menu and wine list
INTERN'TL.	**Caesar's Palace** Av Revolucion at Calle 4a Elevator to 2nd floor; over Le Drug Store	88-27-94	— L D					$	ALL	Elegant modern decor Continental & American cuisine with large wine list Live music and dancing (F/Sa)
MEXICAN	**Bol Corona** 520 Av Revolucion North of Second St (Woolworth's)	(706) 685-47-08	B L D	Y	✓	$	$		MC V AE	One of TJ's oldest & most popular restaurants Downstairs: busy family style eatery Upstairs: two rooms and open-air balcony
	Cafe La Especial 718 Av Revolucion (Gomez Arcade) Btwn Calle 3a and 4a - down one level	-----	B L D		✓	$			MC V	Very casual hangout for residents and visitors Traditional Mexican dishes
	Cilantro's In Viva Tijuana Shopping Center at borde Next to pedestrian footbridge; 2nd level	82-83-38	— L (Tu-Su) D (Tu-Su)					$	MC V AE	Opened June 1990, High tech modern decor Menu features classic dishes from Puebla, Yucatan, Veracruz and Oaxaca
	La Costa 150 Calle 7a - Glez. Ortega (7th St) West of Av Revolucion - near Jai Alai	(706) 685-84-94	— L D	Y				$	MC V AE	Long time TJ visitor favorite Seafood specialties
	La Placita 783 Av Revolution Btwn Calle 3a and 4a	88-27-04	B L D	Y	✓		$		MC V AE	Attractive patio-style decor Wide variety of Mexican dishes
	Las Mananitas 222 Puente Mexico Plaza San Angel (3 blocks from ped.brdg)	---	— L D				$		MC V	Outdoor seating in the Plaza or in courtyard Traditional Mexican dishes Native dancers perform on Sa & Su (1p to 6p)
	Margaritas Village 702 Av Revolucion btwn 3a and 4a-east side-one level down	85-38-60	— L D				$		MC V	Casual cantina is active, noisy and very festive Famous for selection of 24 flavors of margaritas Sunday brunch specials, Music and dancing
	Tequila Circo Calle 3a - Carrillo Puerto (3rd St) Corner with Av Revolucion - 2nd floor	(706) 685-02-75	— L D			$			MC V	Bar and restuarant is always full of activity Volley ball court and competitions held here Disco dancing (W-Su); Live entertainment
	Tia Juana Tilly's 701 Av Revolucion Corner of Fronton Palacio Jai Ala	85-06-24	— L D	Y				$	MC V	This non-stop action bar is a tourist favorite Restaurant serves a diverse menu
SEAFOOD	**Pedrin's** 1115 Av Revolucion N of Calle 8a (St); Across from Jai Alai	(706) 685-40-62	— L D	Y				$	MC V	Very popular, charming multi-level restaurant Over 60 seafood entrees
SPANISH	**Chiki-jai** 1050 Av Revolucion On corner with Calle 7a	(706) 685-49-55	— L D			$			MC V AE DC	Unpretentious setting in an insider's favorite Classic Spanish cuisine Paella special on Sunday
	El Mason Espanol 1838 Calle 4a - Diaz Miron (4th St) Btwn Av Constitucion & Av Ninos Hereos	(706) 688-24-16	— L D				$		MC V AE	Traditional Spanish decor and cuisine Live music (organ)
STEAK HOUSE	**La Leña** 816 Av Revolucion Between Calle 4th & 5th	88-09-08	— L D					$	MC V	New; downtown branch of popular restaurant by same name on Blvd. Agua Caliente in Leisure Row Dining Area

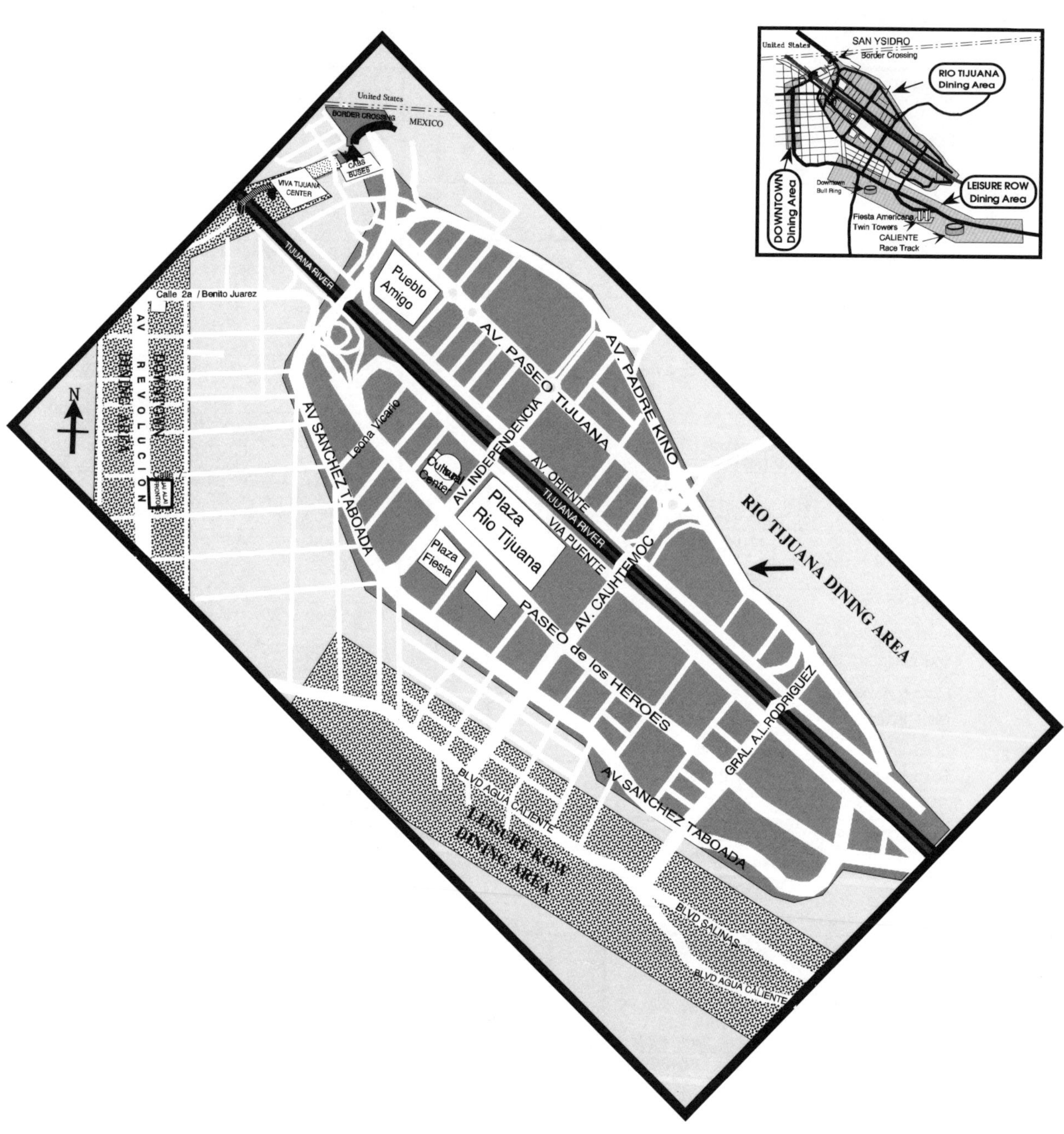
United States
BORDER CROSSING
MEXICO
CABS
BUSES
VIVA TIJUANA
CENTER
TIJUANA RIVER
Calle 2a / Benito Juarez
Pueblo
Amigo
AV. PASEO TIJUANA
AV. PADRE KINO
AV. REVOLUCION
N
AV. SANCHEZ TABOADA
Leona Vicario
Cultural
Center
AV. INDEPENDENCIA
AV. ORIENTE
TIJUANA RIVER
Plaza
Rio Tijuana
VIA PUENTE
RIO TIJUANA DINING AREA
Plaza
Fiesta
AV. CAUHTEMOC
PASEO de los HEROES
GRAL. A.L. RODRIGUEZ
BLVD AGUA CALIENTE
AV. SANCHEZ TABOADA
LEISURE ROW
DINING AREA
BLVD SALINAS
BLVD AGUA CALIENTE
SAN YSIDRO
Border Crossing
United States
RIO TIJUANA
Dining Area
DOWNTOWN
Dining Area
Downtown
Bull Ring
LEISURE ROW
Dining Area
Fiesta Americana
Twin Towers
CALIENTE
Race Track

Cuisine (NOTES)	Restaurant — COMMUNITY - Street — Located Near	PHONE — Country Dialing Code 011 - 52 - 66	Serving (B=Brkfst, L=Lunch, D=Dinner; X=Closed)	Late Night Din.	Su. Brk/Brunch	Under $10	$5 to $15	$15-$25+	Credit Cards	SPECIAL FEATURES
ARGENTINEAN	**El Gaucho** — 1420 Av Leona Vicario — North of Independencia Blvd	(706) 634-1039	-- / L / D	Y				$	MC V	Dine on the elegant garden patio Beef specialties with an Argentine flair Piano music
CHINESE	**Dragon Plaza** — In Plaza Rio Tijuana — Near Cultural Center	84-19-64	-- / L / D	Y		$				Intriguing decor in this well-known restaurant Mandarin Cuisine
CONTINENT'L	**Alcazar Del Rio** — 56-4 Paseo de los Heroes — at Av Rodriguez; in OH! Disco Building	(706) 684-2672	-- / L / D	Y			$		MC V AE	Elegant modern decor; Sophisticated menu with large wine list Piano and violin music (Tu-Sa)
	Capistrano Grill — #1205 Paseo Tijuana — Near Pueblo Amigo	84-10-84	-- / L / D	Y				$	MC V	Lavish, sophisticated decor Live music/entertainment in restaurant and bar Dancing nightly
	Las Espuelas — In Plaza Rio Shopping Center — Near front/center of center	(706) 684-0157	B / L / D		✓		$		MC V AE	Very popular richly appointed restaurant Menu features a wide variety Salad bar
FRENCH	**El Puente** — Paseo de los Heroes — in Hotel Lucena - at A.L.Rodriguez	84-01-15	B / L / D	Y				+		Sophisticated and up scale Tijuana restaurant French and Continental cuisine Alternative restaurant in Hotel is El Acueducto
INTERNAT'L	**Freeday** — 9311 Paseo de los Heroes — Across from Plaza Rio Tijuana	34-14-06	-- / L / D	Y				$	MC V AE	Brand new, the place to go Modern and very upscale decor
JAPANESE	**Komasa** — Blvd. Sanchez Taboada — At Orozco St.	84-23-63	-- / L / D	Y			$		MC V	Interesting decor surrounds the Sushi Bar Extensive Japanese menu wiritten in Spanish
MEXICAN	**Carnitas Uruapan Rio** — Paseo de los Heroes — Near circle with Lincoln statute		-- / L / D	Y			$		MC V	Rio area branch of well known La Mesa parent Classic Mexican menu Mariachi bands in evening
	Giragril — 9 Blvd. Sanchez Taboada — West of Blvd. Rodriguez	84-01-47	-- / L / D					$		New; Polished California ``grill'' environment Fixed Price buffet only - served at table Mostly Spanish spoken
	Guadalajara Grill — 19 Diego Rivera — East of Paseo de los Heroes	(706) 684-2043					$		MC V AE	Mexican village decor & atmosphere Traditional Mexican dishes are served Live mariachis and guitar music
	Hacienda Del Rio — 6 Av. Leona Vicario — near Cultural Center	34-10-39	-- / L / D				$		ALL	Well known restaurant Classic Mexican and Spanish dishes Dancing on two dance floors on weekends
	Hacienda El Abajeno — 79 Blvd. Sanchez Toboado — at Antonio Casa Blvd- near Plaza Rio	684-2791	B / L / D		✓		$		MC V	Attractive Hacienda setting Traditional menu Mariachis
	La Espadana — 10813 Blvd. Sanchez Taboada — West of Blvd. Rodriguez (Opposite Giragril)	34-14-88	-- / L / D					$	MC V	New; shares several owners with famous La Lena Attractive decor - California Grill style
	Senor Frog's — 60 Via Oriente — In Pueblo Amigo	82-49-58	-- / L / D	Y				$	ALl	Super casual, party-bar/restaurant atmosphere Walking distance from border (Follow the Frogs) Popular tourist destination
SEAFOOD	**El Faro De Mazatlan** — 10106 Blvd. Sanchez Taboada — Two block from Plaza Rio Tijuana	84-88-82	-- / L / D					$	MC V	New Modern stylish colorful decor Drawing attention of up scale local residents
	Ochoa's — 61 Paseo del los Heroes — One block from Hotel Lucerna	84-18-57	-- / L / D	Y			$		MC V	Modern up-scale decor Popular restaurant & bar Music and Dancing
	Popeye's Seafood — 60 Via Oriete — In Pueblo Amigo	none	-- / L / D				$		MC V AE	Attractive, modern decor Wide variety of seafood dishes Popular with tourists and local residents
STEAK HOUSE	**La Fogata** — 114 Paseo del los Heroes — Near Cultural Center	---	-- / L / D				$			Attractive congenial environment Steak (carne asada) dish specialties Popular piano bar
TAPAS BAR	**La Taberna Espanola** — 18A Plaza Fiesta Shopping Center — Across from Rio Tijuana Shopping Center	84-75-62	-- / L / D	Y				$	None	Classic Spanish Tapas Bar (drinks & ``snacks'') Popular attractive hangout for locals & visitors

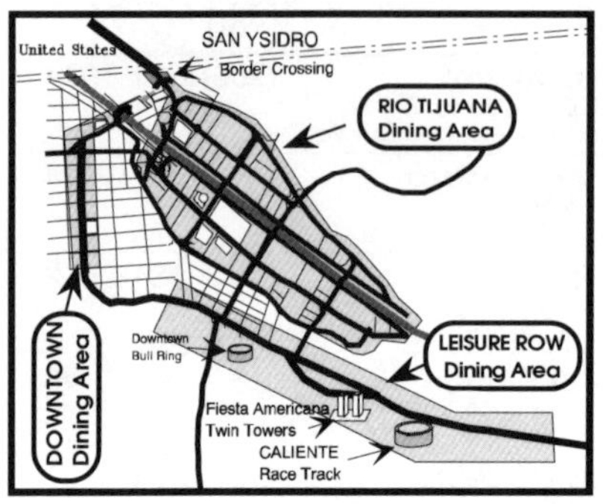

United States
SAN YSIDRO
Border Crossing
RIO TIJUANA
Dining Area
DOWNTOWN
Dining Area
LEISURE ROW
Dining Area
Downtown
Bull Ring
Fiesta Americana
Twin Towers
CALIENTE
Race Track

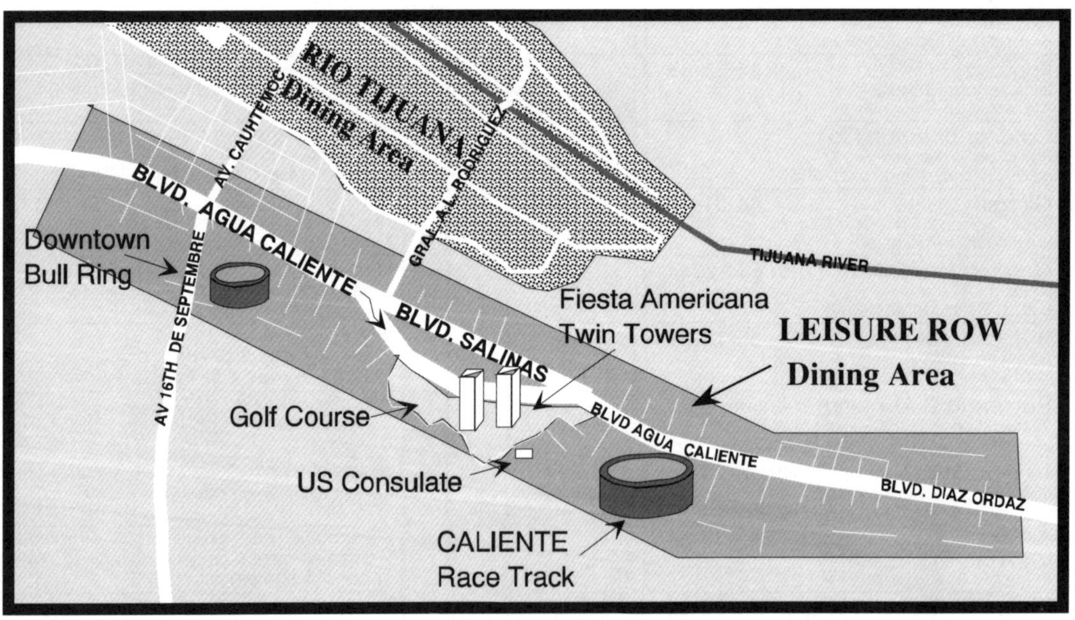

RIO TIJUANA
Dining Area
AV. CAUHTEMOC
GRAL. A. L. RODRIGUEZ
TIJUANA RIVER
BLVD. AGUA CALIENTE
Downtown
Bull Ring
AV 16TH DE SEPTEMBRE
BLVD. SALINAS
Fiesta Americana
Twin Towers
LEISURE ROW
Dining Area
Golf Course
BLVD AGUA CALIENTE
US Consulate
BLVD. DIAZ ORDAZ
CALIENTE
Race Track

Cuisine (NOTES)	Restaurant COMMUNITY - Street Located Near	PHONE Country Dialing Code 011 - 52 - 66	Serving (B L D, X=Closed)	Late Night Din.	Su. Brk/Brunch	Under $10	$5 to $15	$15-$25+	Credit Cards	SPECIAL FEATURES
ARGENTINE	**Rinciocito Gaucho** 1490 Blvd. Agua Caliente On south side (look for medieval tower)	86-55-66	L D	Y		$				Comfortable environment Argentine specialties
CHINESE	**Palacio De Oro Cafe** 1601 Blvd. Agua Caliente Across from the Rinoncito Gaucho rest.	---	L D	Y			$			Attractive decor Traditional menu Carry-out available
CONTINENTAL	**Boccacio's** 2500 Blvd. Agua Caliente (north side) past Fiesta Americana	86-22-66	L D	Y				$	MC V	White tablecloth atmosphere; fine reputation Italian & Continental specialties; wine list Guitar (M-Su)
	La Escondida No.1 Santa Monica Past Racetrack, R on Las Palmas, L on SM	(706) 681-4458	L D	Y				$	MC V AE	Popular, sprawling hidden hilltop hacienda Five dining rooms, two gardens Outdoor children's area
FRENCH	**Place De La Concorde** 4500 Blvd. Agua Caliente Lower promenade - Hotel Fiesta Americana	(706)681-7000	D	Y				$	MC V AE DC	Elegant atmosphere, European service Gourmet French specialties Piano player, jacket and tie required
GREEK	**Dionnysos** 218 Pio Pico At corner with Blvd. Agua Caliente	84-85-08	L D	Y				$	MC V	Neat, attractive classic Greek restaurant decor Small two-story layout; Greek & Arabian dishes Fairly new with growing local clientele
INTERN'T.	**Giuseppi's** 700-10 Blvd. Agua Caliente Near Bull ring	84-10-18	L D			$			MC V	Very popular local family-style Italian restaurant Extensive menu features choices of Mexican, Italian, and other International dishes
MEXICAN	**Carnitas Uruapan** 550 Blvd. Diaz Ordaz 6 blocks past Track (N side)	(706) 681-61-81	B L D	Y	✓	$			MC V AE	Famous for their Carnitas (Broiled Pork) Bench & table atmosphere; mariachis Carry-out available
	Jacaranda 213 Av 16 de Septiembre In The Hotel Palacio Azteca	(706) 681-8100	B L D		✓			$	MC V DC	Interesting decor Beef & Seafood specialties Special brunch on Sundays, Live music
	La Flamita 6000-A Blvd. Agua Caliente Next to Mr Fish- near Plaze Fiesta Hotel	(706) 681-7805	L D	Y		$			MC V AE	Small immaculate, family-owned restaurant Traditional homemade Mexican foods
	La Fonda Roberto's 356-6 Av 16 de Septiembre In La Sierra Motel (off Agua Caliente)	86-46-87	B L D		✓			$		Owned by Roberto Reyes, of Chula Vista's Roberto's Attractive spacious room - Mexican style cuisine Primarily local clientele
	El Capitan 1393 Blvd. Agua Caliente Across from Bull Ring	81-70-85	L D	Y				$	MC V	Dressy, wide range of items on menu Primarily Spanish spoken
SEAFOOD	**Los Arcos** 201 Blvd. Salinas (North side) At Calle Escuadron	(706) 686-3171	L D				$		MC V	Nautical decor; tropical music Popular seafood and steak spot
	Mr Fish 6000 Blvd. Agua Caliente At Blvd Salinas	(706) 686-3603	L D				$		MC V AE	Casual dining, Polynesian decor Wide variety of seafood dishes Live music (guitar or organ)
SPANISH	**Paellas Tonico** 230 Av Jalisco Turn east off Blvd. Agua Caliente	84-09-41	L D			$			MC V	Small but popular Specialty is Paella Simple decor
STEAK HOUSE	**El Rodeo** 1777 Blvd. Salinas near Fiesta Americana hotel	86-56-40	L D	Y			$		MC V AE	US Old West decor in this steak house favorite Other location in La Mesa area with same name
	El Rodeo De La Mesa 8 Av Los Chabros Off Blvd. Diaz Ordaz (2 mi E- Caliente R.Trk.)	(706) 681-6808	L D	Y			$			Traditional Mexican menu Well known for their carne asada Piano & singer (nightly)
	La Leña 4560 Blvd. Agua Caliente Just past Fiesta American Hotel	86-29-20	L D	Y			$		MC V	Very popular with visitors and local diners Mesquite-grilled beef and chicken specialties
	Don Quijote 1771 Blvd. Agua Caliente In Hotel Conquistador	81-79-60	B L D		✓			$		Well known for their steaks Unhurried atmosphere Pianist in the evening

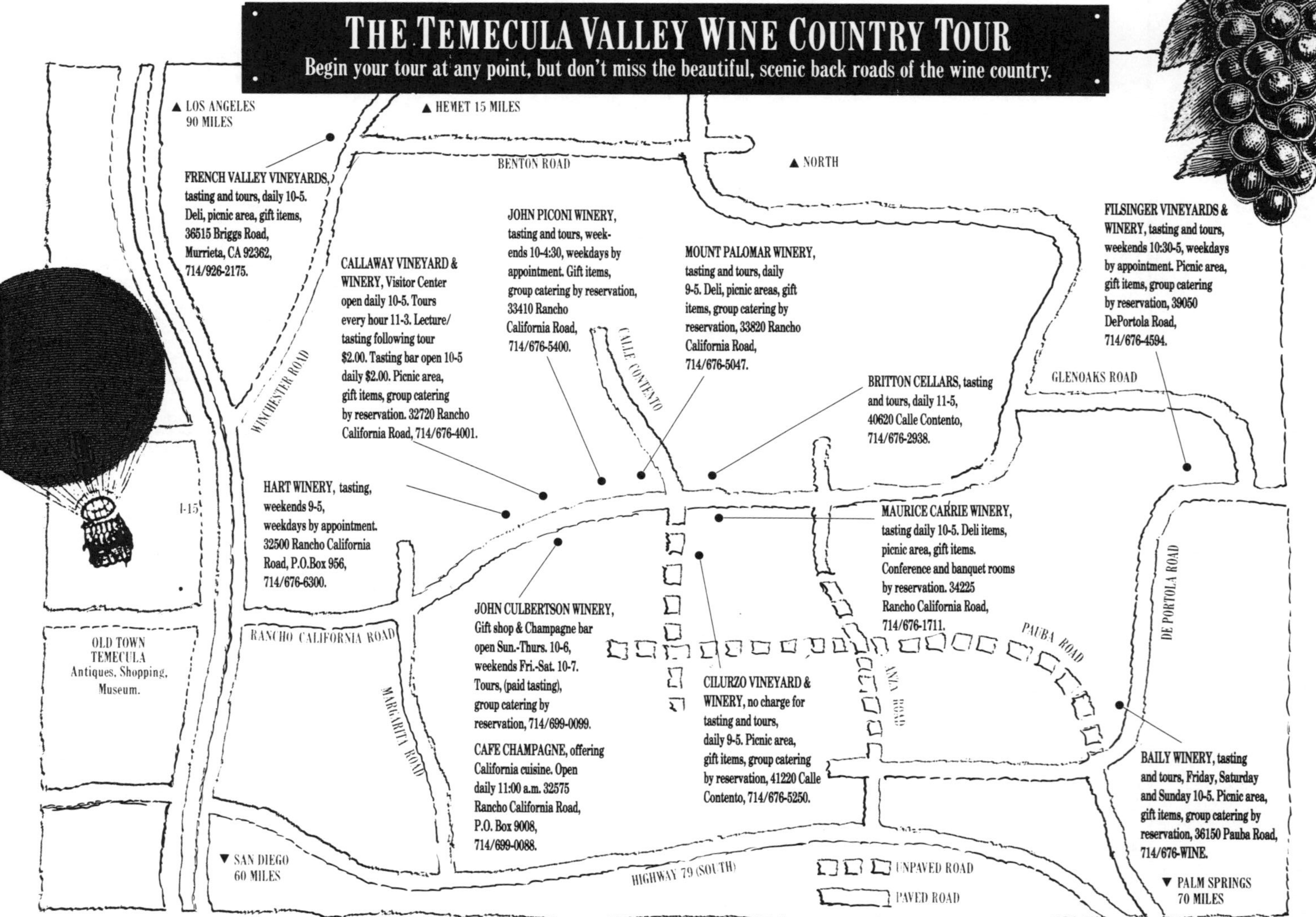

THE TEMECULA VALLEY WINE COUNTRY TOUR
Begin your tour at any point, but don't miss the beautiful, scenic back roads of the wine country.

LOS ANGELES 90 MILES
HEMET 15 MILES
NORTH
BENTON ROAD

FRENCH VALLEY VINEYARDS, tasting and tours, daily 10-5. Deli, picnic area, gift items, 36515 Briggs Road, Murrieta, CA 92362, 714/926-2175.

CALLAWAY VINEYARD & WINERY, Visitor Center open daily 10-5. Tours every hour 11-3. Lecture/ tasting following tour $2.00. Tasting bar open 10-5 daily $2.00. Picnic area, gift items, group catering by reservation. 32720 Rancho California Road, 714/676-4001.

JOHN PICONI WINERY, tasting and tours, weekends 10-4:30, weekdays by appointment. Gift items, group catering by reservation, 33410 Rancho California Road, 714/676-5400.

MOUNT PALOMAR WINERY, tasting and tours, daily 9-5. Deli, picnic areas, gift items, group catering by reservation, 33820 Rancho California Road, 714/676-5047.

FILSINGER VINEYARDS & WINERY, tasting and tours, weekends 10:30-5, weekdays by appointment. Picnic area, gift items, group catering by reservation, 39050 DePortola Road, 714/676-4594.

CALLE CONTENTO

BRITTON CELLARS, tasting and tours, daily 11-5, 40620 Calle Contento, 714/676-2938.

GLENOAKS ROAD

WINCHESTER ROAD

I-15

HART WINERY, tasting, weekends 9-5, weekdays by appointment. 32500 Rancho California Road, P.O.Box 956, 714/676-6300.

MAURICE CARRIE WINERY, tasting daily 10-5. Deli items, picnic area, gift items. Conference and banquet rooms by reservation. 34225 Rancho California Road, 714/676-1711.

PAUBA ROAD

DE PORTOLA ROAD

OLD TOWN TEMECULA Antiques, Shopping, Museum.

RANCHO CALIFORNIA ROAD

JOHN CULBERTSON WINERY, Gift shop & Champagne bar open Sun.-Thurs. 10-6, weekends Fri.-Sat. 10-7. Tours, (paid tasting), group catering by reservation, 714/699-0099.

ANZA ROAD

CILURZO VINEYARD & WINERY, no charge for tasting and tours, daily 9-5. Picnic area, gift items, group catering by reservation, 41220 Calle Contento, 714/676-5250.

MARGARITA ROAD

CAFE CHAMPAGNE, offering California cuisine. Open daily 11:00 a.m. 32575 Rancho California Road, P.O. Box 9008, 714/699-0088.

BAILY WINERY, tasting and tours, Friday, Saturday and Sunday 10-5. Picnic area, gift items, group catering by reservation, 36150 Pauba Road, 714/676-WINE.

SAN DIEGO 60 MILES
HIGHWAY 79 (SOUTH)
UNPAVED ROAD
PAVED ROAD
PALM SPRINGS 70 MILES

All wineries are located in Temecula, CA 92390 unless otherwise noted. Holiday hours may vary. Call for information. Map not to scale.

PALM SPRINGS
&
THE DESERT COMMUNITIES

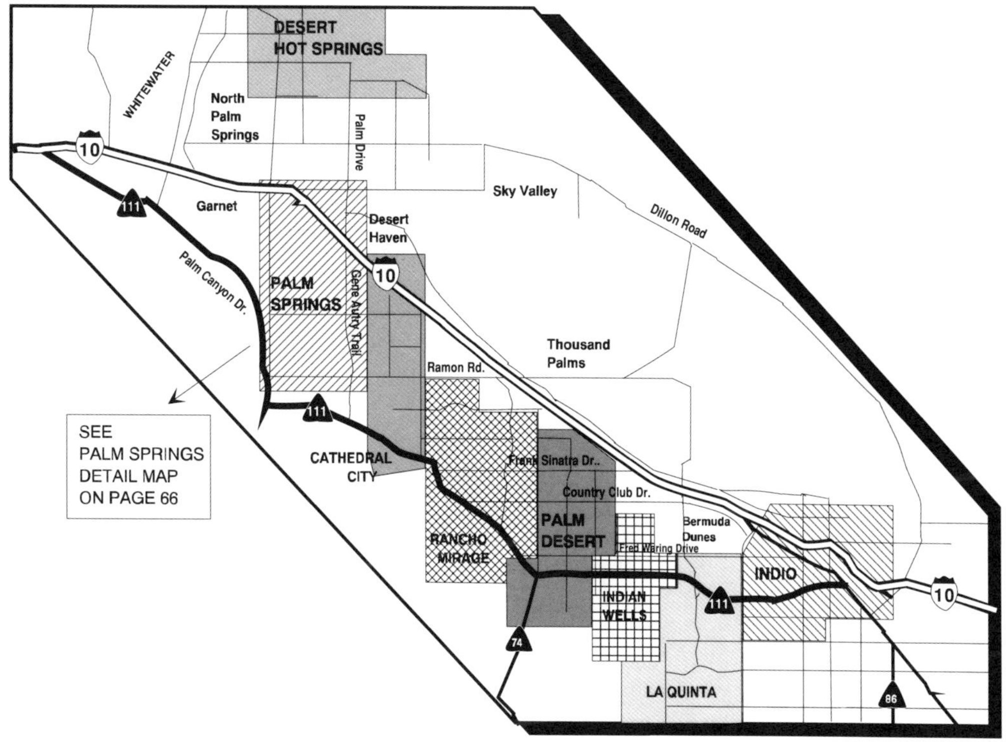

WEEKEND EXCURSION INFORMATION
For people interested in fine dining, the wineries of Temucula make a great day trip from Palm Springs, San Diego or Los Angeles or a nice stop off on a trip between the cities. Here are quick profiles of some of the sights to see there.

PALM SPRINGS

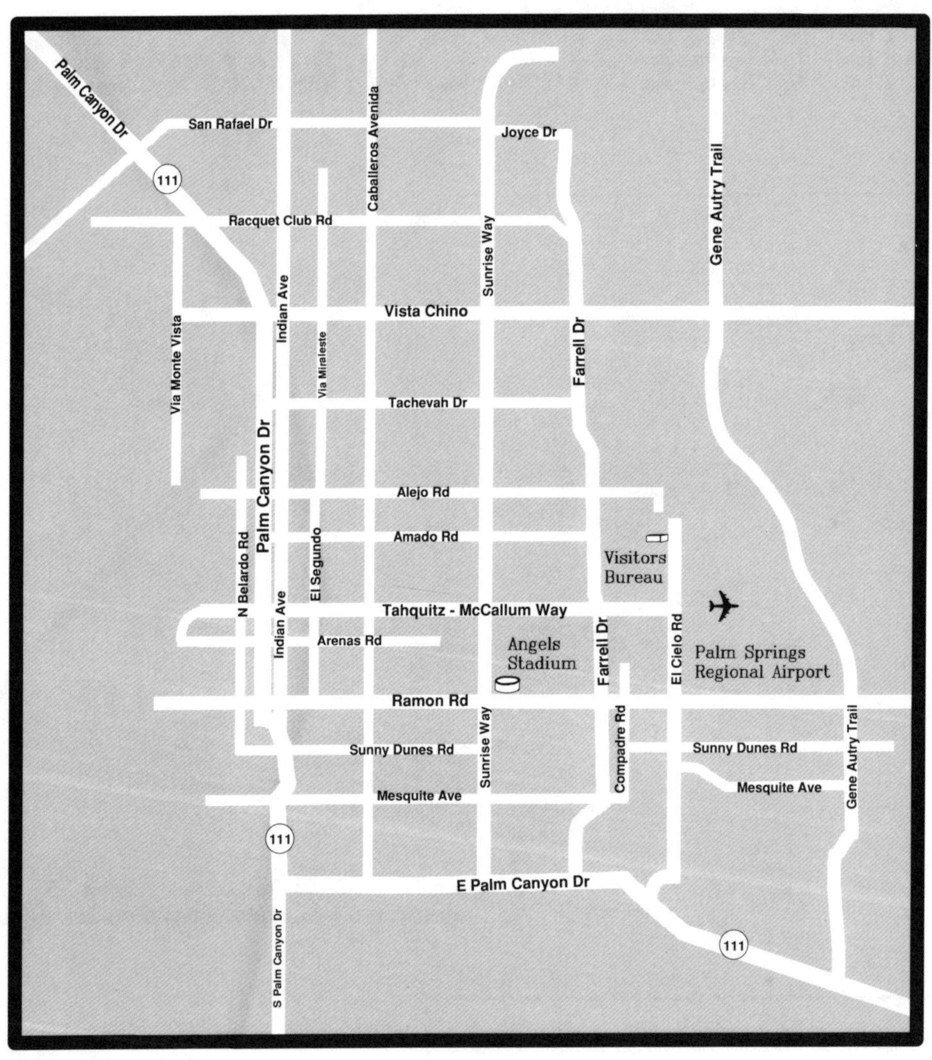

ALPHABETIC INDEX

NAME	CUISINE CATEGORY
A Sensu Restaurant	JAPANESE
Aerial Tramway	AMERICAN
African Queen	AMERICAN
Alfredos Italian Garden	ITALIAN
Appley's	SOUTHWESTERN
Banducci's Bit Of Italy	ITALIAN
Billy Reed's	AMERICAN
Bobby A's Restaurant & Nightclub	SEAFOOD
Bolero's	INTERNAT.
Bono	ITALIAN
Cafe Jardin	AMERICAN
Cafe St. James	INTERNAT.
Cedar Creek Inn	AMERICAN
Chen Ling Garden	CHINESE
Chez Zizi	FRENCH
Cinnamon's	AMERICAN
Comedy Haven At Brussels	CONTINENTAL
Don Quixote Room	CONTINENTAL
Easa de Alfredo	ITALIAN
El Mirasol	MEXICAN
Europa	CONTINENTAL
Eveleen's	FRENCH
Fairchild's	CONTINENTAL
Ferraro's	ITALIAN
Flower Drum, The	CHINESE
Gaity Deli, The	AMERICAN
Garden Court	AMERICAN
Georgio's Ristorante	ITALIAN
Great Wall, The	CHINESE
Jeremiah's Steak House	AMERICAN
Kiyosaku	JAPANESE
Laff Stop/Rock Around The Clock	AMERICAN
Lam's Garden Chinese Restaurant	CHINESE
Las Casuelas	MEXICAN
Las Casuelas Terraza	MEXICAN
Le Vallauris	FRENCH
Livreri's Italian Restaurant	ITALIAN
Lou Calen	FRENCH
Louise's Pantry	AMERICAN
Lyon's English Grille	ENGLISH
Moody's	CONTINENTAL
Nate's Deli	AMERICAN
Otani - A Garden Restaurant	JAPANESE
Papa Joe's	ITALIAN
Paul D'amico's Steak House	AMERICAN
Pepper's Thai Cuisine	THAI
Perrinas	ITALIAN
Raphael's Trattoria	ITALIAN
Rennick's	CALIFORNIAN
Riccio's	ITALIAN
San Gennero	ITALIAN
Siamese Gourmet	THAI
Silk Road	JAPANESE
Sombrero Room	MEXICAN
Sorrentino's	SEAFOOD
Tapestry Room	CONTINENTAL
Vin De France	FRENCH

Cuisine (NOTES)	Restaurant / COMMUNITY - Street / Located Near	PHONE (619)	Serving: B/L/D (X=Closed)	Late Night Din.	Sunday Brunch	Under $10	$10 to $20	$20 to $30+	Credit Cards	Reservations	SPECIAL FEATURES
AMERICAN	**Aerial Tramway** PALM SPRINGS - Tramway Rd At N. Palm Canyon Dr	325-1391	-- L D		✓		$		MC V AE	No 250	Spectacular mountain view, Combo Ride'N'Dine package / Last car up in Winter 8p/ Summer 9p / Cocktail lounge
	African Queen PALM SPRINGS - 2665 East Palm Canyon Dr East of Sunrise Way	322-0990	-- -- D	Y			$		MC V AE D	Rec	Tropical decor, relive with Hepburn and Bogart / Daily special, homemade pastries, incredible popovers / Piano F/Sa, Silver Medal/SCRW
	Billy Reed's PALM SPRINGS - 1800 North Palm Canyon Dr North of Vista Chino	325-1946	B L D	Y	✓		$		MC V AE D	No 50	Varied menu which is served all day / from prime rib to pot roast to swordfish / Silver Award/SCRW
	Cafe Jardin PALM SPRINGS - 888 East Tahquitz Way In The Wyndham Hotel	322-6000	B L D	Y			$		MC V AE DC	Rec 80	Indoor/outdoor patio dining, soft pastel colors / Serving three different menus, breakfast, lunch & dinner / Appley's is the hotel's gourmet dining room
	Cedar Creek Inn PALM SPRINGS - 1555 South Palm Canyon Dr South of Sonora Rd	325-7300	-- L D		✓		$		MC V	Yes	Ayers Family hospitality in Country French decor / Everything is homemade, chili, incredible desserts / B&W, Silver Medal/SCRW
	Cinnamon's PALM SPRINGS - 2800 South Palm Canyon Dr In The Ramada Resort Hotel	327-3744	B L D				$		MC V AE DC	Rec 350	Light and airy, done in peach tones / California cuisine with a Continental flair / Silver Medal/SCRW
	Gaity Deli, The PALM SPRINGS -448 South Indian Av	323-5691									Clowns cover the walls in this deli / Typical Kosher food / Carry-out counter
	Garden Court PALM SPRINGS - 150 South Indian Av In The Marquis Hotel	322-2121	B L D	Y	✓			$	MC V AE	Yes 500	Italian and American cuisine / Seafood specials and hamburgers for lunch / B&W, Dinner specials 4 items for $11.95
	Jeremiah's Steak House PALM SPRINGS - 1201 East Palm Canyon Dr West of Sunrise Way	327-1469	-- -- D	F / Sa			$		MC V	Yes	Casual atmosphere with hanging plants / Decorated with wood and stained glass / Prime rib, prime steak, seafood and spirits
	Laff Stop/Rock Around the Clock PALM SPRINGS - 1000 East Thaquitz Way In The Palm Springs Entertainment Ctr	327-8889	-- -- D	Y			$		MC V AE DC	Rec 220	Food available in both rooms, cover charge for comedy / Appetizer type menu featuring hamburger, veggie & dip / Live bands on the weekends
	Louise's Pantry PALM SPRINGS - 124 South Palm Canyon Dr South of Tahquitz Way	325-5124	B L D			$			NONE	No	40's coffee shop featuring counter & booths / Freshly baked danish, cakes & pies / Big portions of hearty American food, always a line
	Nate's Deli PALM SPRINGS - 100 South Indian Av South of Tahquitz Way	325-3506	B L D		✓	$			MC V AE DC D	No 75	"Mister Corned Beef of Palm Springs" / Family owned & operated since 1948 / 9 course dinner from 4-6, carry out, B&W
	Paul D'amico's PALM SPRINGS - 1180 South Palm Canyon Dr South of Mesquite Av	325-9191	-- L (X:Su) D	Y			$		MC V	Must	Family oriented, catering to the locals / in the dessert for 19 years / Silver Medal/SCRW, piano T-Sa
CALIFORNIA	**Rennick's** PALM SPRINGS - 100 North Indian Av In The Spa Hotel	325-1461	B L D				$		MC V AE DC	Rec 600	Outdoor patio dining / Spa cuisinefor the health conscious / Early bird specials
CHINESE	**Chen Ling Garden** PALM SPRINGS - 787 North Palm Canyon Dr North of Val Monte	322-0039	-- L D				$		MC V	Rec	Mandarian & Szechuan cuisine using only fresh vegetables / Low fat vegetable oil, low sodium, fresh herbs & spices / No msg, B&W, One Star/CRWA
	Flower Drum, The PALM SPRINGS - 424 South Indian Av North of Ramon Rd	323-3020	-- L D	Y			$		MC V AE	Rec 100	Waterfall in restaurant, NYC favorite for 25 yrs / Cooking all five cuisines with changing seasonal menu / No msg, low sodium, oriental dancers, Silver Medal/SCRW
	Great Wall, The PALM SPRINGS - 362 South Palm Canyon Dr South of Bristol Rd	322-2209	-- L D	F / Sa	✓		$		MC V AE DC	160	Szechuan, Mandarin & Hunan cuisine / Mongolian BBQ
	Lam's Garden PALM SPRINGS - 622 North Palm Canyon Dr South of Tamarisk Rd	325-8860	-- L D			$			MC V AE DC		Cantonese, Mandarin, & Szechuan dishes / Family style dinners / B&W, carry-out, One Star/CRWA
CONTINENTAL	**Comedy Haven** PALM SPRINGS - 1450 North Indian Av South of Vista Chino; at Brussels Cafe	320-7855	B L D		✓			$	MC V AE	Rec 150	Contintental cuisine with an Italian flair / Dessert Restaurant Award for Shrimp Scampi / Comedy show Th-Su, music & dancing in lounge nightly
	Don Quixote Room PALM SPRINGS - 444 Av Caballeros In The La Mancha Hotel	323-1773	B L D (F&Sa)				$		MC V AE	Must 30	California & European cuisine / 6 course prix fixe / Jacket required

Cuisine (NOTES)	Restaurant / PHONE / COMMUNITY - Street / Located Near	SERVING: Brkfst / Lunch / Dinner (X=Closed)	Late Night Din.	Sunday Brunch	Under $10	$10 to $20	$20 to $30+ (Dinner/Person)	Credit Cards	Reservations	SPECIAL FEATURES
CONTINENTAL (Con't)	**Europa** 327-2314 *PALM SPRINGS* - 1620 Indian Trail In The Villa Royale	-- L (X:M) D (X:M)				$		MC V	Rec 45	Country inn atmosphere with outdoor dining Dine fireside or under the stars on daily specials B&W, Promising Newcomer/SCRW
	Fairchild's 327-1263 *PALM SPRINGS* - 1001 South El Cielo Rd South of Ramon Rd	B L D (F&Sa)		✓			$	MC V AE	Rec 125	Lake setting at Bel Air Greens featuring outdoor dining Jacket and tie for dinner Entertainment nightly
	Moody's 323-1806 *PALM SPRINGS* - 1480 South Palm Canyon Dr South of Sonora Rd	-- -- D	Y				$	MC V AE	Must 40	Supper club with show tunes, party atmosphere Tributes to Cole Porter, George Gershwin Late night cabaret with hosts Phil & Grace Moody
	Tapestry Room 320-6868 *PALM SPRINGS* - 400 East Tahquitz Way In The Sheraton Plaza Hotel	-- -- D (X:M)	T / Su				$	MC V AE DC	Must 60	Banquettes, crystal chandeliers, prix fixe menu Elegant dining Named ''Restaurant of the Year'' by Palm Springs Life
ENGLISH	**Lyon's English Grille** 327-1551 *PALM SPRINGS* - 233 East Palm Canyon Dr West of Via Salida	-- -- D	Y			$		MC V AE DC	Must 100	Unique English restaurant since 1946 Featuring large booths with banner & pub sign decor Traditional menu of prime ribs and steaks, Silver/SCRW
FRENCH	**Chez Zizi** 320-3375 *PALM SPRINGS* - 276 North Palm Canyon Dr South of Amado Rd	-- L (X:M) D (X:M)					$	MC V AE DC	Rec 40	Mediterranean specialties, from Italian to Greek to Spanish, and even Classic French Silver Award/SCRW
	Eveleen's 325-4766 *PALM SPRINGS* - 664 North Palm Canyon Dr North of Alejo St	-- -- D (X:M,Tu)					+	MC V AE	Rec 50	Intimate and romantic atmosphere dining indoor or out Classic French Cuisine, private room Tie & jacket, Gold Award/SCRW, 3 Star/CRWA
	Le Vallauris 325-5059 *PALM SPRINGS* - 385 West Tahquitz Way West of Palm Canyon Dr	-- L D	Y	✓			+	MC V AE DC	Rec 250	Historic building featuring patio dining Daily blackboard menu, nouvelle cuisine, chef's special Winner of multiple Awards, piano bar
	Lou Calen 327-1196 *PALM SPRINGS* - 445 North Palm Canyon Dr	B (F-Su) L (X:M) D (X:M)		✓			$	MC V AE DC	Yes	Small French cafe Provencal and Nouvelle cuisine
	Vin De France 322-2202 *PALM SPRINGS* - 123 North Palm Canyon Dr North of Tahquitz Way	-- L (M-F) D (F-Su)				$		MC V AE	No	Very casual, patio dining under unbrellas Nicoise salads, montrachet salads, pasta dishes B&W
INTERN'TI	**Bolero's** 327-8311 *PALM SPRINGS* - 1600 North Indian Av In The Radisson Resort	B L D	Y			$		MC V AE	Rec 150	View of San Jacinto mountains American, California, and Mexican foods Entertainment and dancing
	Cafe St. James 320-8041 *PALM SPRINGS* - 254 South Palm Canyon Dr South of Arenas Rd	-- -- D(X:M,Tu)	W - Su		$			MC V	Rec	Bistro decor with balcony seating, cappucino & wine bar Daily menus, private luncheons available B&W, Silver Award/SCRW
ITALIAN	**Alfredo Italian Garden** 325-4060 *PALM SPRINGS* - 285 South Palm Canyon Dr South of Arenas Rd	-- -- D	Y			$		MC V AE	Yes 35	Bistro decor with balcony seating, cappucino & wine bar Daily menus, B&W Private luncheons available, Silver Award/SCRW
	Alfredo's Ristorante 320-1020 *PALM SPRINGS* - 292 East Palm Canyon Dr West of Calle Palo Fierro	-- -- D	Y			$		MC V AE	Yes	Casual & comfortable, typical Italian restaurant Italian dishers from pizza to buffalo wings to steak alfredo No bar
	Banducci's Bit Of Italy 325-2537 *PALM SPRINGS* - 1260 South Palm Canyon Dr South of Mesquite Av	-- -- D	Y			$		MC V AE	Rec	Outdoor dining at the home of mamas authentic recipes ''an Italian restaurant where Italians go'' since 1964 Piano bar cocktail lounge
	Bono 322-6200 *PALM SPRINGS* - 1700 North Indian Av At Vista Chino	-- L (M-F) D	Y				$	MC V	Rec 200	Casual comfortable dining in this lively, upbeat spot Popular with the locals, owned by mayor of Palm Springs Sicilian cooking, piano bar
	Ferraro's 327-7344 PALM SPRINGS - 150 East Vista Chino East of N. Palm Canyon Dr	-- -- D	Y			$		MC V AE	No	Family-owned featuring Southern Italian recipes Pizza, B&W Food to go, dancing
	Georgio's Ristorante 325-2821 PALM SPRINGS - 1115 North Palm Canyon Dr South of Vista Chino	-- -- D	F / Sa			$		MC V AE DC	Yes	Complimentary bottle of wine to the ladies Happy hour every hour, pizza bread on the hour Piano bar W-Sa
	Livreri's 327-1419 PALM SPRINGS - 350 South Indian Av North of Ramon Rd	-- -- D (X:Tu)	W - M			$		MC V AE	Rec 110	Seafood specialties and American dishes Lounge with entertainment
	Papa Joe's 320-9511 PALM SPRINGS - 1111 East Palm Canyon Dr West of Sunrise Way	-- L D	F / Sa			$		MC V	Yes 500	Casual and quaint with 12 foot ceilings Pizza, pasta plus a full Italian menu Jazz - 7 days

Cuisine (NOTES)	Restaurant / COMMUNITY - Street / Located Near	PHONE	Brkfst / Lunch / Dinner / X=Closed	Late Night Din.	Sunday Brunch	Under $10	$10 to $20	$20 to $30 +	Credit Cards	Reservations	SPECIAL FEATURES
ITALIAN (Con't)	**Perrinas** / PALM SPRINGS - 340 North Palm Canyon Dr / North of Amado Rd	325-6544	-- / -- / D (X:M)	Tu - Su			$		MC V / AE DC / 12	Rec	Same location since 1980 / Continental specialties / Piano bar
	Raphael's Trattoria / PALM SPRINGS - 266 South Palm Canyon Dr / South of Arenas Rd	320-8344	-- / L (X:Su) / D		$				MC V / AE / CB	Rec	Very small, sits 18 inside and 16 outside / Northern Italian cuisine, all dinner complete with / caesar salad and garlic bread, B&W
	Riccio's / PALM SPRINGS - 2155 North Palm Canyon Dr / North of Vista Chino	325-2369	-- / L (M-F) / D	Y			$		MC V / AE DC / 30	Rec	Elegant European service / Northern & Southern Italian food, seafood specialties / Piano lounge, Silver Medal/SCRW, 3 Star/CRWA
	San Gennero / PALM SPRINGS - 777 East Tahquitz Way / East of Calle El Segundo	322-9322	-- / L / D	Y		$			MC V / DC / 200	Rec	Modern High Tech/ Sports bar / Pizza, Pasta, Grilled items / Weekend show Cabaret style
JAPANESE	**A Sensu Restaurant** / PALM SPRINGS - 265 South Palm Canyon Dr / South of Arenas Rd	322-0090	-- / L (X:M) / D (X:M)	Tu - Su	✓	$			MC V / AE DC / 108	Rec	Sushi and sake bar, B&W / Daily specials, no msg, deep fried ice cream / Carry out
	Kiyosaku / PALM SPRINGS - 1420 North Palm Canyon Dr / South of Vista Chino	327-6601	-- / L (X:Su) / D	Y		$			MC V / 45	Rec	Sushi bar, traditional menu with special dishes / Traditional menu with special dishes, B&W / Live lobsters and crab
	Otani - A Garden Restaurant / PALM SPRINGS - 1000 Tahquitz Way / East of Sunrise Way	327-6700	-- / L / D		✓		$		MC V / AE DC / 30	Rec	Sushi and Yakitori bar / Tempura bar / Catering, Promising Newcomer/SCRW, 2 Star/CRWA
	Silk Road / PALM SPRINGS - 169-A North Indian Av / North of Tahquitz Way	322-6452	-- / L / D	Y		$			MC V / AE / 100	Rec	Black, silver, white cosmopolitan high tech decor / ``New Age Oriental Cuisine, Thai, Chinese & Japanese / Shogun room is very traditional, B&W
MEXICAN	**El Mirasol** / PALM SPRINGS - 140 East Palm Canyon Dr / West of Calle Palo Fierro	323-0721	-- / L (X:Su) / D (X:Su)		$				MC V / 20	Yes	Northern Central Mexico decor with patio dining / Regional Mexican specialties, lunch specials under $5 / Mole poblano, carnitas, B&W
	Las Casuelas / PALM SPRINGS - 368 North Palm Canyon Dr / South of Alejo Rd	325-3213	B (Sa/Su) / L / D	Sa / Su	$				MC V / AE DC	Yes	Original location dowtownm established 1958 / Cal-Mex home cooking, food all made by hand
	Las Casuelas Terraza / PALM SPRINGS - 222 South Palm Canyon Dr / South of Arenas Rd	325-2794	-- / L / D		✓	$			MC V / 75	Rec	Out door patio dining / Third generation of the Delgado Family / Flamenco guitar
	Sombrero Room / PALM SPRINGS - 4200 East Palm Canyon Dr / Palm Canyon Dr & Gene Autry Trail	328-1171	B / L / D		✓	$			MC V / AE DC / D / 110	Rec	Pool and garden dining, hors doeurves 4-6p / Accents of Italian and Cajun cooking / Dress code after 6p, dancing & entertainment
SEAFOOD	**Bobby A`s** / PALM SPRINGS - 1900 East Palm Canyon Dr / North of Hwy 111	321-1060	-- / -- / D (X:M,Tu)	F / / Sa		$			MC V / AE	Yes	Chef Johnny Costa preparing Italian favorites, seafood / Dancing and live entertainment, B&W
	Sorrentino's / PALM SPRINGS - 1032 North Palm Canyon Dr / South of Vista Chino	325-2944	-- / -- / D	Y		$			MC V / AE DC	Rec	Palm Springs casual, seafood with an Italian flair / now in its 22nd season of serving the freshest seafood / Entertainment Tu-Su, Silver Award/SCRW
SOUTHWEST	**Appley's** / PALM SPRINGS - 888 East Tahquitz Way / In The Wyndham Hotel	322-6000	-- / -- / D (Tu-Sa)				$		MC V / AE DC / CB / 200	Yes	Innovative American cuisine with a French accent / Adventurous appetizers, Open Sept through May / Classical guitar, Gold Award/SCRW, 3 Stars/CRWA
THAI	**Pepper's Thai Cuisine** / PALM SPRINGS - 495 North Palm Canyon Dr / At Alejo Rd	322-1259	-- / L / D	F / / Sa		$			MC V / DC / 40	Rec	Patio dining at this family run restaurant / Lunch and seafood specials, coconut milk curry / B&W, Carry out
	Siamese Gourmet / PALM SPRINGS - 4711 East Palm Canyon Dr / West of Gene Autry Trail	328-0057	-- / L (X:Su) / D	Y		$			MC V / AE DC / 85	Rec	Traditional Thai dishes, / Curry & seafood specials, early bird 4:30-6:30 / B&W, Carry out

THE DESERT COMMUNITIES

CATHEDRAL CITY

DESERT HOT SPRINGS

INDIAN WELLS

INDIO

LA QUINTA

PALM DESERT

RANCHO MIRAGE

THE DESERT COMMUNITIES

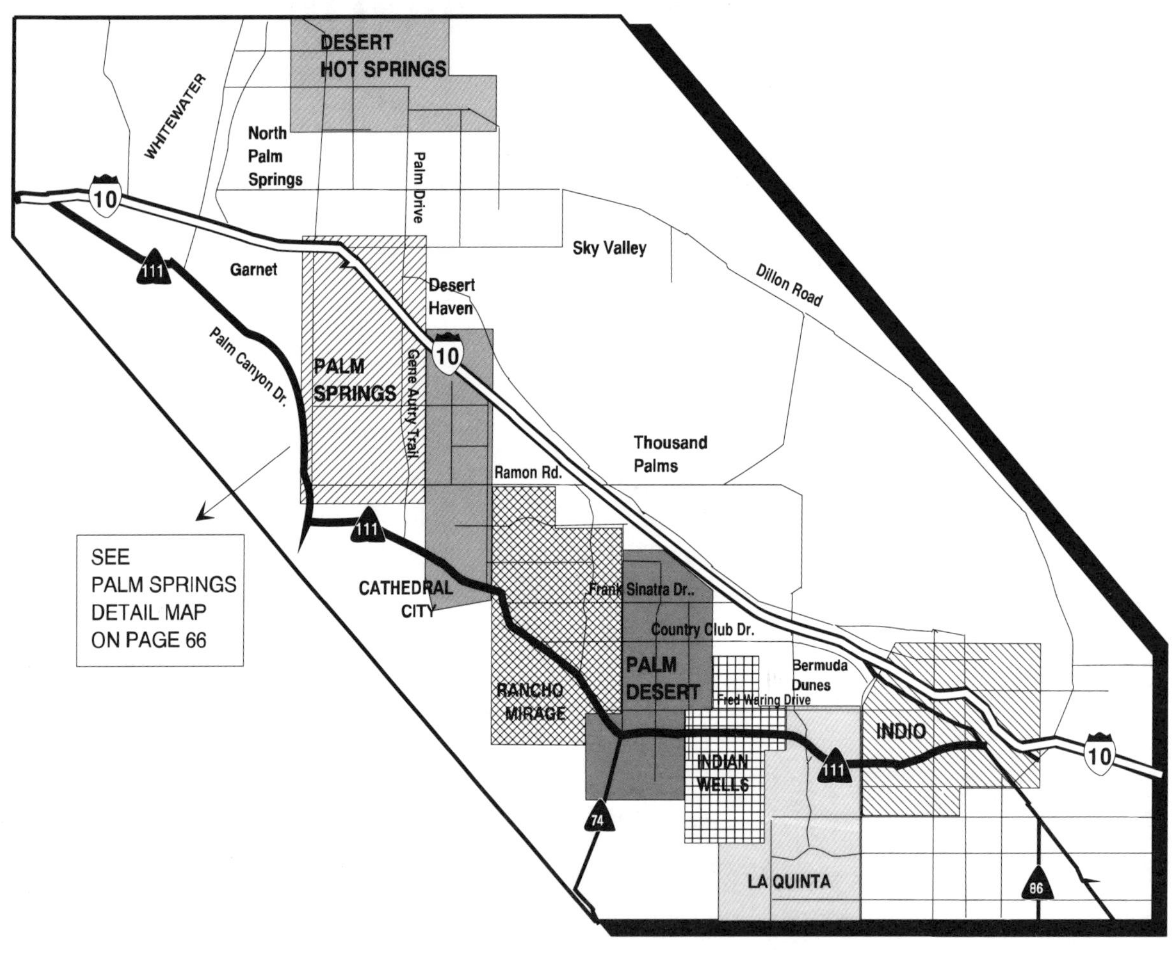

LISTING BY COMMUNITY (Look under CUISINE LISTINGS for details)

RESTAURANT (CUISINE)

DESERT HOT SPRINGS
Budapest Inn (HUNGARIAN)
Mission Lakes Country Club (AMERICAN)
Sunshine Cafe (AMERICAN)

CATHEDRAL CITY
Cactus Corral (AMERICAN)
Cattails (CONTINENTAL)
Mandarin Palace (CHINESE)
Mr. Wong's (CHINESE)
No Finer Diner (AMERICAN)
Olympic Cafe (GREEK)
Paoli's Pizzeria And Pasta House (ITALIAN)
Princess Room, The (CALIFORNIA)
Promenade Cafe (AMERICAN)
Wilde Goose, The (CONTINENTAL)

RANCHO MIRAGE
Alberto's (ITALIAN)
Beach House Inn (AMERICAN)
Cabrillo Room (CONTINENTAL)
Cafe, The (AMERICAN)
Chaplin's (CONTINENTAL)
Charley Brown's (AMERICAN)
Chart House (AMERICAN)
Dar Maghreb (MOROCCAN)
Dining Room, The (CONTINENTAL)
Dominick's (CONTINENTAL)
Fountain Court (AMERICAN)
House Of Bamboo (CHINESE)
Kobe Japanese Steak House (JAPANESE)
La Cave (FRENCH)
Las Casuelas Nuevas (MEXICAN)
Lord Fletcher's Inn (ENGLISH)
Maria Bonita (MEXICAN)
Mario's (CONTINENTAL)
Michael's Bistro (ITALIAN)
Pirate 'n Bull (SEAFOOD)
Prevue (AMERICAN)
Red Dragon (CHINESE)
Scoma's of San Francisco (SEAFOOD)
Wally's Desert Turtle (CONTINENTAL)
Zorba's (GREEK)

PALM DESERT
A Touch Of Mama's (ITALIAN)
Andreino's ``King'' of Fettuccine (ITALIAN)
B.B. O'Brien's Sports Cafe (AMERICAN)
Bob & Manon Sorrentino's (ITALIAN)
Bogie's Grill (AMERICAN)
China Gardens (CHINESE)
Club 74 (FRENCH)
Cuistot (FRENCH)
Desert Wharf (SEAFOOD)
Dominick Mancuso's Trattoria (ITALIAN)
Don O's (AMERICAN)
El Cafe de Mexico (MEXICAN)
Elephant Bar & Restaurant (AMERICAN)

RESTAURANT (CUISINE)

Gold Phoenix (CHINESE)
Lake View Restaurant (CONTINENTAL)
Le Paon (FRENCH)
Louise's Pantry (AMERICAN)
Mancuso's (ITALIAN)
Marinello Italian Restaurant (ITALIAN)
Midori (JAPANESE)
Mikado (JAPANESE)
Mille Fleurs (FRENCH)
Mitage At The Oasis Country Club (AMERICAN)
Monterey Country Club (AMERICAN)
Papa Dan's (ITALIAN)
Papagayo Room (AMERICAN)
Pietro's (ITALIAN)
Red Onion (MEXICAN)
Renzo's Bistro (CONTINENTAL)
Reuben's (AMERICAN)
Ristorante Mamma Gina (ITALIAN)
Romano's (ITALIAN)
Ron's In The Desert (CONTINENTAL)
Rusty Pelican (SEAFOOD)
Sea Grille (SEAFOOD)
Smoky's (AMERICAN)
Sonoma Grille (CALIFORNIA)
Spiaggia Seafood Ristorante (ITALIAN)
T.G.I. Friday's (ECLECTIC)
Tai Ping (CHINESE)
Tony Roma's (AMERICAN)
Tuscany's Ristorante (ITALIAN)
Tutti Gusti (ITALIAN)
Victor's Bistro (CONTINENTAL)

INDIAN WELLS
Charisma (CALIFORNIA)
Charlie's (SOUTHWEST)
Don Diego's of Indian Wells (MEXICAN)
Erawan Room (CONTINENTAL)
Jasmine (CALIFORNIA)
Nest, The (CONTINENTAL)
Orient Express (CHINESE)
Sirocco (MEDITERRANEAN)
Sunshine Meat, Fish & Liquor Co.
Sutter Street Bar & Grill (AMERICAN)
Trattoria California (AMERICAN)
Vicky's Of Santa Fe (AMERICAN)

LA QUINTA
Adobe Grill (MEXICAN)
Beef & Brew (AMERICAN)
Cunard's of La Quinta (CONTINENTAL)
Huntsman Restaurant of the Desert (CONTINENTAL
La Mirage Room (CONTINENTAL)
Morgans (AMERICAN)
Robi (CONTINENTAL)
Sandbar (AMERICAN)

INDIO
Teresa's Cafe (MEXICAN)

Cuisine (NOTES)	Restaurant / COMMUNITY - Street / Located Near	PHONE (619)	SERVING: Brkfst / Lunch / Dinner / X=Closed	Late Night Din.	Sunday Brunch	Under $10	$10 to $20	$20 to $30+	Credit Cards	Reservations	SPECIAL FEATURES
AMERICAN	**B.B. O'Brien's Sports Cafe** *PALM DESERT* - 72-185 Painters Path West of El Paseo	346-5576	-- L (Sa/Su) D (M-F)	M - F			$		MC V AE	Yes 6p+ 140	Filled with sports memorabilia 3 satelites, 2 big screen tv, 11 monitors Signature item, BBQ Baby Back Ribs, pizzas,
	Beach House Inn *RANCHO MIRAGE* - 70-115 Hwy 111 South of Frank Sinatra Dr	328-6585	-- -- D	Y	✓		$		MC V AE	Rec 350	Casual warm atmosphere in Cape Cod type beach house 3 chefs cooking seafood and steaks nightly Seafood and oyster bar, Silver Medal/SCRW
	Beef & Brew *LA QUINTA* - 78-483 Hwy 111 West of Washington St	564-6224	-- L (X:S,Su) D				$		MC V DC	Yes 60	Cozy, big booths, happy hour 4-7 Sports lounge, 2 satelites, 2 big screen TVs Steak, seafood, chicken, Appetizers only S/Su
	Bogie's Grill *PALM DESERT* - 76-200 Country Club Dr In The Palm Valley C.C.	345-2737	-- -- D				$		MC V	 350	Golf course and mountain views Dinner only served in the main dining room
	Cactus Corral *CATHEDRAL CITY* - 67-501 Hwy 111	321-8558	-- -- D (X:M)				$		MC V AE DC	Rec 250	Contemporary Country Music and dancing to live bands Free dance lessons Th & Su, cover charge W-Su "black tie to blue jeans", hors d'oevures till 2am
	Cafe, The *RANCHO MIRAGE* - 68-900 Frank Sinatra Dr In The Ritz-Carlton Hotel	321-8282	B L D	F / Sa	✓		$		MC V	Yes	Hearty American cuisine, lavish Sunday Brunch American Heart Assoc. firness approved menu Soft piano background music for lunch & dinner
	Charley Brown's *RANCHO MIRAGE* - 70-190 Hwy 111 South of Frank Sinatra Dr	328-3131	-- -- D		✓		$		MC V AE DC	Yes	Family type restaurant Prime rib, USDA prime steaks, fresh seafood Prime time special from 5-7p for $9.95
	Chart House *RANCHO MIRAGE* - 69-934 Hwy 111 North of Frank Sinatra Dr	324-5613	-- -- D	F / Sa				$	MC V AE DC	Yes 30	Small menu, mostly grilled beef and seafood, Salad bar with over 60 items
	Don O's *PALM DESERT* - 42-455 Washington St South of 42nd Av	345-6588	-- -- D (X:M)				$		MC V	Yes 50	All American menu such as Yankee pot roast Nightly specials for $10.95 Entertainment Th-Sa for six seasons: Foster Edwards
	Elephant Bar & Restaurant *PALM DESERT* - 73-833 Hwy 111 At San Lui Rey	340-0456	-- L D	Y			$		MC V AE D	Rec 6p+	Safari decor creates a casual atmosphere for Both indoor and outdoor dining Eclectic menu, carry out
	Fountain Court *RANCHO MIRAGE* - 41-00 Bob Hope Dr In The Marriott Rancho Las Palmas Resort	568-2727	-- L D	F / Sa	✓		$		MC V AE DC	Yes	Early California atmosphere in family dining room Featuring golf course views Twilight dinners from 4:30-7p, lavish Sunday Brunch
	Louise's Pantry *PALM DESERT* - 44-491 Town Center Way North of Hwy 111	346-1315	B L D			$			NONE	No	Homesyle cooking
	Mission Lakes Country Club *DESERT HOT SPRINGS* - 8484 Clubhouse Blvd South of Augusta Av	329-6481	-- L (X:M-F) D (X:M-W)		✓		$		MC V	150	Most beautiful view of desert and golf course Entertainment & dancing (F/Sa)
	Mirage at the Oasis *PALM DESERT* - 42-300 Casbah Way In the Oasis Country Club	345-2717	-- -- D (X:M)				$		MC V DC CB	Yes	Casual elegance overlooking the golf course Entertainment W-Sa
	Monterey Country Club *PALM DESERT* - 41-500 Monterey Av North of Fred Waring Dr	568-9311	B (W-Su) L (X:M,Tu) D (F,Sa)		✓		$		MC V	Rec 200	Golf and mountain views All American menu with a Continental flair
	Morgans *LA QUINTA* - 49-499 Eisenhower Dr In La Quinta Hotel	346-2904	B L D		✓		$		MC V AE DC	Rec	Cafe type atmosphere with photos of famous guests and movies that were filmed on site Dancing & entertainment Sa/Su; Silver Award/SCRW
	No Finer Diner *CATHEDRAL CITY* - 35-955 Date Palm Dr North of Hwy 111	324-7707	D L D		✓	$			MC V	Rec 10p+	'50's diner, serving breakfast all day Comfort food, typical american cooking Daily specials include chicken pot pies, frank n beans
	Papagayo Room *PALM DESERT* - 77-333 Country Club Dr In Palm Desert Resort C.C.	345-2781	-- -- D (X:M-F)				$		MC V	180	Fri twilight golf and dinner special Desert Weekly's Silver Palm Award/1988
	Prevue *RANCHO MIRAGE* - 42-490 Bob Hope Dr In The Rancho Las Palmas Ctr	346-7113	-- L (X:Su) D (X:Su)	F / Sa				$	MC V AE DC	Rec 70	Contemporary black & white decor European bistro menu Pre-theatre prix fixe menu
	Promenade Cafe *CATHEDRAL CITY* - 67-967 Vista Chino In the Doubletree Inn	322-7000	B L D		✓			$	MC V AE DC	Yes	Traditional American favorites Old fashioned fountain specialties, champagne brunch Dancing & entertainment in the Oasis Lounge

Cuisine (NOTES)	Restaurant / COMMUNITY - Street / Located Near	PHONE	Serving (B/L/D, X=Closed)	Late Night Din.	Sunday Brunch	Under $10	$10 to $20	$20 to $30 +	Credit Cards	Reservations	SPECIAL FEATURES
AMERICAN (Con't)	**Reuben's** / PALM DESERT - 72-291 Hwy 111 / At Fred Waring Dr.	568-9388	-- / -- / D			$			MC V AE DC	Rec	Steak & prime rib, $10.95 complete diner
	Sandbar / LA QUINTA - 78-120 Calle Tampico / East of Eisenhower Dr	564-3660	-- / -- / D		F / / Sa	$				Rec	Casual homespun family atmosphere / Nightly specials including ground round and short ribs / Live entertainment nightly
	Smoky's / PALM DESERT - 74-450 Hwy 111 / East of Portola Av	346-1323	-- / L (X:Su) / D			$			MC V D	Yes 20	Casual dress, family style home cooking / Southern pan fried chicken, best burgers
	Sunshine Cafe / DESERT HOT SPRINGS - 10-805 Palm Dr / In The Desert Hot Springs Spa	329-6495	B / L / D			$			MC V AE	Yes	Outdoor dining, California Spa cuisine / Hearty breakfast, Belgian waffles / Entertainment and dancing
	Sunshine Meat, Fish & Liquor Co. / INDIAN WELLS - 74-985 Hwy 111 / West of Cook St	341-3211	-- / L / D			$			MC V	No	Oyster bar, appetizers, shell fish and lighter meals / Regular dining room features fresh fish and Black Angus beef / Library bar, entertainment, guitarist 7 nights
	Sutter Street Bar & Grill / INDIAN WELLS - 76-661 Hwy 111 / In The Ramada Inn	345-6466	B / L / D			$			MC V AE DC	Rec 450	Overlooking swiming pool and golf course / Featuring Chateaubriand for one / Entertainment and dancing(F-Sa)
	Tony Roma's / PALM DESERT - 73-155 Hwy 111	568-9911	-- / L / D	Y			$		MC V AE DC	No	Family favorite with children's menus / World famous original baby back ribs, onion ring loaf / Late night dining, carry out, delivery
	Trattoria California / INDIAN WELLS - 44-600 Indian Wells Lane / In The Hyatt Grand Champions Resort	341-1000	B / L / D		✓		$		MC V AE	Yes 15	European bistro atmosphere serving the flavor of Italy / with a California flair, pizza, pastas, salads / Mesquite grilled entrees, Sunday Brunch
	Vicky's Of Santa Fe / INDIAN WELLS - 45-100 Club Dr / Between Eldorado & Washington	345-9770	-- / -- / D	Y			$		MC V	No	Daily changing menu in this pleasant decor / Entertainment
CALIFORNIA	**Charisma** / INDIAN WELLS - 44-400 Indian Wells Lane / In The Stouffer Esmeralda Resort	773-4444	-- / -- / D	Y			$		MC V AE DC	Yes 50	Casual dining featuring breakfast and lunch buffets / Lobby court lounge features piano entertainment / Promising Newcomer/SCRW
	Jasmine / INDIAN WELLS - 44-660 Indian Wells Lane / In The Hyatt Grand Champions Resort	341-1000	-- / -- / D (X:M)					+	MC V AE DC	Rec	Intimate dining surrounded by modern art / Nouvelle Cuisine menu with oriental flair changes weekly / Gold Award/SCRW, Exceptional Dining/CRWA
	Princess Room, The / CATHEDRAL CITY - 67-967 Vista Chino / In The Doubletree Resort	322-7000	-- / -- / D	Y			$		MC V AE DC	Rec 20	Elegant setting features chinois haute cuisine / Daily chef specials and freshly baked breads
	Sonoma Grille / PALM DESERT - 74-700 Hwy 111 / In The Embassy Suites Hotel	340-2499	-- / L / D		✓	$			MC V AE DC	Rec 380	Innovative menu with Continental flair / Entertainment W-Sa, Silver Medal/SCRW for American Food
CHINESE	**China Gardens** / PALM DESERT - 73-196 Hwy 111 / East of Hwy 111	346-4624	-- / L (season) / D (season)	Y		$			MC V	Yes 5p+	Casual, cooking all Chinese cuisines / (Closed Mondays: June - Sept.)
	Gold Phoenix / PALM DESERT - 72-655 Hwy 111 / In Palms to Pines Center	346-4426	-- / L (X:M) / D (X:M)			$			MC V	Yes	Family-owned, featuring Mandarin, Cantonese & Szechuan / Specials: Seafood-in-a-basket, Mongolian Beef / B&W, carry out, 2 Star Winner/CRWA
	House Of Bamboo / RANCHO MIRAGE - 71-265 Hwy 111 / South of Country Club Dr	346-3834	-- / -- / D	Y		$			MC V	Rec	Szechuan, Mandarin & Cantonese dishes / Early dinner specials from 4-6pm / Carry-out
	Mandarin Palace / CATHEDRAL CITY - 67-555 Hwy 111 / West of Date Palm Dr	328-0848	-- / L / D		F / / Sa ✓	$			MC V	Rec 130	Mandarin, Szechuan, and Hunan dishes
	Mr. Wong's / CATHEDRAL CITY - 68-345 Hwy 111 / West of Cathedral Canyon Dr	321-2279	-- / L (X:Su) / D			$			MC V	Rec 20	Small family-owned restaurant / B&W, carry-out
	Orient Express / INDIAN WELLS - 76-477 Hwy 111 / In The Erawan Grand Hotel	346-8021	-- / -- / D (X:M)			$			MC V	Yes	Oriental cuisine featuring Thai, Mongolian and Japanese dishes
	Red Dragon / RANCHO MIRAGE - 71-691 Hwy 111 / South of Country Club Dr	340-6630	-- / L / D			$			MC V AE	Rec 6p+	Family-owned serving Cantonese, Mandarin, Szechuan / Specials include Sizzling Shrimp / B&W

Dinner/Person covers the three price columns (Under $10 / $10 to $20 / $20 to $30+).

Cuisine (Notes)	Restaurant / COMMUNITY - Street / Located Near	Phone	Serving (B/L/D, X=Closed)	Late Night Din.	Sunday Brunch	Under $10	$10 to $20	$20 to $30+	Credit Cards	Reservations	Special Features
CHINESE (Con't)	**Tai Ping** PALM DESERT - 45-299 Lupine Lane South of Hwy 111	340-1836	-- / -- / D					$	MC V AE	Yes 30	Cantonese, Hunan, and Szechuan dishes Each dish is individually prepared Specialty is Chinese Chicken Salad
CONTINENTAL	**Cabrillo Room** RANCHO MIRAGE - 41-00 Bob Hope Dr In The Marriott Rancho Las Palmas Resort	568-2727	-- / -- / D (X:M,Tu)		✓			$	MC V AE DC	Rec	French accent, tableside service, jacket suggested Everything from Beluga Caviar to Souffle Rothschild Entertain: dancing W-Sa, Gold Award/SCRW, 3 Star/CRWA
	Cattails CATHEDRAL CITY - 68-369 Hwy 111 At Melrose Av	324-8263	-- / -- / D (X:Tu)					+	MC V	Must 85	Casually elegant, small intimate dining rooms Daily blackboard menu featuring International Cuisine Wine list, exciting desserts, Silver/SCRW, 2 Star/CRWA
	Chaplin's RANCHO MIRAGE - 69-950 Frank Sinatra Dr At Hwy 111	328-2427	-- / -- / D	Y			$		MC V AE	Rec	Bar & Bistro French, Swiss & American fare, late night brasserie Silver Award/SCRW, One Star/CRWA
	Cunard's of La Quinta LA QUINTA - 78-045 Calle Cadiz	564-4443	-- / -- / D		✓			$	MC V AE	Yes	Combination of French, continental, Northern Italian 15,000 bottles in Wine Cellar, Jacket required Pasta/break/desserts baked on premise, piano player
	Dining Room, The RANCHO MIRAGE - 68-900 Frank Sinatra Dr In The Ritz-Carlton Hotel	321-8282	-- / -- / S	Y				+	MC V	Rec	Pampered service in this elegant atmosphere Haute cuisine with California accent Piano, jacket required, Gold Medal/SCRW, 2 Star/CRWA
	Dominick's RANCHO MIRAGE - 70-030 Hwy 111 At Frank Sinatra Dr	324-1711	-- / -- / D	Y			$		MC V AE DC	Rec 100	South Seas decor Italian and American specialties Piano entertainment nightly
	Erawan Room INDIAN WELLS - 76-447 Highway 111 In the Erawan Garden Hotel	346-8021	B / L / D	F / Sa			$		MC V AE	Yes	See the big dragon who breathes fire Soft pastel shades of mauve and gold, patio dining
	Huntsman LA QUINTA - 78-477 Hwy 111 West of Washington St	564-2448	-- / -- / D					$	MC V AE D	Yes 100	Classic cuisine, wild game, venison, rack of lamb Live Maine lobster, dancing to live bands 5 nights Michelin Award winner, other location in Ireland
	La Mirage Room LA QUINTA - 49-499 Eisenhower Dr In The La Quinta Hotel	564-4111	-- / -- / D (X:M)		✓			$	MC V AE DC	Rec	Californian accent Sunday buffet brunch Entertainment and dancing
	Lake View Restaurant PALM DESERT - 74-855 Country Club Dr In The Marriott Desert Springs Resort	341-2211	B / L / D		✓			$	MC V AE DC	Rec 200	Lake view, California and Spa cuisine, fine wine list Special sundowner dinner, lavish sunday brunch Dancing at night
	Mario's RANCHO MIRAGE - 71-730 Hwy 111 North of Rancho Mirage Lane	346-0584	-- / -- / D					$	MC V AE DC	Rec 220	Italian specialties, opera & broadway entertainment Singing waiters, the Mario Singers, continuous from 6pm
	Nest, The INDIAN WELLS - 75-188 Hwy 111 East of Cook St	346-2314	-- / -- / D	Y			$		MC V AE DC D	30	Italian, Swiss, French home-style cuisine Trademark bottomless black soup kettle, newspaper menus Famous piano bar and noisy jolly clientel
	Renzo's Bistro PALM DESERT - 73-725 El Paseo East of Hwy 74	568-0300	-- / -- / D					$	MC V AE	Rec 80	Casual intimate atmosphere Seafood specialties with an Italian flair Silver Medal/SCRW
	Robi LA QUINTA - 78-085 Av La Fonda West of Washington St	564-0544	-- / -- / D (X:Su)					+	MC V AE	Rec 40	Like dining at home at a 7 course prix fixe dinner Gallery Robi exhibits art, chance to meet the chef Private rooms, jacket suggested, B&W
	Ron's In The Desert PALM DESERT - 73-703 Hwy 111 West of Portola Av	773-3766	-- / L (X:Su) / D	Y	✓			$	MC V AE DC	Rec 70	Kenn Duncan Red Shoe Photo Collection Patio and indoor dining, entertainment nightly American dishes with an Italian accent
	Victor's Bistro PALM DESERT - 72-850 El Paseo West of Palms Hwy	346-1727	-- / -- / D (X:Su)	Y	✓		$		MC V	Yes 50	Yugoslavian specialties, desert casual Continental: steaks, prawns, fish Pasta of the day
	Wally's Desert Turtle RANCHO MIRAGE - 71-775 Hwy 111 At The Veldt	568-9321	-- / L (F only) / D	Y				+	MC V AE	Rec	Elegant sunken dining room where socialites gather Classic cuisine in elegant presentations Fashion shows on Friday, piano player
	Wilde Goose, The CATHEDRAL CITY - 67-938 Hwy 111 West of Date Palm Dr	328-5775	-- / -- / D					$	MC V AE C	Rec 110	Casual dress in this European country atmosphere Specializing in wild game, featuring 6 kinds of duck Dessert and cognac carts, Piano bar
ECLECTIC	**T.G.I. Friday's** PALM DESERT - 72-620 El Paseo West of Palms Hwy	568-2280	-- / L / D	Y			$		MC V AE	None	Memorabilia fills the walls, waitstaff are always fun Extensive menu with everything from snacks to full meal

Cuisine (NOTES)	Restaurant / COMMUNITY - Street / Located Near	PHONE	Brkfst / Lunch / Dinner / X=Closed	Late Night Din.	Sunday Brunch	Under $10	$10 to $20	$20 to $30 +	Credit Cards	Reservations	SPECIAL FEATURES
ENGLISH	**Lord Fletcher's Inn** / RANCHO MIRAGE - 70-385 Hwy 111 / South of Frank Sinatra Dr	328-1161	-- / -- / D (X:Su)				$		MC V	Rec	Old English decor / Traditional menu of prime rib and daily specials / Since 1966, Silver Medal/SCRW
FRENCH	**Club 74** / PALM DESSERT - 73-061 El Paseo / At Hwy 74	568-2782	-- / L (X:Tu) / D					$	MC V AE	Yes / 18	Opened by owners of Evelen's / Elegant surroundings include marble entry / Crystal chandeliers, pampered service
	Cuistot / PALM DESERT - 73-111 El Paseo / In The El Paseo Galleria	340-1000	-- / I (X:M) / D (X:M)					+	MC V AE	Must / 120	Contemporary decor, courtyard dining, casual dress / Open kitchen, chef trained by Paul Bocuse & Roger Verge / Silver Medal/SCRW
	La Cave / RANCHO MIRAGE - 70-064 Hwy 111 / South of Frank Sinatra Dr	324-4673	-- / -- / D (X:M)	Y				+	MC V AE DC	Rec	Dining by piano music and candlelight in banquettes / Classic cuisine presented on hand written menus / Lower level of Medium Rare
	Le Paon / PALM DESERT - 45-640 Hwy 74 / South of Hwy 111	568-3651	-- / -- / D	Y				$	MC V AE DC	Must / 200	Classic Cordon Bleu Continental Cuisine, big wine list / Tableside carts, luxurious prepartions / Entertainment, pianist and singer since 1980
	Mille Fleurs / PALM DESERT - 73-101 Hwy 111 / East of Palms Hwy	773-3337	-- / L (X:S,Su) / D	Y			$		MC V AE	Yes	Opened by Bertrand Hug of Mille Fleurs in neighboring / Rancho Santa Fe
GREEK	**Olympic Cafe** / CATHEDRAL CITY - 68-375 Hwy 111 / Btwn Melrose Ave & Cathedral Canyon Dr	321-1525	-- / L (X:Su) / D (X:Su)		$				NONE	Yes / 55	Belly dancing night, also Greek dancers, B&W
	Zorba's / RANCHO MIRAGE - 42-434 Bob Hope Dr / North of Hwy 111	340-3066	-- / L / D				$		MC V AE DC	Rec / 140	Patio dining in this family-owned restaurant / Live Greek & contemporary music, Greek & belly dancers / Greek happening:Mon, Silver Medal/SCRW, 2 Star/CRWA
HUNGARIAN	**Budapest Inn** / DESERT HOT SPRINGS - 11349 Palm Dr / North of Pierson Blvd	329-8050	-- / -- / D (X:Su)	✓		$					Traditional Hungarian menu / Senior discount, early bird specials
ITALIAN	**A Touch Of Mama's** / PALM DESERT - 74-063 Hwy 111 / East of Portola Av	568-1315	-- / -- / D				$		MC V AE	Rec / 40	Romantic dining by candlelight, small intimate / Continental dishes, homemade pasta, B&W / Strolling violins, other location: Dino's in Acapulco
	Alberto's / RANCHO MIRAGE - 71-416 Hwy 111 / South of Country Club Dr	346-3221	-- / -- / D (X:M)					$	MC V	Yes	Attractive, cheerful atmosphere / Northern Italian specialties featuring Milanese cuisine / Two Star/CRWA, eighth award winning season
	Andreino's / PALM DESERT - 73-098 Hwy 111 / East of Palms Hwy 74	773-3365	-- / -- / D				$		MC V AE	Rec	Patio dining / Northern Italian cuisine, extensive wine list, B&W / Silver Medal/SCRW, Two Stars/CRWA
	Bob & Manon Sorrentino's / PALM DESERT - 73-725 El Paseo / East of Hwy 111	568-0300	-- / -- / D				$		MC V AE D	Yes / 80	Casual intimate atmosphere / Pasta & seafood specialties
	Dominick Mancuso's / PALM DESERT - 73-520 El Paseo / At San Pableo	346-0445	-- / F / / D	Sa			$		MC V AE	Must / 35	New / Northern Italian menu with a continental flair / Piano lounge, VIP Room for private parties
	Mancuso's / PALM DESERT - 72-281 Hwy 111 / South of Bob Hope Dr	340-6610	-- / -- / D	Y			$		MC V AE DC	Rec / 60	French & Northern Italian dishes / Family-owned, from Scottsdale and Paradise Valley, AZ / Piano lounge, 3 Star/CRWA for Wine Cellar
	Marinello / PALM DESERT - 73-609 Hwy 111 / East of Palms Hwy	346-4165	-- / -- / D (X:M)								Complete Italian menu / Wide variety of pizzas / Carry-out
	Michael's Bistro / RANCHO MIRAGE - 70-065 Hwy 111 / East of Frank Sinatra Dr	328-5650	-- / -- / D				$		MC V AE	Must / 35	Now in its 12th season, formerly Bistro III / Northern Italian, seafood, Chicago charbroiled steak / Over 120 wines on list
	Paoli's / CATHEDRAL CITY - 68-977 Hwy 111 / West of Date Palm Dr	324-3737	-- / L (X:M-F) / D	Sa / / Su			$		MC V	Yes / 6p+ / 75	Intimate, friendly, serving traditional Italian menu / Gourmet pizzas and great desserts / B&W, delivery and carry-out
	Papa Dan's / PALM DESERT - 73-131 Country Club Dr / East of Monterey Av	568-3267	-- / L / D	F / / S		$			MC V	Yes / 6p+ / 20	Casual Italian dining / Pasta & pizza / Carry out and delivery
	Pietro's / PALM DESERT - 72-221 Hwy 111 / West of Palms Hwy	568-0202	-- / -- / D				$		MC V AE	Rec / 120	Family style, seafood specialties, gourmet pasta bar / Family recipes, piano bar - music of the ``40's / Silver Medal/SCRW, Two Star/CRWA, early bird specials

Cuisine (NOTES)	Restaurant / COMMUNITY - Street / Located Near	PHONE	Serving Brkfst Lunch Dinner X=Closed	Late Night Din.	Sunday Brunch	Under $10	$10 to $20	$20 to $30+	Credit Cards	Reservations	SPECIAL FEATURES
ITALIAN (Con't)	**Ristorante Mamma Gina** *PALM DESERT* - 73-705 El Paseo San Luis Rey Av	568-9898	-- -- D (X:Su)					$	MC V AE DC	Must 80	Northern Italian menu, featuring Tuscan specialties Piano lounge, antipasto & desert carts, Awards for both Dining and Wine, also in Florence Italy
	Romano's *PALM DESERT* - 72-795 Hwy 111 West of Palms Hwy	340-4600	-- L D	F / Sa		$			MC V	No	Reasonable prices with very large portions Pizza, spaghetti, manicotti, veal & peppers Calzones, sub sandwiches, B&W
	Spiaggia Seafood Ristorante *PALM DESERT* - 72-760 El Paseo West of Palms Hwy	773-5753	-- L D				$		MC V AE DC D	Rec 400	Outdoor patio dining from daily blackboard specials Unique combination of fresh seafood and pasta Piano bar, private room, Two Stars/CRWA
	Tuscany's Ristorante *PALM DESERT* - 74-855 Country Club Dr In The Marriott Desert Springs	341-1725	-- -- D				$		MC V AE DC D	Rec 150	Mountain and lake views Northern Italian cuisine Promising Newcomer/SCRW
	Tutti Gusti *PALM DESERT* - 73-030 El Paseo East of Hwy 74	341-3451	-- L (X:Tu) D (X:Tu)	W - Su			$		MC V AE	Yes 35	Patio dining, in this upbeat trendy bistro Gourmet pizza cooked in wood burning pizza oven, B&W Pasta and seafood cooked in exhibition kitchen
JAPANESE	**Kobe** Japanese Steak House *RANCHO MIRAGE* - 69-838 Hwy 111 North of Frank Sinatra Dr	324-1717	-- D	Y			$		A L L	Yes	Decor of Japanese country inn with Koi fish ponds Sushi bar, teppan grills, traditional Japanese feast Multi-level dining area, piano bar in cocktail lounge
	Midori *PALM DESERT* - 73-759 Hwy 111 East of Palms Hwy	340-1466	-- L D	F / Sa			$		MC V AE	Rec 30	Sushi bar B&W Catering services available
	Mikado *PALM DESERT* - 74-855 Country Club Dr In The Marriott Desert Springs Resort	341-2211	-- -- D		✓			$	MC V AE DC	Must 32	Situated on an island reached by boat, waterfall view Overlook Japanese gardens, teppan grills Sundowner dinner 5:30-6:30p
MEDITERRANEAN	**Sirocco** *INDIAN WELLS* - 44-400 Indian Wells Lane In The Stouffer Esmeralda Resort	773-4444	-- -- D	Y			$		MC V AE DC D	Rec 12	Traditional & comtemporary Mediteranean cuisine Entertainment, 3 Star Award/CRWA
MEXICAN	**Adobe Grill** *LA QUINTA* - 49-499 Eisenhower Dr In La Quinta Hotel	346-2904	-- L D					$	MC V AE DC	Rec 40	Mountain view Regional specialties Private room, 2 Stars/CRWA
	Don Diego's of Indian Wells *INDIAN WELLS* - 74-969 Hwy 111 Southwest corner at Cook St.	340-5588	-- L D		✓		$		MC V	Rec 130	Champagne buffet brunch, Gold Medal in Fajita Cookoff Regional cuisines, tamales Recommended Dining/CRWA
	El Cafe de Mexico *PALM DESERT* - 73-325 Hwy 111 East of Palms Hwy	346-2639	-- L (X:Su) D		✓	$			MC V	No 14	Authentic Mexican decor featuring hand painted murals Daily lunch specials, menudo, chili con carne Machaca, desserts such as flan and churros
	Las Casuelas Nuevas *RANCHO MIRAGE* - 70-050 Hwy 111 At Frank Sinatra Dr	328-8844	-- L D	F / Sa			$		MC V AE DC	Rec 350	Outdoor garden terrace to view the social scene Over sixty entrees on the menu Mariachis
	Maria Bonita *RANCHO MIRAGE* - 71-900 Hwy 111 North of Bob Hope Dr	568-6557	-- I (X:Su) D (X:Su)		✓	$			NONE	Yes 25	Small family-owned, serving authentic Mexican cuisine Hand-made tamales in the traditional manner Relienos, B&W
	Red Onion *PALM DESERT* - 72-840 Hwy 111 West of Palms Hwy	340-0029	-- L D				$		MC V AE DC	Rec 75	Southwest decor Happy hour 4-9p, 2-for-1 drinks, free buffet Live DJ playing top '40's
	Teresa's Cafe *INDIO* - 45-682 Towne South of Indio Blvd	347-7411	B L D		✓	$			NONE	No	Home cooking from huevos rancheros, steak & eggs to menudo, machaca, Beer
MOROCCAN	**Dar Maghreb** *RANCHO MIRAGE* - 42-300 Bob Hope Dr North of Hwy 111	568-9486	-- -- D	Y	✓			$	MC V DC	Must 185	A dining adventure with sofas or floor cushions Prix fixe menu, silverware on request Belly dancers
SEAFOOD	**Desert Wharf** *PALM DESERT* - 72-839 Hwy 111 West of Hwy 74	568-3474	B B D				$		NONE	No	Order at counter and food is brought to you Seafood is cooked on a charbroiler grill, B&W Fish market
	Pirate 'n Bull *RANCHO MIRAGE* - 71-380 Hwy 111 South of Country Club Dr	346-9037	-- L (X:Su) D (X:Su)	M - Sa		$			MC V	No	English pub type setting features fish & chips Hamburgers
	Rusty Pelican *PALM DESERT* - 72-191 Hwy 111 Btw Fred Waring Dr & Bob Hope Dr	346-8065	-- -- D				$		MC V AE DC	Yes 50	Casual relaxed dining atmosphere Fresh seafood specials, sushi and seafood bar Entertainment & dancing F/Sa

Cuisine (NOTES)	Restaurant COMMUNITY - Street Located Near	PHONE	Brkfst Lunch Dinner X=Closed	Late Night Din.	Sunday Brunch	Under $10	$10 to $20	$20 to $30 +	Credit Cards	Reservations	SPECIAL FEATURES
SEAFOOD (Con't)	**Scoma's** of San Francisco *RANCHO MIRAGE* - 69-620 Hwy 111 North of Frank Sinatra Dr	**328-9000**	-- -- D		Y			$	MC V AE DC	Must 20	San Franciso landmark from Pier 47 Wharf favorites and some Italian specialties Piano bar, Gold Medal/SCRW, Exceptional Dining/CRWA
	Sea Grille *PALM DESERT* - 74-855 Country Club Dr In The Marriott Desert Springs Resort	**341-2211**	-- -- D					$	MC V AE DC	Rec	Extensive menu, water view, open kitchen, oyster bar Fresh pizza
SOUTHWEST	**Charlie's** *INDIAN WELLS* - 44-600 Indian Wells In Hyatt Grand Champrions	**341-1000**	-- L (F-Su) D					$	MC V AE	Yes	Cactus with warm earth tones Combination of California and Southwest Grill Veal chops, lamb chops, paella, pasta

ADDITIONS

ORDER CARD FOR COMPLIMENTARY POCKET EDITION

☐ Please send me a complimentary copy of the 3" by 5" *Flashfacts System*[sm] **POCKET EDITION** which covers <u>all three</u>

TIJUANA DINING AREAS
- Downtown
- Rio Tijuana
- Leisure Row

____
Name (PLEASE PRINT)

____

____
Street

____
City /ST /ZIP

☐ I'd also like to receive information on how to purchase 3" by 5" *Flashfacts System*[sm] **POCKET EDITIONS** covering <u>other</u> Dining Areas from the San Diego/Tijuana/Palm Springs GUIDE.

____

____

____

☐ Please send information about quantity purchases of the 3" by 5" *Flashfacts System*[sm] **POCKET EDITIONS** for use as business gifts.

☐ Please send information about quantity purchases of *Flashfacts System*[sm] **DINING GUIDES** for use as gifts.

FEEDBACK CARD

FROM:

____
Name (PLEASE PRINT)

____

____
Street

____
City/ST/ ZIP

☐ I'd like to receive information about *Flashfacts System*[sm] **DINING GUIDES** for other cities. The ones I'm most interested in are:

#1 _______________________________

#2 _______________________________

☐ Please send information about custom imprinted *Flashfacts System*[sm] **DINING GUIDES** for use as Business Gifts.

I wish to nominate the restaurant(s) listed below for inclusion in the next edition of the *SAN DIEGO/ TIJUANA/PALM SPRINGS GUIDE* :

1) Restaurant: _______________________________

Address: _______________________________

City/ST/ZIP: _______________________________

Telephone: _______________________________

2) Restaurant: _______________________________

Address: _______________________________

City/ST/ZIP: _______________________________

Telephone: _______________________________

BUSINESS REPLY MAIL

FIRST CLASS MAIL   PERMIT NO. 4618   NEW YORK, NY

POSTAGE WILL BE PAID BY ADDRESSEE

Flashfacts System
RRN Inc. Fulfilment Center
22 West 21Street
New York, NY   10010-6904

NO POSTAGE
NECESSARY
IF MAILED
IN THE
UNITED STATES

BUSINESS REPLY MAIL

FIRST CLASS MAIL   PERMIT NO. 4618   NEW YORK, NY

POSTAGE WILL BE PAID BY ADDRESSEE

Flashfacts System
RRN Inc. Fulfilment Center
22 West 21Street
New York, NY   10010-6904